Trade Warriors

States, Firms, and Strategic-Trade Policy in High-Technology Competition

Commercial rivalries in high technology are among the most heated in today's global economy. From robotics to aerospace, states are subsidizing their national champions and competing for market share in the "industries of tomorrow." This book explains why states intervene and (or) retaliate in some high-technology industries but not in others, and how these commercial rivalries are likely to unfold. Professor Busch argues that states subsidize national champions in industries promising externalities that domestic industries are primed to make use of, spend more on subsidies where these benefits do not escape national borders, and are more likely to bring these commercial rivalries back from the brink of a trade war where strategic-trade policies leave both states worse off. This book is among the first to argue specifically about externalities and to evaluate how they have, or have not, shaped decisions for strategic trade in several of the most important commercial rivalries in high technology. Drawing on new and previously unreported documentation from governments, firms, industry associations, and expert observers in Europe, Japan, and the United States, Busch sheds new light on the high-technology rivalries in civil aircraft, semiconductors, high-definition television, robotics, and superconductors.

Marc L. Busch is an associate professor of Government and Social Studies at Harvard University. His publications, which appear in *American Journal of Political Science, International Organization, Journal of Conflict Resolution,* and several edited volumes, include research on nontariff barrier protectionism, the debate over absolute and relative gains in international relations, and the causes and consequences of regional economic integration. Professor Busch is Director of Graduate Student Programs at the Weatherhead Center for International Affairs at Harvard, and a faculty associate at Harvard's John M. Olin Institute for Strategic Studies. He has also been a John M. Olin National Faculty Fellow, a Fellow at the Center for Social Science at Columbia University, and the recipient of fellowships from the John D. and Catherine T. MacArthur Foundation and the Institute for the Study of World Politics.

Trade Warriors

States, Firms, and Strategic-Trade Policy in High-Technology Competition

MARC L. BUSCH
Harvard University

CAMBRIDGE
UNIVERSITY PRESS

PUBLISHED BY THE PRESS SYNDICATE OF THE UNIVERSITY OF CAMBRIDGE
The Pitt Building, Trumpington Street, Cambridge, United Kingdom

CAMBRIDGE UNIVERSITY PRESS
The Edinburgh Building, Cambridge CB2 2RU, UK
40 West 20th Street, New York, NY 10011-4211, USA
10 Stamford Road, Oakleigh, Melbourne 3166, Australia
Ruiz de Alarcón 13, 28014 Madrid, Spain
Dock House, The Waterfront, Cape Town 8001, South Africa

http://www.cambridge.org

© Marc L. Busch 1999

First published 1999
First paperback edition 2001

Printed in the United States of America

Typeface Sabon 10/13 pt.   *System* DeskTopPro$_{/UX}$® [BV]

A catalog record for this book is available from the British Library

Library of Congress Cataloging in Publication data is available

ISBN 0 521 63340 0 hardback
ISBN 0 521 79938 4 paperback

For Zachary and Lelia,
and in memory of their great-grandfather, Jack

Contents

Figures

Acknowledgments

I am indebted to the many people who helped see this book through to its completion. Jack Snyder, chair of my dissertation committee, read countless drafts and always offered encouragement while critiquing my work. His intellectual input made this a better book; his dedication as a teacher and advisor made my years at Columbia so rewarding. Helen Milner pushed me to refine my argument at every turn, giving generously as my teacher, colleague, and friend. She has mentored me from the day she inherited me as her teaching assistant, and I have cherished working with her ever since. Robert Jervis stimulated my interest in international relations, and taught me far more about the field than I have been able to convey in the pages of this book.

I am also grateful to Ken Oye, whose input and encouragement have been invaluable in completing this book, and to Eric Reinhardt, whose unwavering support and friendship since graduate school made all the difference. I also thank my colleagues at Harvard, notably Lawrence Broz, who provided extensive comments on the manuscript, and Jeffry Frieden and Gary King, who suggested how to improve the argument and presentation of the book more generally. James Brander, Rachel Bronson, Kurt Dassel, Chris Gelpi, Bob Keohane, Ed Mansfield, Lisa Martin, John Matthews, Richard Nelson, Ronald Rogowski, Steve Rosen, David Yoffie, seminar participants at the Program on International Politics, Economics and Security at the University of Chicago, the anonymous reviewers who read the book for Cambridge University Press, and my editors, Alex Holzman and Brian MacDonald, all provided helpful guidance and instructive criticism on various parts of the book. For research assistance, I thank Gabriel Aguilera, Daniel Alexandre, Dev Ghosh, Sam Sternin, Stephen Weinburg, and especially Melissa Freeman, who shared her Sarah McLachlan CDs and pursued each case study with expertise. Generous financial support was provided by the John M. Olin Foundation, which sponsored a year's leave to finish writing this book, and by Harvard's Center for International Affairs, the Graduate School of Arts and Sciences' Clark Fund at Harvard University, the Harvard-MIT Data Center, the Harvard-MIT Research Training Group in Positive Political Economy, the Graduate School of Arts and Sciences' Gillian Lindt Fellowship at Columbia University, the Center for Social Sciences at Columbia, the John D. and Catherine T. MacArthur Foundation, and the Institute for the Study of World Politics. Finally, I owe my biggest debt to my wife, Xenia, whose patience, perspective, and love helped make this book possible. The dedication is to our children, Zachary and Lelia, and to the memory of their great-grandfather, Jack, who would have been so proud of them both.

1

Introduction

In 1990, the president of the Semiconductor Industry Association urged Congress not to abandon his membership in its trade dispute with Japan. In an impassioned plea before a receptive audience, this influential witness testified that there was a difference between semiconductor chips and potato chips that mattered for the nation as a whole.[1] His plea did not fall on deaf ears. Few on Capitol Hill thought of the semiconductor rivalry as just another trade dispute. These chips, after all, are the underpinnings of the information age, the kind of high-technology industry in which governments might invest to leverage their economic growth and competitiveness. Perhaps not surprisingly, Washington reaffirmed its commitment to "level the playing field" in chips by funding U.S. firms and by seeking to renew the Semiconductor Trade Agreement.

At about the same time, the American Electronics Association's vice-president argued before Congress that his membership, too, needed help if it was to compete with Japan in high-definition television (HDTV).[2] Like those who had pleaded the case for government intervention on behalf of the semiconductor industry, proponents of HDTV explained that there were too many key technologies at stake to let U.S. firms fend for themselves. One sympathetic lawmaker put the matter more succinctly than most, claiming that the fight over HDTV had "become a symbol of America's willingness to compete in a tough new world in which foreign competitors target every aspect of modern industrial technology."[3] And yet, this plea fell on deaf ears. Indeed, not only did Washington deny the industry start-up funding, but there was no attempt to push for an agreement limiting what Japan spent on *its* "na-

1

tional champions," leaving U.S. firms to go it alone against subsidized competitors abroad.

Why such different trade policy outcomes across these two industries, despite all they have in common? Most notably, semiconductors and HDTV were both argued to be on the cutting edge of high technology, the expectation being that they would help stimulate entire sectors of the American economy. Moreover, since the contours of these industries limit competition to only a handful of firms, and favor larger producers over smaller ones, Washington might have been expected to use trade policy *strategically* to help American firms win market share from Japan in HDTV, just as in semiconductors. Further, there may have been good reason to expect Washington to follow through, since by subsidizing the exports or research and development (R&D) of its national champions, protectionism might well have been profitable, enticing the government to overrule the market's verdict on HDTV.

The way in which the semiconductor and HDTV battles have been fought sheds light on some of the most heated commercial rivalries unfolding today, as well as on how some highly anticipated commercial rivalries will likely be waged in the future. From satellites and rockets to biotechnology, developed and developing states have been jockeying for a foothold in high-technology industries, the spoils of which may be had by just a few lucky winners. These commercial rivalries are fueled by concerns that gains and losses may be path-dependent, and that success in these industries may confer an insurmountable lead in building the "economy of tomorrow." Against this backdrop, a state might be expected to fight for its national champions across the board in high technology,[4] and yet the United States chose not to fight for HDTV. Why?

One likely explanation centers on the threat of foreign retaliation. Where a rival state provides its national champions with offsetting subsidies, for example, both sides end up worse off than if neither had interfered in the market. Fear of a trade war is sure to weigh heavily in decisions for strategic trade, deterring government forays into the market where the expected costs of intervention outweigh the anticipated benefits. Framed in this light, a state might thus be unwilling to fight for its national champions across the board in high technology, and yet the United States fought for semiconductors. Why?

This book provides answers to these questions. It examines the way in which strategic-trade policy strains relations among states, pinpointing the conditions under which trade wars are likely to arise, as well as conditions under which these trade wars are likely to be resolved. The challenge is to explain more than just a government's decision to intervene or not. In semiconductors, for example, Washington opened up the public purse, but was hardly as generous as the industry had hoped. Similarly, the Japanese government showed a good deal of restraint in subsidizing its national champions in HDTV, despite the fact that the United States had no intention of retaliating. In explaining why, the book offers fresh insights into the strategic-trade "calculus" of states.

THE PUZZLE

The puzzle is that, on the one hand, states do not fight for their national champions as often as proponents might hope, but, on the other hand, they fight for them far more often than critics would lead us to expect. Taking the first part of this puzzle first, we find at least two reasons to expect more government intervention in high-technology industries than we, in fact, witness. First, these industries often promote the well-being of related firms and industries, stimulating a nation's economic growth and competitiveness in ways not fully accounted for by the market. For example, when an end user purchases a large volume of an input from its supplier, this can help the supplier achieve economies of scale and realize lower unit costs as a result,[5] a benefit undervalued by the price of this transaction. Second, and relatedly, the supplier may learn to adopt, assimilate, and employ a product, process, or management skill as it tailors products to meet an end user's needs – benefits that escape the market's attention. A state might thus intervene to correct for these market "failures," particularly in high-technology industries where, as Chapter 2 explains, it might be profitable to do so.[6] Posed this way, it is difficult to see why a state would ever be reluctant to fight for its national champions.

The wrinkle in the story, of course, is that a foreign state might retaliate, giving rise to a trade war that would leave both sides worse off. Governments abroad may be unwilling to leave the fate of their national champions to the market, fearful of conceding industries that feed the high-technology "food chain." As competing states increase what they spend on subsidies, however, they impose ever higher costs on each other while accomplishing less in the marketplace. Posed this way, it is difficult to see why a state would ever fight on behalf of its national champions.

A look at the real-world practice of strategic-trade policy reveals why it is important to think systematically about this puzzle. States do fight for national champions, but not in all industries, and certainly not always with the same investment of resources. And even where states fight, they sometimes cooperate with each other to ease trade tensions, but at other times not. The civil aircraft rivalry has been more heated than most, for example, in that both the United States and Europe have spent lavishly on their national champions. Yet both sides have shied away from other fights, the United States from HDTV and Europe from semiconductors.[7] Continuing with civil aircraft, both the United States and Europe have sought to ease trade tensions in this industry through a series of agreements. Yet, as in the case of satellites and rockets, both sides have let other fights go largely unchecked. This begs three questions. Why do states risk trade wars by fighting for their national champions in some high-technology industries but not in others? Why do states subsidize certain national champions at higher levels than others? And why, when states commit to a fight, do they cooperate with each other to ease trade tensions in some cases but not others?

THE ARGUMENT

In seeking to maximize their *national* welfare gains, states weigh the expected benefits from intervention against the potential costs of initiating a trade war. On the benefits side of the equation, states calculate the anticipated return to investing in a national champion. This involves gauging whether efforts to subsidize a national champion's push into world markets might leverage economic growth and competitiveness more generally. Again, this can result where relations between suppliers and end users result in scale efficiencies "upstream" or "downstream," giving rise to what is more formally referred to as a *linkage externality*, and where technology diffuses among related industries, or what is commonly referred to as a *spillover externality*. The first part of the argument, then, is that the return to investing in a national champion depends on whether related industries are positioned to benefit from these externalities. In determining this, states evaluate the extent to which their economies host the relevant upstream-downstream relations, not only because access to these linkage externalities hangs in the balance, but because the spillovers exhibited by a national champion also tend to diffuse upstream and downstream, tying these external benefits together.

If these externalities are likely to help leverage economic growth and competitiveness upstream and downstream, the next step is for states to determine whether this payoff is strictly national. The concern, of course, is that if these linkage and spillover externalities reach beyond its borders, then it is doubtful a state would fight as hard for its national champion, or fight at all, since industries abroad may benefit as much from this helping hand as industries at home. For example, if foreign competitors are closely bound together in these upstream-downstream relations, then both sides will share in these externalities, regardless of which state subsidizes its national champions. The incentive here is thus to free-ride rather than to outspend a trade rival.

The third step in the argument is to go beyond the calculations states make about their own economies, and to bring in the calculations they make about how trade rivals abroad stack up in terms of being able to exploit these same externalities. In deciding whether to fight for a national champion and, if so, with what investment of resources, states assess the likelihood that a trade rival abroad will fight back and, if so, with what investment of its own resources. Because competing economies may not be equally primed to make use of the externalities exhibited by an industry, the will to fight for national champions need not be symmetrical across states, giving rise to some one-sided battles. This suggests that the risk of initiating a trade war is not a constant and that, at times, states may weigh in on the side of their national champions with impunity. At other times, however, state forays into the market are certain to elicit retaliation. The book's theory identifies the conditions under which these outcomes are likely, as well as the conditions under which more varied outcomes are to be expected, including the decision on the part of both sides not to wage battle at all.

The first two parts of the preceding argument touch on the theory's independent variables. The question of whether an economy is primed to make use of the externalities that a national champion exhibits taps the logic of what the book refers to as the *consumption* variable. The question of whether these externalities yield strictly national benefits taps the logic of what the book terms the *internalization* variable. All things equal, states are more likely to subsidize national champions in industries that exhibit externalities that the domestic economy can consume, and to spend more on subsidies if the resulting benefits are internalized within national borders. The third part of the argument says that in the end, decisions for strategic trade ultimately reflect how competing states measure up on these two independent variables. Finally, the theory's dependent variable concerns the outcome of a commercial rivalry, scored in terms of which of three strategic-trade policies states practice in competing with each other: *full intervention, limited intervention,* or *nonintervention.* Briefly, the theory makes the following predictions.

If both states can consume the externalities at stake, and these externalities are nation-specific, then both are likely to act on the incentive to subsidize their national champions. This gives rise to a trade war in which states try to outspend each other. Here, states may seek to cooperate by jointly *lowering* their spending (i.e., practice limited intervention), rather than escalate their spending on subsidies (i.e., practice full intervention). Chapter 3 explains the U.S.-Europe civil aircraft rivalry in this light.

If both states can consume the externalities at stake, and yet these externalities leak out beyond national borders, then the incentive is to free-ride on whatever subsidies the other provides to *its* national champions. In other words, since the external benefits that result diffuse internationally, any subsidies help firms abroad as much as they do domestic ones. States thus hurt each other by spending *too little,* rather than too much. Here, states may seek to cooperate by jointly *increasing* their spending (i.e., practice limited intervention), rather than free-riding (i.e., practicing nonintervention). Chapter 4 explains the U.S.-Japan rivalry in semiconductors this way.

If one state can consume and internalize the externalities at stake, and the other cannot make use of these external benefits, then the former will be expected to purge the industry of competitors abroad, without fear of retaliation. This case has long generated interest in strategic-trade theory, even if the literature has been at a loss to identify conditions under which a foreign state might choose *not* to retaliate. The book predicts when an outcome of this sort is to be expected, revealing why foreign retaliation does not make sense in this case.

If one state can consume but cannot internalize the externalities at stake, and the other is not positioned to make use of these external benefits, then the former has incentive to subsidize its national champion, but with a lesser investment of resources (i.e., practice limited intervention). More to the point, even though the interventionist state has little to worry about in terms of a fight now, it may one day get a fight if its foreign trade rival can exploit a "late mover" advantage, sharing in technologies the interventionist state helps to underwrite. Chapter 5 describes the U.S.-Japan HDTV rivalry along these lines.

Finally, if neither state can consume or internalize the externalities at stake, then there is no incentive for either to fight for this industry. This is not a trivial outcome; studies of strategic trade typically see the threat of foreign retaliation as the *only* reason why a state might leave the fate of its national champions to the workings of the market (i.e., practice nonintervention), yet this is misleading. Indeed, the book identifies the conditions under which *two* rival states might back away from a fight in high technology, absent any threat of foreign retaliation. More generally, the book argues that nonintervention is a strategic-trade *policy*, rather than a failure of strategic trade.

The book's theory offers new insights into the puzzle of strategic-trade policy. It says that the way in which these commercial rivalries unfold depends on how competing states measure up in terms of being able to make use of the externalities for which they fight, as well as on the scope of these benefits. In certain cases, strategic-trade practices are likely to give rise to heated trade wars, but in other cases to some one-sided battles or to no battle at all.

IMPLICATIONS OF THE ARGUMENT

The causes and consequences of trade wars have long been of interest to political scientists and economists alike.[8] As a *cooperation problem* among states, trade wars are among the most salient sources of conflict in international relations. Much of the interest in trade wars traces back to optimal tariff theory, which says that under certain strict conditions, a state can export the cost of curbing imports, and therefore profit from protection.[9] This insight figures prominently in discussions of hegemonic stability theory, for example, and in theories of the political economy of trade more generally.[10] For all the interest, though, the necessary market power to employ an optimal tariff curtails the reach of this theory.[11] Strategic trade theory breathes new life into a similar dynamic, but boasts far greater reach, emphasizing market structure as opposed to market power.[12] It thus brings into play the same "beggar-thy-neighbor" dynamic popularized by optimal tariff theory, but insists that this dynamic is relevant across a wider range of industries. One of the main

goals of this book is to explain when trade wars of this sort are likely to
unfold, as well as when they are likely to be resolved cooperatively.

Few observers doubt that externalities carry considerable weight in
the state's calculus of strategic trade.[13] And yet, to insist that externalities
matter is a point of departure, not an argument. This book offers one of
the first systematic arguments about the conditions under which externalities are likely to sway policymakers to fight for national champions
in high technology, and with what investment of resources. In this way,
the book marks a substantial improvement on the literature, which tends
instead to invoke externalities as a way of mopping up any (and all)
unexplained variance in strategic trade outcomes.[14] The most important
implication of the consumption variable, of course, is that not all national champions exhibiting externalities are worth fighting for, since
some promise little payoff for the domestic economy. As argued in
Chapter 5, this variable casts considerable doubt on the lessons that
have been drawn about the U.S.-Japan rivalry in HDTV.[15] More to the
point, and certainly most provocatively, it speaks to the criticism that
states lack sufficient information to "pick winners," since in evaluating
the score on the consumption variable, states let the *market* pick their
winners for them.

The internalization variable provides a second cut at the puzzle of
strategic trade. The intuition behind this variable is that the level of
resources invested in a national champion depends on whether the payoff is strictly national. If foreign competitors enjoy access to the externalities that result, the incentive is to let others incur the cost of subsidizing their national champions, and to free-ride on these external benefits.
To be sure, Avinash Dixit muses that, under these conditions, rivals are
likely to retaliate for each other's forays into the market with a "note of
thanks."[16] It would be wrong, moreover, to dismiss this as a theoretical
quip; this concern proved to be a stumbling block in Washington's
debate over funding for the Semiconductor Manufacturing Technology
(Sematech) consortium, just as it had in Tokyo's deliberations over the
Very Large Scale Integration (VLSI) projects. As argued in Chapter 4,
this variable offers a fresh new look at the U.S.-Japan semiconductor
rivalry. Put more boldly, by drawing out the implications of the internalization variable, the book can hardly be accused of telling the same
old story about chips.

Putting these pieces together, the book's theory has implications for
broader questions about the political economy of trade policy. Endoge-

nous protection theory, in particular, has done much to popularize an interest group politics approach to the study of tariffs and nontariff barriers. The underlying argument is that elected officials act on the demands of politically influential constituents, looking for returns at the ballot box.[17] The expectation is thus that protectionism is given to those industries vested with sufficient electoral clout and incentive to lobby.[18] As persuasive as this account is in explaining broader trends in tariffs and nontariff barriers, it falls short in explaining subsidy practices in high technology. Indeed, many high-technology industries that receive subsidies fare poorly on most measures of electoral clout, and some even get more help than they ask for. Other high-technology industries, flush with political capital and highly motivated to lobby, fail to get what they ask for, or fail to get anything at all. The book argues that these patterns are within reach of a state-centered theory of strategic trade, one in which policies in line with the "national interest" prevail over interest group politics, given unique opportunities and constraints that serve to shape trade protectionism in high technology.

OUTLINE OF THE BOOK

The book proceeds as follows. Chapter 2 explains and operationalizes the book's theory, takes up issues of evidence and case selection, and sets up a competing explanation with a hold on the case studies presented in the chapters that follow.

Chapters 3 through 5 then present the book's three primary case studies, including the U.S.-Europe civil aircraft rivalry, the U.S.-Japan semiconductor rivalry, and the U.S.-Japan HDTV rivalry. Each case study is divided into three sections: the first looks at the economics of the industry, the purpose of which is to show that an assortment of market imperfections bring the case within reach of strategic-trade theory; the second evaluates the independent variables; the third scores the dependent variable and assesses whether the book's theory does a better job explaining the case than does the competing explanation.

Chapter 3 argues that both the United States and Europe[19] consume and internalize the externalities exhibited by the civil aircraft industry and that, as a result, the temptation is to practice full intervention on behalf of their national champions. This puts them at risk of a trade war, fear of which has long motivated both sides to pursue agreements intended to curb subsidies. In contrast to the competing explanation and much of the literature on this case, Chapter 3 insists that the heated tone of this commercial rivalry owes to the fact that the states involved, rather than their national champions, have been calling the shots in civil aircraft, and that externalities, rather than votes, are the currency of this fight.

Chapter 4 argues that the United States and Japan consume, but do not internalize, the externalities exhibited by the semiconductor industry. The ease with which these external benefits diffuse beyond national borders has long dampened the enthusiasm on both sides of the Pacific for subsidizing chip vendors. Instead, the incentive in this commercial rivalry has been to free-ride on the help the other gives to its national champions. Cooperation in the semiconductor industry has thus required getting the United States and Japan to spend *more* on their domestic industries, not less. This distinguishes the battle in chips from the battle in civil aircraft, making it clear that the competition in semiconductors is anything but a representative case of "managed" trade.

Chapter 5 argues that the United States could not consume the externalities of HDTV through the 1970s and 1980s, when intervention was hotly debated, whereas Japan has long been able to consume, but not internalize, these external benefits. Since the United States was absent or underrepresented in almost every segment of consumer electronics, HDTV was not a fight worth waging, given the lack of a bridge to semiconductors, displays, and fiber optics, among other industries. In contrast, consumer electronics has paved the way for Japan to leverage these same industries by sponsoring HDTV. Yet, in light of the migration toward digital technologies in consumer electronics, American competitiveness in logic chips, and expectations that most HDTV receivers will be built in export markets, Japanese policymakers were concerned that the United States was poised to exploit a late-mover advantage in this industry, accessing subsidized externalities that diffused beyond that country's borders. As a result, Japan waged a surprisingly restrained fight against an American industry left to fend for itself.

Chapter 6 revisits the scope of the book's theory, taking a brief look at three additional cases, including robotics, superconductors, and wheat. Robotics and superconductors are among the most widely anticipated commercial rivalries in high technology, the contours of which should be within reach of the book's theory. Wheat has also received attention in the strategic-trade literature, although this case is beyond the book's reach for reasons it can fully explain. Indeed, because the factors privileging national interest considerations in high-technology trade are not at work in this case, it shares little in common with any of the other cases in this study. The U.S.-Europe wheat rivalry is thus particularly instructive in gauging the scope of the book's theory.

Chapter 7 concludes by drawing out the book's more salient implications, assessing its limitations, and probing some of the policy prescriptions that follow.

2

The Argument

Why do states fight for national champions in some high-technology industries but not in others? Why do states invest more resources waging certain of these fights? And why, when they fight, do states sometimes cooperate with each other to ease trade tensions but at other times not? The book argues that states fight for national champions in industries exhibiting external benefits that other domestic industries can make use of, that they fight harder where these benefits tend not to diffuse beyond national borders, and that they are more likely to seek to ease trade tensions where both sides are made worse off as a result of these strategic-trade policies. In short, the book explains when commercial rivalries in high technology are likely to heat up, how these commercial rivalries are likely to unfold, and which ones are likely to be brought back from the brink of a trade war.

This chapter is in two parts. The first section explains and operationalizes the argument and takes up issues of evidence and case selection. The next section offers a competing explanation drawn from endogenous protection theory, and details hypotheses with a claim on each of the case studies presented in the chapters that follow.

THE CALCULUS OF STRATEGIC TRADE

In explaining why states might intervene on behalf of their national champions in high technology, scholars focus either on *rents* or *externalities*. Rents are returns to an input in excess of what that same input could earn in another activity.[1] They entail "supernormal" profits that persist because various market imperfections keep them from being competed away by would-be entrants. Rents figure prominently in most accounts of strategic trade.[2] To exploit these market imperfections, and capture the rents at stake, national champions are expected to demand export and (or) R&D subsidies from their elected representatives who, in turn, are expected to act on the demands of politically influential firms, looking for rewards at the ballot box. Moreover, where firms compete over output (rather than price), these export or R&D subsidies can potentially more than pay for themselves, the upshot being that, much like an optimal tariff, this type of protectionism may be profitable. The logic is that these subsidies not only help a firm increase exports or perform more R&D, but gain a scale advantage over unsubsidized firms abroad who, by lowering their own output in response, fall further behind in these increasing-returns industries. In this way, protectionism might yield dividends well into the future.

This account takes its cues from a model by James Brander and Barbara Spencer, and informs much of the strategic-trade literature.[3] Though intriguing, the model, like most of the studies it inspires, says little about the prospects for foreign retaliation. Rather, critics and proponents alike tend to interpret strategic-trade rivalries as Prisoner's Dilemma (PD) games, taking the risk of foreign retaliation as given.[4] Under threat of a trade war, a state would thus either have to be irrational (i.e., in a single-shot or finitely iterated PD) or optimistic about its chances for cooperating with a trade rival on subsidy levels (i.e., in an infinitely iterated PD) to fight for its national champions. Put another way, strategic-trade policy would either have to be a mistake, or nonconflictual. The evidence paints a rather different picture. Why this gap between theory and practice?

In reflecting on what the literature has had to say about his model, Brander provides an important clue. Pointing to the real-world practice of strategic-trade policy, he argues that it is "naïve" to take foreign retaliation as given, since this fails to "address the question of what to do in the face of existing predatory policies by other countries, and fails to take account of the *basic incentive structure of the international environment*."[5] With this as its point of departure, the book argues that the PD is not the only or even necessarily the most accurate depiction of strategic-trade policy preferences. Rather, the book anticipates the contours of five different strategic-trade rivalries, some of which are expected to give rise to heated trade wars, others to one-sided battles or to no battle at all. To get beyond the PD, the book develops a supply-side argument about externalities, offering a demand-side argument about rents as a competing explanation.

Externalities come in two types: *linkages* and *spillovers.*[6] A linkage externality arises where interdependencies between upstream and downstream industries yield benefits that are undervalued by the market. Demand for an input by a downstream industry may help an upstream industry achieve scale economies, for example, such that the returns to this transaction would not be fully market-mediated. Linkage externalities figure centrally in accounts of increasing-returns competition, since trade in inputs helps upstream industries exploit scale efficiencies and pass on savings downstream. The relationship between the semiconductor and computer industries is a case in point. Greater demand for memories on the part of the computer industry helps semiconductor firms by more than the amount tallied by the market, because cost reductions owing to aggregate output are substantial in chip manufacturing. States might thus be expected to fight for those national champions anchoring these upstream-downstream relationships, seeking to ensure that important linkage externalities are not undersupplied.

Spillover externalities arise when the "know-how" embedded in products, processes, or management skills cannot be fully appropriated by those who invest in them. Referred to as "pure" or technology externalities, they reflect the gap between the private and social returns to investing in R&D.[7] Along these lines, the semiconductor industry tends to underinvest in R&D as viewed from the perspective of the computer industry, in that returns at the device level are largely realized at the systems level.[8] States might thus subsidize a national champion invested in R&D promising returns for wide sectors of the economy, particularly one deterred from making a more "socially" optimal investment by subsidized competitors abroad.

This setup implies that strategic-trade policy reflects "national interest" considerations, as opposed to interest group politics. In sponsoring a more optimal supply of linkage and spillover externalities, the assumption, in other words, is that decisions for strategic-trade policy are reached *as if* by a rational unitary state seeking to maximize its national welfare gains. Put another way, the state is assumed to order its preferences hierarchically and to choose that option holding out the highest expected payoff. By "black boxing" the state, the book is able to provide a more cogent account of the contours of different strategic-trade rivalries. Of course, whether strategic-trade policies are more in line with the national interest than with interest group politics is an empirical question. Chapters 3 through 6 offer evidence with which to make this assessment, as well as hypotheses about interest group politics to contrast with the book's argument. Still, there are two reasons why it is useful to treat the state as a rational unitary actor in theorizing about externalities and strategic trade, even if the assumption is oftentimes less useful in theorizing about protectionism more generally, or about industrial policy.[9]

First, political scientists and economists widely agree that correcting for failures of the market is one of the most axiomatic functions that states perform, and that in this respect, concern for aggregate welfare prevails over distributional politics.[10] Likewise, the undersupply of linkage and spillover externalities affords the state a compelling interest in high-technology trade, advancing the cause of a national constituency, rather than acting at the behest of firms flush with political clout. Indeed, concern for market failure, which goes hand in hand with a focus on externalities, helps distinguish the book's theory of strategic trade from more general theories of protectionism, and narrows its scope, a point taken up more fully in Chapter 6.

Second, the market imperfections characteristic of high-technology industries help bring the risk of foreign retaliation more sharply into focus, since firms and the states that subsidize them compete directly with each other, rather than against world prices. Most studies of protectionism explain patterns of tariffs or (less frequently) nontariff barriers in perfectly competitive industries, where overall market conditions, and not particular trade rivals, inform these decisions. The risk of foreign retaliation, which tends to privilege the state in economic (and security) issues, is thus far less salient in theories of protectionism more generally. Similarly, because industrial policy typically involves measures aimed at infrastructure or nontraded industries, the threat of foreign retaliation does not discipline these initiatives, in this way leaving considerable latitude for "pork barrel" politics.

For these two reasons, the rational unitary actor assumption is useful in thinking about externalities and the incentive for states to intervene or retaliate on behalf of their national champions. These, after all, are the most important pieces of the puzzle, pieces that have long eluded the literature on strategic-trade policy.

Independent Variables

To get at these pieces of the puzzle, the book's theory builds up from two independent variables, referred to as the potential for a state's economy to *consume* and *internalize* the externalities exhibited by a national champion.

The *consumption* variable taps whether an economy is sufficiently primed to gain from the external benefits exhibited by a national champion. The intuition behind this variable is that the payoff to helping a national champion depends on whether industries upstream or downstream are in place to anchor the relevant linkage externalities and, in doing so, share in the spillover externalities that follow in their wake. First, and most obvious, a presence upstream and (or) downstream is required to participate in the relevant linkage externalities. For example, if widgets are made from carbon composites, and there are no domestic vendors upstream in advanced materials, then there will be little opportunity to exploit this linkage externality, lessening the returns to fighting for the widget industry. Moreover, spillover externalities are likely to prove elusive in this case as well, since technological know-how tends to diffuse among suppliers and end users independently engaged in complementary R&D.[11]

Linkage and spillover externalities are seldom paired in this way. Observers routinely focus more on the former than the latter, not least because upstream-downstream relations leave a more explicit paper trail for doing empirical research. Some of this literature even taps the intuition behind the consumption variable, insisting that a presence upstream and downstream encourages states to target specific industries for strategic-trade policy.[12] Spillover externalities, on the other hand, have not received the same kind of systematic treatment. Rather, they more often get play where predictions drawn from arguments about rents or (less frequently) linkage externalities fall short.[13] The problem is not that observers think spillover externalities unimportant. Rather, the challenge is to find proxies with which to evaluate *how* important they are. Interestingly, some clues to this question can be had by tracing the more observable fingerprints left by linkage externalities.

A considerable amount of econometric evidence suggests that regions experiencing so-called Silicon Valley effects tend to be populated by industries independently pursuing similar R&D.[14] This is a provocative finding, not least because it challenges widely held beliefs about the role technology plays in sparking economic growth and competitiveness. What appears to be happening is that by independently engaging in complementary R&D, related industries build up "absorptive capacity," by which the Organisation for Economic Co-operation and Development (OECD) means the skills to adopt, assimilate, and employ the technology exhibited by a source industry.[15] The big picture is that related industries do *not* ride entirely for free, "reverse-engineering" at zero cost what a national champion produces, or exploiting the know-how that leaks beyond a national champion's doors. Quite the opposite – the less R&D these related industries do on their own, the lower will be the return to locating near an externality-exhibiting industry. This suggests, more generally, that these spillover externalities do not reach as widely throughout the economy as is often thought but that, instead, they follow in the path of linkage externalities, given that industries upstream and downstream are more likely to be independently invested in similar R&D, feeding different parts of the high-technology "food chain." By tracing the flow of linkage externalities, we thus get a better sense for where to look for spillover externalities and, in the process, uncover more overt benchmarks with which to gauge their importance. In this regard, the book's theory offers a window on spillover externalities by giving pride of place to linkage externalities.

Piecing this together, the import of the consumption variable is evident in a variety of works tapping a similar theme. In a study comparing Silicon Valley's success through the 1980s versus Route 128's relative stagnation, for example, Annalee Saxenian stresses the importance of agglomeration effects, but points out that technology sharing is more likely among firms with the skills and resources to learn from others.[16] Studies of the impact of National Aeronautics and Space Administration (NASA) facilities on regional economies across the United States similarly find that areas populated by firms with complementary R&D interests thrive in their presence.[17] Finally, the logic of the consumption variable is evident in the concerns voiced by industry about public R&D in general. In testimony before the Subcommittee on Science, for example, a representative of the Ford Motor Company explained that "the auto industry has found it difficult to *absorb* technology from the National Laboratories."[18] This comment goes to the very heart of the consumption variable.

The logic of the consumption variable plays out internationally as it does domestically. Recent studies indicate, for example, that levels of domestic R&D influence the degree to which trading nations are likely to benefit from foreign R&D, with important implications for North-South trade, in particular.[19] These findings challenge the view that technology diffusion benefits developed or developing states at little cost to themselves, or that "late industrializers" get a free ride on the R&D performed by others. Rather, related firms and industries must independently pursue complementary R&D in order to make sense of the products, processes, and management skills to which they are exposed, and to employ this know-how in turn. The consumption variable thus offers a first cut at the list of national champions for which a state might fight. *A state is more likely to intervene or retaliate on behalf of national champions in industries exhibiting externalities that can be consumed, all other things equal.*

In operationalizing the consumption variable, the first step is to map out the national champion's industry and identify the flow of inputs and outputs upstream and downstream. A domestic presence upstream and (or) downstream is crucial in this respect, such that these industries might anchor the linkage externalities at stake. The greater this volume in trade in inputs and (or) outputs, the more likely industries upstream or downstream are to invest in complementary R&D to meet demand, and to keep pace with changes in specifications and standards, for example. Trade flows, world market shares, and R&D investment as a percentage of total sales are among the general metrics considered in making this assessment. Other sources tapped include reports and expert testimony on behalf of government agencies, firms, and business associations, interviews with managers, and data from financial institutions and from international organizations with a hand in monitoring patterns in trade protectionism.

The *internalization* variable taps whether these same external benefits diffuse beyond national borders. The intuition behind this variable is that states are likely to be reluctant to subsidize a national champion if the externalities that result help foreign firms as much as they do domestic ones.[20] Rather, the expectation is that, if externalities tend to diffuse internationally, states will "race to the bottom" in terms of their subsidy practices, looking to free-ride on each other's spending (so long as they are able to consume the externalities at stake).[21] The Congressional Budget Office explains it this way: "if these [high-technology] industries are to warrant governmental support, *their external benefits must accrue in disproportionate measure within national boundaries. To the extent that the benefits are shared internationally, the strategic nature of the industry diminishes.*"[22]

Why are some externalities largely nation-specific and others primarily international in scope? The consensus is that certain externalities are localized within a region or country where proximity to a source industry is essential for the purpose of "learning by doing." The complexity of design and production processes shapes patterns of this sort. The task of integrating large complex systems, for example, promotes tighter "clusters" than more standardized manufacturing, where common specifications and "off-the-shelf" inputs give rise to a different score on the internalization variable.[23] Along these lines, a concentration of knowledge often results where related firms and industries not only contribute "design-ins" for subsystems but have a hand in piecing these subsystems together. Historically, this has encouraged contractors to source locally, given the need to reengineer inputs through production, for example, and the incentive to stay with suppliers whose experience on past projects has moved them farther along their learning curve. As in the past, similar trends in certain industries today limit the extent to which trade extends the reach of these linkage and spillover externalities beyond national borders. Moreover, trade does not necessarily "internationalize" technology: the evidence suggests that spillovers are often slow to diffuse abroad, and that the know-how embodied in traded goods can be extremely difficult to tap by foreign competitors, for reasons having to do with the score on the consumption variable.[24] The internalization variable thus informs the levels at which a state might subsidize its national champions. *A state is more likely to invest greater resources fighting on behalf of national champions in industries exhibiting externalities that can be internalized, all other things equal.*

In operationalizing the internalization variable, there are several metrics with which to evaluate the diffusion of externalities beyond national borders. These include the share of imported inputs (with an emphasis on design-ins), the complexity and design intensity of production, the nature of corporate alliances, levels of foreign direct investment, and the share of R&D performed by national champions in export markets.[25] These metrics help to gauge the amount and quality of access that foreign firms have to the relevant linkage externalities, and the spillover externalities that follow in their path. Other sources include studies by government agencies, business groups, firms, and professional organizations charged with monitoring technology diffusion, as well as reports by experts in the field, interviews with managers, and the testimony of those lobbying both for and against strategic-trade policy.

Before proceeding, the book's theory makes three simplifying assumptions. First, the independent variables are treated as though they were dichotomous: that is, externalities can be consumed or not, and internalized or not. Although both variables are more accurately continuous, this simplifying assumption eases the presentation of the theory, and does not deprive it of explanatory leverage, since the objective is to predict *qualitative* differences in the strategic-trade policies of states. Second, and for somewhat obvious reasons, it is assumed that a state cannot internalize those externalities it cannot consume. Indeed, the factors contributing to the localization of externalities are doubtful to be at work where an absence of industries upstream or downstream places these external benefits beyond reach. Third, if both states can consume the externalities at issue, they must also realize the same score on the internalization variable. This symmetry traces to the book's emphasis on the underlying technologies and the means by which they diffuse (or not), as opposed to any "technonationalist" policies that states might pursue to stem this diffusion, which are beyond the scope of the book.[26] More generally, the scores on the independent variables are taken as being exogenous, meaning that *states do not invest in a capacity to consume or internalize these externalities.* This tack is theoretically necessary in the sense that, if this part of the story was endogenized, the book's argument would be unfalsifiable.

Dependent Variable

The dependent variable concerns the strategic-trade policies practiced by the two rival states. In other words, the unit of analysis is the state-state dyad. States fight with export and (or) R&D subsidies. In order to get a sense not only for whether states fight, but with what investment of resources, three outcomes on the dependent variable are posited along a continuum of subsidy levels, from *full intervention* (F) through *limited intervention* (L) to *nonintervention* (N). Full intervention involves the highest level of subsidies and is aimed at helping national champions gain market share at the expense of foreign rivals. Limited intervention, on the other hand, involves moderate subsidy levels, and is intended to help national champions gain or maintain a foothold in an industry. Last, nonintervention involves withholding subsidies from national champions, leaving their fate to the market. Few studies present nonintervention as a strategic-trade *policy*, rather than as a failure of strategic trade per se.[27] The book's theory and case studies reveal why it is essential to do so.

These are qualitative and not quantitative distinctions; the point is to draw attention to the objectives of the strategic-trade policies implemented. Each of the case study chapters provides data on subsidies and codes the dependent variable in light of the economics of that industry. This is necessary because the same investment in subsidies in one industry may accomplish less in another, given differences in the costs of production, for example. To round out the analysis of the dependent variable, the case study chapters also examine the political debates over strategic-trade policy, looking to understand how states weighed their options, and why they acted as they did.

Two final points about the dependent variable. First, states need not practice the same strategic-trade policy. Indeed, a central claim of the book is that not all of the cooperation problems that strategic trade gives rise to are symmetrical. Second, the book follows convention in defining *cooperation* as policy adjustments on the part of rival states to realize a mutually preferable (Pareto-superior) outcome, where the equilibrium they would otherwise reach falls short in this respect.[28]

Strategic-Trade Rivalries

To begin, we can match up the independent and dependent variables in thinking about state *preferences* for strategic trade, which in turn feed into the story about strategic-trade *outcomes*. Recalling the three simplifying assumptions, the independent variables pair up in anticipating the *maximum* level of subsidies states would prefer to supply their national champions, as depicted in Figure 2.1.

The logic behind these strategic-trade policy preferences is straightforward: the level at which a state may be willing to subsidize its national champions depends on the extent to which it can appropriate its return on investment. The consumption variable offers a first cut at this. If a state cannot consume the externalities that result, then it will not spend on subsidies (lower left corner). If a state *can* consume these externalities, attention turns to the internalization variable. Subsidy levels will be lower if these external benefits diffuse beyond national borders (upper left corner) than if they are national in scope (upper right corner), all other things equal.

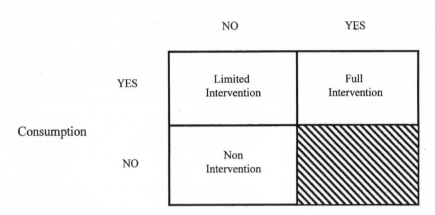

Figure 2.1 Strategic-trade policy preferences.

The next step is to move from preferences to outcomes by bringing the "strategic" part of the story back in. Working with two dichotomous independent variables, and keeping in mind the three simplifying assumptions noted earlier, the book's theory predicts *five* different strategic-trade rivalries. Figure 2.2, which pairs the competing states, gives an overview of these strategic-trade rivalries.

Figure 2.2 reveals a more interesting picture of strategic-trade policy than the one painted by critics or proponents. On the one hand, the book predicts more state intervention than critics would have us expect. On the other hand, the book predicts more variation across these rivalries than proponents suggest, and even predicts nonintervention in the absence of threats of foreign retaliation. Take the four rivalries in which intervention is expected: in two cases, one state concedes the industry (the Predation and Cautious Activist games), while in the other two, a trade war arises, one involving overspending (the Beggar-Thy-Neighbor PD), the other underspending (the Favor-Thy-Neighbor PD). Finally, the fifth rivalry (the Free Market game) reveals a case in which competing states have incentive to leave the fate of their national champions to the market. The big picture is that the risk of foreign retaliation is *not* a constant, *not* always a deterrent to strategic trade, and *not* the only explanation for nonintervention. Predictions concerning how these five rivalries are expected to unfold can be drawn from the simple game models that follow.

STATE B

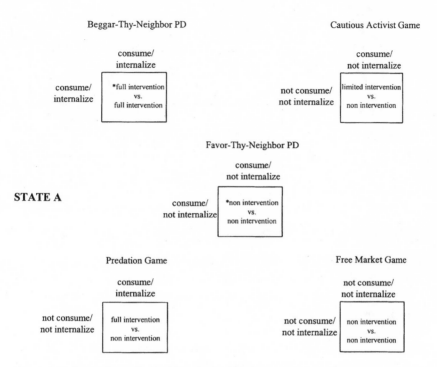

Figure 2.2. Strategic-trade rivalries. Asterisk indicates Pareto suboptimal.

Beggar-Thy-Neighbor PD. Both states can consume and internalize the industry's externalities. Most observers have this case in mind in thinking about high-technology trade wars among the advanced industrial states. The decision variable for both states concerns whether to practice full or limited intervention. Nonintervention is "dominated" out since neither state wishes to do without the more optimal level of externalities that their economies are primed to consume. Each state prefers to practice full intervention if the other limits its subsidies, thus gaining market share at the other's expense. Each state also prefers not to be on the losing side of this scenario. And finally, both states prefer mutually restrained to mutually unrestrained spending, as in Figure 2.3.

To avert a trade war, which in this case involves a race to the top over subsidies, states may negotiate a ceiling to cap spending, so long as they do not overly discount the future. States may well disagree over the specifics of a given subsidy ceiling, since different caps entail different

State B

		N	L	F
	N	3,3	2,8	1,9
State A	L	8,2	6,6	4,7
	F	9,1	7,4	(5,5)

Figure 2.3. Beggar-Thy-Neighbor PD.

distributions of private gain, leading to conflict along the Pareto frontier.[29] These issues are taken up in detailing the U.S.-Europe civil aircraft rivalry in Chapter 3.

Favor-Thy-Neighbor PD. Both states can consume but cannot internalize the industry's externalities. This is the case observers have in mind in arguing that states might respond to foreign subsidies with a "note of thanks."[30] The decision variable concerns whether to practice limited intervention or nonintervention. Full intervention is dominated out, given the diffusion of the externalities at stake in this commercial rivalry. Nonintervention involves *free riding*: each state prefers for the other to incur the cost of sponsoring these externalities. Limited intervention, on the other hand, entails contributing to an *international* public good in light of the scope of the external benefits exhibited. Each state prefers to practice nonintervention if the other practices limited intervention, and not to be on the losing side of this scenario. Each state also prefers for both to practice limited intervention, as opposed to nonintervention, since these states would rather not forgo externalities that they can consume. This game is as shown in Figure 2.4.

To avert a trade war, which in this case involves a race to the bottom over subsidies, states may negotiate a subsidy floor to increase spending above a certain level. This may involve establishing property rights in

State B

		N	L	F
	N	3,3	8,2	9,1
State A	L	2,8	6,6	7,4
	F	1,9	4,7	5,5

Figure 2.4. Favor-Thy-Neighbor PD.

the form of market shares, for example. Allocating property rights no doubt involves a distributional conflict over private gain, but given the temptation to free-ride on each other's subsidies, concern for market failure may prove to be the greater obstacle to cooperation in this case. These issues are taken up in Chapter 4, which presents the U.S.-Japan semiconductor rivalry in a new light.

Free Market Game. Neither state can consume or internalize the industry's externalities. There is more to this case than meets the eye. The expectation is that both states practice nonintervention, an intriguing prediction for two reasons. First, externalities do not carry sway in this case because neither state boasts an economy primed to make use of them. Most studies imply that externalities are an across-the-board justification for strategic trade, although the Free Market game sets out conditions under which not just one, but both states choose to leave the fate of their national champions to the market. Second, these states are expected to practice nonintervention despite the absence of any threat of foreign retaliation. Many studies suggest that foreign retaliation is the only deterrent to strategic trade, and yet the Free Market game sets out conditions under which both states stay out of this commercial rivalry, given their score on the consumption variable. Figure 2.5 presents the Free Market game.

State B

		N	L	F
	N	(7,7)	8,4	9,1
State A	L	4,8	5,5	6,2
	F	1,9	2,6	3,3

Figure 2.5. The Free Market game.

State B

		N	L	F
	N	3,9	2,6	1,3
State A	L	7,8	6,5	4,2
	F	(9,7)	8,4	5,1

Figure 2.6. The Predation game.

Predation Game. State A can both consume and internalize the industry's externalities, whereas State B cannot consume or internalize these externalities. State A's decision variable is whether to practice limited or full intervention against a foreign rival lacking any incentive to fight for the industry, as in Figure 2.6.

This is the case that generated so much interest in strategic-trade theory but seemed so unrealistic in a world of strategic states – unrealistic, that is, because states are assumed to be unwilling to concede industries to trade rivals abroad, not least where externalities are thought to be at stake. The Predation game suggests otherwise; foreign retaliation makes little sense where investing in a national champion holds out little return for upstream or downstream industries. On the one hand, critics might be content that of the five strategic-trade rivalries anticipated by the book, this is the only case in which a state subsidizes its national champions so lavishly, and with impunity. On the other hand, proponents might be satisfied to find even a single case of this sort.

Cautious Activist Game. State A can consume but cannot internalize the industry's externalities, whereas State B cannot consume or internalize these externalities. Both states must decide whether to practice limited intervention versus nonintervention. In contrast to the Favor-Thy-Neighbor PD, only State A has an incentive to fight for its national champions. Yet State A is in a bind: if it could internalize the industry's externalities, it would practice full intervention; if State B could consume these externalities, it would practice limited intervention. Because neither policy is within reach here, State A most prefers to practice limited intervention if State B follows suit, gaining market share and benefiting from State B's subsidies as well. Notice that the difference between this game and the Favor-Thy-Neighbor PD is that free riding is no longer a viable option. The Cautious Activist game is presented in Figure 2.7.

State A least prefers to practice nonintervention if State B is similarly inclined, since this means forgoing a more optimal supply of externalities at home and the opportunity to benefit from State B's subsidies. State A also prefers limited intervention to nonintervention if State B practices nonintervention, rather than be caught practicing nonintervention if State B, in turn, follows suit.

For its part, State B most prefers to practice nonintervention if State A is so inclined, in which case its national champions get the industry's residual demand, and least prefers to incur the cost of subsidizing if State A practices nonintervention, since it would rather not fund externalities it cannot consume. State B also prefers to practice nonintervention if State A practices limited intervention, so that its national champions get the industry's residual demand (at a much lower cost than if State A practices nonintervention), rather than incur the cost of limited subsidies if State A follows suit.

State B

		N	L	F
	N	7,9	6,6	1,1
State A	L	(8,8)	9,7	3,2
	F	4,5	5,4	2,3

Figure 2.7. The Cautious Activist game.

Here, State A practices limited intervention, and State B nonintervention. Since State A cannot internalize the resulting benefits, though, State
B may benefit over time from its rival's subsidies. State A must concern
itself with the possibility that its interventionist impulses may backfire,
influencing State B's ability to consume the relevant externalities at some
point in the future. This game should appeal to cautious activists[31] because State A subsidizes at levels conducive to an agreement like the one
anticipated in the Favor-Thy-Neighbor PD, at least where State B can
one day consume, but not internalize, these externalities.

Case Selection

The merits of the book's argument are evaluated through a series of case
studies. This is an appropriate methodology for gauging whether different states have consistently held to the book's expectations across industries and over time. Since selection bias would do much to undermine
this effort, it is important to be clear on the criteria with which certain
case studies were chosen over others. Three criteria held sway in selecting
civil aircraft, semiconductors, and high-definition television as the book's
main case studies. First, the industries had to be *imperfectly competitive,*
with *output* the main decision variable. This criterion is a useful re-
minder that the book's theory speaks to a small subset of commercial
rivalries in the global economy. In particular, these imperfections, in-

cluding steep learning curves, large economies of scale and scope, and high fixed costs of production, limit entry into the industry and insulate rents, such that firms – and the states that subsidize them – compete directly with each other, rather than against world prices. In this respect, high technology, which is typically defined in terms of R&D as a percentage of sales, is widely offered as a shorthand for imperfect competition more generally, although expectations for spillovers, beyond the linkages in increasing-returns industries, tend to distinguish definitions of high technology more specifically.[32] Where competition centers over output, moreover, export and R&D subsidies can result in a net national welfare gain at the expense of a trade rival, tying the cases back to the Brander-Spencer insight, which informs the puzzle of strategic trade.

Second, the industries had to be *commercially viable*. This criterion touches on two related concerns. The first concern was to select industries that are primarily commercial, as opposed to being strictly of military significance, since issues of defense preparedness and alliance commitments might afford certain states a greater incentive to fight for their national champions. The second concern was to select industries that promise products in the marketplace, rather than simply basic science. Indeed, where commercial applications are unlikely, more general arguments about externalities would win out over arguments about rents by default.

Third, there had to be sufficient data on the industries, particularly with respect to technology diffusion and government subsidies. The three main case studies span several decades for Japan, Europe, and the United States, offering ample opportunity to assess the book's argument against the claims of the competing explanation.

In the end, however, three case studies do not constitute a full test of the theory. Since the book's dependent variable concerns the strategic-trade policies of the *two* rival states, the cases *do* provide more information than would be true if the goal was simply to explain the protectionist practices of one or the other. Moreover, each chapter offers a case within a case, explaining the strategic-trade policies of states on the sidelines of these commercial rivalries, and Chapter 6 briefly sketches three additional case studies, covering industries that the theory should be expected to explain, as well as an industry it should not be expected to explain. Still, the book can claim only to provide a partial test, setting the stage for further research.

THE COMPETING EXPLANATION

Endogenous protection theory offers some useful building blocks with which to piece together a competing explanation. Cast at either a national or sectoral level, it argues that elected officials act on *demands* for protection (including subsidies) in order to maximize their electoral fortunes, especially when these demands are made by industries flush with political capital.[33] This story is the basis for claims that states "can't pick winners," since electoral concerns, rather than the national interest, are expected to cloud the judgment of policymakers. In measuring an industry's electoral clout, four variables are emphasized in the literature: employment size, geographic concentration, political dispersion, and industrial concentration.[34] Employment size speaks to the *number* of votes that an industry might potentially deliver. The challenge is that lobbying requires that firms overcome the collective action problem inherent in making demands for protection. Geographically concentrated industries may have greater success monitoring and sanctioning firms that free-ride on the lobbying efforts of others (where transaction costs fall with spatial proximity), and thus be likely to deliver on the votes they promise. Politically dispersed industries, in turn, are likely to have more representatives pleading their case the more spread out they are across electoral districts. Finally, firms in more concentrated industries – that is, those in which market share is disproportionately held by only a few vendors – are especially likely to invest in lobbying, since they capture a larger share of the rents secured through protection. These four variables, drawn from endogenous protection theory, serve to ground the competing explanation in an interest group politics model of strategic trade.

Two questions still need to be addressed in setting out the competing explanation: why subsidies over tariffs or nontariff barriers? And why would a subsidized industry ask for an international agreement limiting their levels? Helen Milner's account of how a firm's export-dependence and multinationality shape its preferences on trade policy offers some important clues.[35] First, these industries, which depend on foreign sales, are likely to ask for subsidies over tariffs or nontariff barriers, in that their reliance on offshore operations for important inputs undermines the logic of an "import protection as export promotion" strategy.[36] Under the threat of foreign retaliation, however, these export-dependent and multinational firms are likely to favor international agreements on subsidy levels, looking to avert a trade war, and the loss of market access abroad. This logic helps round out the competing explanation, giving it the building blocks to contest the book's account of the case studies that follow.

CONCLUSION

This chapter has explained and operationalized the book's theory, discussed issues that pertain to evidence and case selection, and provided a competing explanation grounded in the basics of endogenous protection theory. In the chapters that follow, the relative merits of the book's argument, as against the competing explanation, are evaluated in explaining the commercial rivalries in civil aircraft, semiconductors, and high-definition television, as well as in robotics, superconductors, and wheat. The book concludes by drawing out the more salient implications of the argument, assessing the theory's limitations, and deriving several policy prescriptions that follow.

3

●━●

The Civil Aircraft Rivalry

The civil aircraft industry is the stuff of legends. The cost and complexity of building a large commercial airplane sets this industry apart from most others, so much so that the Boeing Company would likely enjoy a monopoly were it not for Europe's efforts to overrule the market.[1] Unwilling to concede this commercial rivalry to the Americans, the four Airbus states have spent lavishly on their national champions, battling for market share in an industry that is widely regarded as the "crown jewel" of high technology. Incumbency, however, has hardly bred apathy on the part of the United States, since even Boeing "bets the store" on each new airplane. Governments on both sides of the Atlantic have, in fact, invested greater resources fighting for civil aircraft than for most other high-technology industries. Yet both sides have also gone out of their way to negotiate agreements to bring this commercial rivalry back from the brink of a trade war. This chapter seeks to explain why.

In the aftermath of World War II, numerous firms entered the market for civil aircraft. Military contractors readily diversified into commercial production, given commonalties in design. The economics of a maturing airline industry changed all this: carriers needed low-maintenance airplanes capable of servicing routes at home and abroad, whereas the military placed increasing emphasis on "performance at all cost." One implication of this greater product differentiation was that civil aircraft firms were less able to count on the "spin-offs" from the military side of the business to ease their financial burden. Exit from the industry was inevitable, though U.S. firms had a considerable leg up on their rivals in Europe. First, the "Buy America" Act limited the access of European firms to the world's largest market, enabling U.S. firms to build up economies of scale and scope from behind protectionist walls. Second, trade barriers within the European Community (EC) further complicated efforts to match U.S. production efficiencies, curtailing the sales of national champions beyond their small domestic markets. Third, U.S. firms gained expertise doing systems integration work on military and space projects, the size and complexity of which were seldom matched in Europe. Several EC consortia were meant to even things out, but not until Airbus – a consortium made up of firms from Britain, France, Germany, and Spain – did Europe set out to compete for every segment of the civil aircraft market, thereby remaking the landscape of the industry.

The Boeing-Airbus competition receives a great deal of attention in the strategic-trade literature. This chapter argues, however, that the literature cannot tell the story it hopes to with the theoretical building blocks it favors. Most notably, it is difficult to blame Boeing or Airbus for the heated tone of this commercial rivalry. Rather, the states involved bear most of the responsibility for escalating this dispute, but also much of the credit for bringing it back from the brink of a trade war. The chapter's argument is that civil aircraft exhibits externalities that the United States and Europe can *consume and internalize*, giving rise to incentive for both sides to practice full intervention on behalf of their national champions. Indeed, the chapter provides some of the first direct evidence bearing on this temptation. Yet threats of escalation, and fear of a trade war, have motivated the United States and Europe to negotiate a number of agreements covering trade in civil aircraft, most notably the 1992 Large Civil Aircraft (LCA) agreement, which curbs direct and indirect subsidies. The literature is surely right that the Prisoner's Dilemma (PD) provides insights into this commercial rivalry, but only because the governments involved, rather than their national champions, have called the shots, and because externalities, rather than votes, are the currency of this strategic-trade rivalry.

The competing explanation also has a strong hold on this case study. The basics of the argument are that civil aircraft firms demand export and (or) R&D subsidies to help them capture rents in this highly imperfect industry, and that policymakers act accordingly with an eye to gaining the industry's votes. In gauging the electoral clout of the civil aircraft industry, the variables of interest include its employment size, geographic concentration, political dispersion, and industrial concentration. There is a lot of mileage to be had from these variables, and yet they come up short. To be sure, the civil aircraft industry in the United States and Europe employs a relatively small number of highly skilled workers concentrated in a handful of geographic regions and political districts. The industry thus does not boast a lot of votes, although it *is* likely to deliver on the votes it promises, since spatial proximity eases the collective action problem inherent in lobbying for protectionism, and political dispersion increases the number of voices the industry enjoys in the legislature. Finally, given the merger of Boeing and McDonnell Douglas, the degree of industrial concentration in civil aircraft – more so than perhaps in any other high technology industry – ensures high returns to lobbying for subsidies. In spite of all this, however, the competing explanation's neglect of the supply side leads it astray. Seldom deterred from acting unilaterally, governments on both sides of the Atlantic have waged this commercial rivalry with passion, often over the objections of the industry itself. In fact, the evidence makes clear that, had firms been the ones calling the shots, this commercial rivalry would have unfolded rather differently. The book's theory helps fill in these gaps where the competing explanation is found wanting.

This chapter proceeds as follows: the first section explains why civil aircraft is within reach of strategic-trade theory, detailing the imperfections of this industry; the second section scores the independent variables; and the third takes up the dependent variable and evaluates whether the book's theory offers a more useful interpretation of this case study than the competing explanation.

THE ECONOMICS OF CIVIL AIRCRAFT

Few industries are as imperfectly competitive as civil aircraft. Would-be entrants face a host of seemingly insurmountable barriers, while even the industry's incumbent, seldom shy of 60% world market share over the past few decades, runs the risk of financial ruin with each new launch. As one influential U.S. government report puts it, "[t]he essential message is that economic failure is the norm in the civil aircraft business."[2] The challenge to doing business in the civil aircraft industry is to exploit sizable learning effects, scale and scope economies, and contend with the high fixed costs of production, both with respect to capital and R&D outlays. These market imperfections are taken up in turn.

The learning curve figures prominently in studies of the civil aircraft industry dating to the early 1930s. Evidence that direct labor costs fall with *cumulative* output is, to say the least, striking.[3] It is estimated, for example, that learning effects account for 80–90% of the reduction in unit costs owing to volume production.[4] Working with this 80% figure, for example, and indexing the number of man-hours required to build the first copy of an airplane at 100, the first 100 copies would average 35 man-hours, while the first 500 copies would average only 20 man-hours. Putting this into some perspective, the first Airbus A300 built in Germany took 340,000 man-hours, whereas the 87th copy was rolled out in 78,000 man-hours.[5] Similarly, whereas Deutsche Airbus required 25 days to complete wing joining on its first A321, the firm estimated that this task would take just 4 days with cumulative experience.[6] Longer production runs clearly help firms exploit these learning effects, and yet the problem is that few large civil aircraft have enjoyed long production runs. Only six models have ever reached the estimated break-even point of 600 sales, including the DC9, the MD80, the 707, 727, 737, and 747.[7] Some models are estimated to have lower break-even points (i.e., 350–400 copies), and even production just shy of these benchmarks can do much to ease cost pressures.[8] Still, in an industry in which failure is the norm, learning effects have been elusive on either side of the Atlantic.

Economies of scale are especially prominent in studies of civil aircraft manufacturing. It is estimated, for example, that for every doubling of *aggregate* output, unit costs fall by 20%.[9] Even lesser gains in production rates can make the difference between profit and financial ruin. In a joint venture with Boeing, for example, subcontractors from Italy and Japan had based their initial cost estimates on an average production rate of ten 767s per month. When production rates fell to two 767s per month, the financial well-being of this collaboration was called into question.[10] Examples along these lines have deterred other subcontractors from working with Boeing, pointing up the importance of scale economies in this industry.

The concern for economies of scale has also made "whitetails" a major issue in U.S.-Europe trade talks. Whitetails are airplanes built with no intended customer, a practice that the United States has long insisted has helped to keep Airbus's production rates high during periods of declining demand. In the mid-1980s, for example, Washington alleged that there were 24 whitetails on the tarmac in Toulouse, a charge the French conceded.[11] A decade later, Boeing's Lawrence Clarkson testified before a House committee that Airbus's production rates had held constant despite a sharp decline in global demand, and warned that "[t]he result could be the continued production of Airbus 'whitetails,' which will then be sold at bargain prices."[12] Airbus points out that airlines sometimes fail to come through on "firm orders," giving rise to accusations of this sort.[13] The bigger picture is that, were it not for the importance of scale economies in civil aircraft, whitetails would garner little attention in U.S.-EC trade talks.

Economies of scope receive surprisingly little attention in most analyses of the Boeing-Airbus rivalry. Instead, the standard account is that Airbus found an untapped market niche, entered with the A300, and built on its success with additional airplanes.[14] The A300 may well have given Airbus some breathing space, yet firms must necessarily offer a "family" of airplanes in order to be competitive. This is because the airlines standardize fleets to reduce operating costs – that is, by cross-certifying pilots and by cross-training maintenance staff – and therefore buy from firms with offerings across different segments of the market.[15] EC policymakers were certainly encouraged by market forecasts for "medium-sized" 120–290 seat airplanes, and the A300 filled this gap.[16] Yet, a year before delivering the first A300, the Airbus states had committed to offer a family of *five*.[17] This commitment, rather than the A300 per se, set Airbus apart from earlier EC projects, most notably the Concorde.[18] Indeed, lacking this commitment to launch a family of aircraft, Airbus would never have stirred the passion it has, testifying to the centrality of economies of scope in this industry.

Finally, the high fixed costs of production serve as one of the most formidable barriers to entry into the civil aircraft industry. Launch costs average $4–5 billion, and half this just for a derivative.[19] At the higher end of this scale, Boeing is estimated to have spent $7 billion taking the 777 from design through to flight testing, or roughly half the amount Airbus is projected to spend on the A3XX, an airplane that will challenge Boeing's "cash cow," the 747.[20] The percentage of sales devoted to R&D sheds considerable light on these figures: Boeing's outlays are 6–9%, but with the inclusion of related aerospace and public funds, this figure may be higher still.[21] Airbus estimated R&D as a percentage of sales at 6% for 1996, but expects a sharp increase in anticipation of the A3XX.[22] Capital investments in civil aircraft are also extraordinary. In 1992, for example, Boeing invested $3.6 billion in support of the 777, primarily for equipment.[23] Like Airbus, Boeing amortizes a share of these costs across commercial and military projects.[24] The need to do so is obvious when considering, for instance, that Boeing's combined investment in the 757 and 767 actually exceeded the firm's net worth.[25] Given that costs may not be recouped for 10–15 years, it is not surprising that one U.S. government report concludes that "launching a new aircraft is tantamount to *betting the entire net worth of the firm on a high risk venture, the rate of return for which may be no more than normally associated with risk-free securities.*"[26]

These market imperfections certainly bring civil aircraft within reach of strategic-trade theory, but tell us little about how this commercial rivalry might unfold. The sections that follow score the independent and dependent variables, shedding new light on the U.S.-Europe civil aircraft rivalry.

THE INDEPENDENT VARIABLES

This section examines the evidence bearing on the argument that the United States and Europe can *consume* and *internalize* the externalities exhibited by civil aircraft. More to the point, it analyzes upstream linkages to materials, design manufacturing equipment, and electronic subsystems (including avionics), and the spillovers that follow, including the systems-integration skills necessary to compete in other large complex industries, like commercial space and energy. This chapter, more generally, argues against the view that industries lobbying for trade assistance play the externalities "card" when all else fails, or that governments blindly act on these demands. Indeed, the evidence reveals that industry can hardly take credit for charging the policymaking process with talk of externalities, nor can policymakers be accused of accepting arguments of this sort on faith alone.

The Consumption Variable

The fight for civil aircraft has always and unambiguously been about externalities. As tensions between the United States and Europe escalated in the mid-1980s, United States Trade Representative (USTR) Ambassador Michael Smith warned a House subcommittee of the stakes at risk. Noting that "the civil aircraft industry has a ripple effect throughout major elements of one's economy, be it ours or the Airbus governments' economies . . . ," Smith went on to insist that "decisions about launch aid and things like that should not be taken lightly, either by the governments involved or by the industries involved."[27] It could hardly be said of Washington, however, that launch aid and "things like that" were taken lightly. Studies assessing the economic impact of civil aircraft on other parts of the economy have long afforded the industry pride of place in policy debates. Representative of this, a report by the National Research Council (NRC) concluded in no uncertain terms that "strength in [civil aircraft] technologies *diffuses throughout industry and contributes substantially to the overall strength and competitiveness of the U.S. economy.*"[28] Along much the same lines, a report prepared for the Department of Commerce argued that "it is possible that the greatest losses to the U.S. economy [resulting from Airbus competition] will come as a result of the loss of significant, beneficial spillover effects for sectors other than aviation as well as in the economy more generally."[29] The rest of this section gives these statements some teeth.

European policymakers have long made clear their intention to keep a foothold in civil aircraft because of the externalities that result.[30] Indeed, the industry is widely seen as an important source of cutting-edge technologies with applications throughout the economy. The Commission of the European Communities, for example, insists in a report that "the stakes are high and crucial to Europe's industrial and technological independence."[31] Similarly, one French official explained that "the money invested in Airbus represents a strategic commitment to maintain a . . . technologically important industry in Europe."[32] In much more dramatic terms, Airbus's director exclaimed that "[w]e are fighting for our children. If we don't have a place in high technology [then] we should be slaves to the Americans and our children will be slaves."[33] If this seems overly passionate, Germany's Independent Council of Economic Advisors lent a little weight to the underlying theme, issuing a report in the late 1980s that public spending on civil aircraft had benefited other economic sectors, and had helped slow the country's "brain drain" more generally.[34] The EC's Aeronautics Task Force identified the more salient externalities at stake, noting that "[c]omputational methods, systems integration, advanced structures and materials have all fed through into any number of advanced applications in hundreds of companies quite removed from aeronautics."[35] One European official put the matter more cogently than most, urging that Airbus is "a luxury we must have."[36] The obvious question is, why *this* particular luxury?

In tracking the variety of industries touched on by civil aircraft manufacturing, studies find their way from cookware to software to systems integration, and sample nearly everything in between.[37] The numbers are simply striking: between 1987 and 1991, Boeing's annual purchase of goods and services exceeded $10 billion from 5,000 suppliers representing all 50 states.[38] Chase Econometrics estimated in 1983 that an increase of $1 billion in sales of civil aircraft would result in a $6.5 billion gain in U.S. gross national product over nine years, a $3.7 billion cut in the federal deficit, and 148,400 full-time equivalent man-years of work, half of which would be registered by labor employed directly by the civil aircraft industry.[39] A more recent study prepared by the U.S. government estimates that each $1 billion increase in sales of civil aircraft leverages $2.31 billion in sales from other sectors, and that for every job created in the industry, 2.03 jobs arise elsewhere in the economy.[40]

By one estimate, 28 industries account for fully 85% of all the inputs used in building civil aircraft, 13 of which are categorized as manufacturing industries, including aircraft parts and equipment; radio and television communications equipment; semiconductors; aircraft engines and parts; electronic components; miscellaneous machinery; blast furnaces and steel mills; aluminum rolling and drawing; miscellaneous plastics; measuring and control instruments; special dies, tools, and accessories; screw machine products; and petroleum refining.[41] Of these, 3 industries account for over half of all direct inputs, including aircraft parts and equipment, radio and television communications equipment, and aircraft engines and parts. In turn, these 3 industries affect a wide variety of other economic sectors. If we return to the earlier example of an increase of $1 billion in civil aircraft sales, for example, 20% of the growth in output realized by these 3 industries would *not* go toward supporting these sales, instead amounting to cheaper inputs and outputs for other sectors of the economy.[42]

In scoring the consumption variable, U.S. and European policymakers thus emphasize the linkages and spillovers pertaining to aircraft parts and equipment, radio and television communications equipment, and aircraft engines and parts. Of the technologies chalked up under aircraft parts and equipment, advanced materials, such as ceramics, metals, and polymers, and the manifold fabrication processes used to work with these materials, are of particular importance. Linkage externalities tying civil aircraft to carbon composites and fiber-reinforced plastics, for example, and computer-aided design and manufacturing (CAD/CAM) equipment stand out in this regard. The aerospace industry – which includes civil and military aircraft, as well as satellites and rockets – is the largest end user of these technologies, and has played an important role in motivating vendors upstream to adopt them in turn, a trend especially pronounced in the case of CAD/CAM equipment.

Carbon composites and fiber-reinforced plastics are used to reduce the weight of the airplane's primary and secondary structures, traditionally made of conventional aluminum alloys. Given their strength-to-weight ratio, these materials are well suited to a variety of applications in other industries. Since 1972, aerospace has accounted for over two-thirds of U.S. output in these materials, and civil aircraft for most of this.[43] Much the same is true in Europe, not least because of Airbus's aggressive use of advanced materials. The A310, for example, was the first airplane with a secondary structure made entirely of composite materials, while the A300–600 and A320 introduced the first primary structures made of these materials.[44] This usage has leveraged economies of scale upstream and has opened opportunities for European suppliers of advanced materials more generally, bestowing a competitive edge in their own markets. EC vendors rival American and Japanese firms in global markets for high-grade fine ceramic powders and advanced fiber reinforcements, among other technologies, all of which find applications in products ranging from rocket nozzles to golf clubs. The United States enjoys the edge in some carbon composites and advanced ceramics, given what the Department of Commerce cites as "*[g]overnment's and industry's continuing commitment to aerospace.*"[45] Indeed, in the post–cold war period, civil aircraft will increasingly determine the competitiveness of countries in this upstream industry.

The reason civil aircraft makes such a difference for those doing business upstream in advanced materials is clear. First, composite materials manufacturers face a wide variety of application barriers, from cost considerations and life cycle confidence to their overall performance reliability.[46] Rising demand on the part of civil aircraft and aerospace firms more generally helps to smooth these obstacles and helps upstream vendors gain currency with other end users, like autos.[47] Indeed, analysts insist that many of these downstream applications would be in doubt, or years away, were it not for this demonstration effect and the cost reductions owing to this linkage externality. Working with advanced materials in piecing together complex systems further imposes a substantial burden on fabrication and testing equipment. To be sure, composite materials are more difficult to employ than are conventional materials, posing new engineering challenges and requiring a different set of process technologies. Testing designs for structural integrity and fatigue, for example, is an exacting task, involving specialized hardware and software, 2 of 28 industries with a hand in civil aircraft manufacturing. The design process is, itself, rather unique, requiring continuous upgrading through production and the integration of various inputs from many hundreds of tiers of subcontractors. CAD/CAM is one of the core process technologies at work in this effort. First debuting in the aerospace industry in the 1950s, CAD/CAM had, by the 1980s, won widespread acceptance among upstream suppliers as well, a trend that is widely credited with helping reduce the cost of a basic system from $1 million in 1960 to less than $10,000 by 1984.[48] In 1993, U.S. vendors supplied two-thirds of the world's demand for CAD/CAM and computer-aided engineering (CAE) equipment, a $2.5 billion market that leverages advances in three-dimensional modeling software and applications, for example, technologies with direct relevance for medical and media industries, among others.[49]

This linkage externality, not surprisingly, has long figured prominently in debates over strategic trade on both sides of the Atlantic. In the mid-1980s, the National Academy of Engineering (NAE) found that design capabilities and supporting infrastructure were comparable in the United States and in Europe, and that the relative "[e]ase of access by foreigners to CAD/CAM hardware and software . . . assures that the European and Japanese aerospace industries can stay competitive in this technology in the future."[50] U.S. civil aircraft firms have tended to utilize CAD/CAM more than their European rivals, the implication being that this know-how is not fully bundled with the equipment.[51] France's Aerospatiale, for example, conceded in 1992 that it lagged Boeing in its use of CAD/CAM, insisting that it tended "to do design on tools that [the firm has] mastered."[52] Computer simulation is also more widely used by U.S. firms, stimulating developments in parallel processing and related software applications.[53] With more design work being done on the computer, the "paperless" airplane has put computer-aided software engineering (CASE) and the like on the map. In the United States, for example, 22% of CASE is expected to be utilized by aerospace firms, the implication being that competitiveness in this upstream industry will largely depend on competitiveness downstream in civil aircraft.[54] Linkages like this carry considerable weight with policymakers on both sides of the Atlantic, giving civil aircraft top billing in U.S.-EC trade talks.

Radio and television equipment includes the electronic subsystems and avionics that draw so much attention to civil aircraft manufacturing. Navigational systems are among these technologies, with applications in a variety of industries, like telecommunications.[55] Much of what is referred to as avionics falls under this category. Though hard to define precisely across firms, Boeing generally defines avionics as technologies bracketed under flight controls and management systems, communications and navigation systems, and electrical and engine controls.[56] Through its R&D, the National Aeronautics and Space Administration (NASA) has helped sponsor gains on each front, the payoffs to which have been realized across wide sectors of the American economy.[57] One key linkage externality binds navigational technologies upstream with civil aircraft. Sensors and satellite-based communications, for example, are used by the naval and auto industries, among others. As the Department of Commerce insists, employment of these navigational tools elsewhere in the economy "follows trends in the aircraft industry."[58] In light of the role of civil aircraft as a key end user of these technologies, states tend to look closely at the industry, particularly since the resulting spillovers generally do not leak out beyond national borders, as will be explained later.

Finally, aircraft engines and parts include the propulsion technologies used in building the "power plants" that lift the airplane off the ground, including technologies of interest to the naval and auto industries. At issue are the various cooling and heating and exhaust systems, pumps, lubricants, and related component parts. The aircraft engine industry has realized remarkable gains in productivity. Advances owe to the use of light materials and other developments that make possible more than 100,000 pounds of thrust, an extraordinary feat when considering the first jet engine's 480 pounds of thrust, and a hunch at that time that engines would not surpass 10,000 pounds of thrust.[59] In 1989, General Electric and Pratt and Whitney combined for over 80% of world orders for aircraft engines, with Rolls Royce tallying much of the rest.[60] France's SNECMA, as well as some European and Japanese firms, also compete in this upstream industry. Interestingly, joint ventures have been on the rise since the late 1980s, as vendors seek out risk-sharing partners to help shoulder the costs of development. Yet, as the U.S. International Trade Commission explains in a study, "U.S. partners *do not believe* that such partnerships transfer important technology that affects their competitive edge."[61] This, of course, begs a closer look at the score on the internalization variable.

As the rivalry in civil aircraft heated up through the mid-1980s, two prominent studies shed light on the consumption variable, focusing attention on the relative standing of U.S. and European firms in aircraft parts and equipment, radio and television communications equipment, and aircraft engines and parts. First, a widely circulated study by the NAE studied the competitive landscape in the areas of aerodynamics, flight controls, advanced systems, avionics, and propulsion. It found the United States to be ahead in aerodynamics and avionics, but concluded that Europe was equal to the task in these other fields.[62] Second, a report by the Department of Commerce compared U.S. and European strengths in aircraft engines and parts, among other technologies. It found U.S. firms to be ahead in engines and engine manufacturing, though not by much.[63] European agencies generally concurred, as did the Airbus members themselves. Taking a closer look at how the Airbus members measure up against each other, in fact, affords an additional angle from which to probe the consumption variable.

The viability of the Airbus consortium has been at risk of falling victim to many of the same factors that plague other European high-technology consortia. In aerospace, efforts ranging from the Concorde to the European Space Research Organization have struggled with the task of allocating work shares among member nations. Typically, the Europeans have doled out pieces of a project in line with partnership shares, themselves a reflection of political compromise – based on gross domestic product, for example – rather than core business competencies. These partnership shares have often bred conflict: smaller states complain about subsidizing larger states who, in turn, object to subsidizing "mediocrity."[64] Along these lines, Airbus has also struggled with this problem of *juste retour*. Founded with equal partnership shares split between Britain and France (37.5%) and a junior role for Germany (25%), the withdrawal and subsequent return of Britain gave rise to a different arrangement, with France and Germany as lead partners (37.9%), Britain assuming the role of junior partner (20%), and Spain purchasing a seat in the consortium (4.2%). These partnership shares, however, have often seemed arbitrary, particularly in light of the charge that, since the launch of the A300, Airbus has largely been a French airplane.[65]

Specialization within Airbus is revealing. The consortium reports the contributions to its offerings as follows: France provides the flight deck, forward fuselage and part of the center fuselage and wingbox sections, engine pylons, and lift dumpers; Britain contributes the main wingbox and, depending on airline preferences, the engines; Germany provides the major fuselage sections, the fin, rudder, tail cone, flaps, spoilers, and flap fairings; and Spain manufactures the tailplane, elevators, nose landing gear doors, and forward cabin entry doors.[66] This list reveals not only France's lead in contributing most of the advanced subsystems, but also France's lead in piecing together the airplane, a task first performed outside of Toulouse in 1993.[67] Systems integration has thus long been a French task, raising concern on the part of the other Airbus states.[68] By the late 1980s, Bonn and London, in particular, were demanding more responsibility for the cockpit and project management.[69] What is interesting about these demands is that the Airbus consortium is widely portrayed as a "club" good, in that these indirect benefits are nonrival among members. This would suggest that any disputes over work shares would be few and far between, yet this has not been the case. Factors that explain why nonmembers do not have access to these external benefits are the same ones that explain why there is considerable competition among the members over work shares, and all of this testifies to the importance of the internalization variable.

Finally, the consumption variable sheds additional light on Japan's apparent absence from the civil aircraft rivalry. U.S. observers in and out of government have long insisted that Japan has targeted this industry as a key source of externalities, but has stopped short of mounting the kind of campaign Europe has waged on behalf of Airbus, given a lack of presence in crucial upstream industries.[70] Firms like Kawasaki Heavy Industries compete in a variety of relevant niches, contributing to the view that "Japan . . . already possesses much of the expertise needed to produce a world class aircraft of its own design *in the future.*"[71] Nonetheless, Japan remains on the sidelines, given its inability to consume the linkages and spillovers at stake. First, observers emphasize Japan's inexperience integrating large complex systems in areas like commercial space and energy.[72] Second, despite its subcontractor status on various Boeing offerings, systems integration skills have *not* diffused to Japan's leading vendors. Once again, the reasons for this pattern merit close scrutiny of the internalization variable.

The Internalization Variable

This section makes the case that civil aircraft externalities are primarily *nation-specific* in scope. The evidence suggests that the process of taking an airplane through production encourages the localization of supplier networks and minimizes foreign content, and that integrating large complex systems curbs the international diffusion of the spillovers that result. Disputes among firms over responsibility for the cockpit and final assembly testify to the scope of these externalities. To be sure, the viability of consortia in civil aircraft hinges on the allocation of work shares, since the returns to the technology tend not to escape national borders.

In assessing the scope of these civil aircraft externalities, patent protection and foreign access to NASA R&D are routinely cited. In fact, neither factor sheds much light on this concern. First, despite weak patent protection in the industry, charges of free riding are unheard of, in part because of the high costs of reverse engineering.[73] Boeing maintains, for example, that "[w]hile the Company owns numerous patents and has licenses under patents owned by others relating to its products and their manufacture, it *does not believe that its business would be materially affected by the expiration of any patents or termination of any patent license agreements.*"[74] Indeed, Airbus's design and application of composite materials in its primary and secondary structures, "fly-by-wire" technology and digital avionics, as well as advances in modular over linear production processes, are seldom traced to Boeing.[75] This is not to imply that American and European firms fail to learn from each other, for competition has pushed Boeing and Airbus in many of the same directions. Yet little technology diffuses beyond a contractor's supplier base, despite this weak patent protection *and* in lieu of joint collaborations.

Second, foreign access to NASA carries little weight in scoring the internalization variable. Airbus has received NASA's help attaching winglets on the A320, for example, and has tested virtually all of its designs in NASA wind tunnels.[76] Similarly, Shin-Meiwa, a Japanese firm, is argued to have learned much of its carbon fiber technology from NASA journals.[77] This access is not inconsequential, but it is also not a competitive liability as viewed from the perspective of U.S. industry. On the one hand, each of the Airbus states has a similar agency mandated to spin off R&D. Yet, even if NASA were the only game in town, there would be little reason to change the score on the internalization variable. As one U.S. scientist insisted with respect to civil aircraft technology, "[i]f you're part of the team that develops it, that beats the hell out of reading it in a paper."[78] The question, of course, is why?

The design intensity of civil aircraft manufacturing serves to distinguish this industry from most others. Whereas a single design can produce a family of microprocessors, for example, a single design may yield as few as 1,000 parts of an airplane.[79] This translates into a long and costly design process stretching through production, a stage at which most other industries, including semiconductors, are focused strictly on manufacturing. Since upstream suppliers participate in this process from start to finish, civil aircraft firms have historically subcontracted on a national basis, keeping this base close enough to minimize the costs of reengineering (engineering change orders number in the tens of thousands on a given project) and to maximize the returns to learning by doing (accounting for 80–90% of the cost reductions owing to volume production).[80]

Current trends point up this national bias in subcontracting. For example, only 4% of Boeing's suppliers are foreign, accounting for roughly 13% of the content by value of its airplanes.[81] U.S. firms, more broadly, spent $34 billion on goods and services in 1991, of which $31.5 billion was spent domestically.[82] Foreign direct investment (FDI) casts little light on this trend: U.S. government restrictions and market incentives to localize one's facilities keep FDI at bay. Much the same is true on the other side of the Atlantic. While Airbus's first A300 looked distinctly American (50% of the content by value according to some estimates), the consortium's airplanes have looked distinctly European since at least the mid-1980s, especially with the launch of the A330 and A340. Not only do U.S. firms "seldom serve as major subcontractors" on foreign aircraft, as the Commerce Department notes, but moreover, Airbus offerings currently rival Boeing's in terms of foreign content by value, estimated at 10–14%.[83] It should be stressed that these trends are *market-driven*, if historically conditioned; the design-intensity of the industry has served to localize these upstream-downstream linkages on a national level.

The process of piecing together an airplane sheds additional light on the scope of these linkage externalities and helps make sense of why the resulting technology spillovers also tend to be nation-specific. The basic story is that the final product is more than the sum of its parts;[84] integrating so many discrete inputs within a vast array of larger systems and subassemblies concentrates technologies among participating suppliers. This is why responsibility for the cockpit and final assembly is so critical. The product, process, and management skills to be had do not leak out beyond the contractor's supplier base, and contractors have long oversampled on domestic suppliers. Systems integration is a U.S. forte, not least because of the expertise Boeing and McDonnell Douglas developed while managing lavishly funded military and space projects through the cold war. Boeing, for example, was responsible for over 40,000 subcontractors building the Minuteman missile, backed by the financial security of a Department of Defense (DoD) "cost plus fixed-fee" contract.[85] The Airbus members have also been deeply involved in military projects and have participated in EC consortia involved in satellites and rockets, for example. Still, systems integration skills have been less evenly distributed throughout Europe; charges that Airbus is really a French airplane trace to Aerospatiale's lead role on this front and to the fact that many key technologies do not diffuse beyond Toulouse as a result.

Joint collaborations in civil aircraft, more generally, boast a poor track record in terms of technology sharing among members. Indeed, proposals for collaborative projects often stumble on disputes over work shares, as in proposals involving Boeing and Aerospatiale, Boeing and British Aerospace, McDonnell Douglas and Airbus, and McDonnell Douglas and the government of Taiwan.[86] Boeing's proposal to collaborate with Aerospatiale, for example, was declined when it became clear that Boeing would fully manage the 777, the concern being that the French aerospace contractor stood to learn little from the project.[87] A 1986 European Commission report taps the basics of this fear, making the case that, in fact, "European industry cannot buy or otherwise obtain this upgraded technological skill from its U.S. competitors."[88] The same conclusion is echoed in U.S. studies. A report prepared for the Office of Technology Assessment (OTA), for instance, concludes unequivocally that "international linkages do result in the transfer of some workshare and technology, *but ownership, R&D, and most of the high-added value work remain at home.*"[89]

The score on the internalization variable has led the Airbus members, as a group, to be more aggressive in their practice of strategic trade than have "second movers" in a host of other industries, including the Japanese in semiconductors, where externalities, by way of contrast, diffuse internationally. Core competencies in civil aircraft have certainly helped in making the case for government export and R&D subsidies, the consortium's financial track record notwithstanding.[90] Pointing to the "Europeanization" of Airbus, for instance, an official testifying on behalf of the Commerce Department told a House subcommittee that "[t]he

Airbus Governments have made it very clear to all of us who have talked to them that *they believe it's their right to have a commercial aircraft industry, whether it's profitable or not, and they seem to be determined to do so in an expanding fashion.*"[91] A McDonnell Douglas official, testifying before a different House subcommittee, found this same trend hardly surprising: "Airbus may be an abysmal failure in generating profits, but [the consortium] has meant jobs, technology, and prestige to the European communities involved."[92] In that Europe consumes and internalizes the many external benefits that the civil aircraft industry exhibits, this resolve to fight for Airbus in an "expanding fashion" is well within reach of the book's theory.

Again, these factors are revealing of Japan's peripheral status in civil aircraft, notwithstanding its many years of subcontracting to Boeing and others. Observers on both sides of the Pacific insist that Japan's inexperience integrating large complex systems has deterred the Ministry of International Trade and Industry (MITI) from engaging in the kind of strategic-trade policies it has practiced in other industries.[93] Moreover, few expect Japan to learn these related skills as a result of collaborations with Boeing or Airbus. Much the same is true on the military side of the business, the FSX project being a case in point. Indeed, despite concerns that this collaboration would serve to strengthen Japan's place in civil aircraft, a General Accounting Office (GAO) report casts doubt on this, finding "no single, causal relationship" between Japan's role on the F15J fighter on the one hand and its subcontracting ties with Boeing and McDonnell Douglas on the other. More generally, while Japanese firms have served as subcontractors on a variety of U.S. civil aircraft projects since 1952, the Aerospace Industries Association (AIA) insists that they "do not pose a competitive threat to any U.S. aerospace products at this time."[94] The internalization variable thus offers new insights into Japan's position in civil aircraft, the ambitions of this "quintessentially activist" state aside.

THE DEPENDENT VARIABLE

Given the scores on the independent variables, the book interprets the U.S.-EC rivalry in civil aircraft as a Beggar-Thy-Neighbor PD, since both can consume and internalize the externalities exhibited by this industry. The decision variable is thus whether to practice full or limited intervention. Full intervention is the dominant strategy, although this risks a collectively suboptimal trade war. Limited intervention would leave both better off but it is hard to hold to, given the temptation to defect. If the future is not overly discounted, states may negotiate a subsidy ceiling as a way to avert a trade war. The remainder of this chapter traces how U.S. and EC policymakers have weighed these strategic-trade policies, examines the competitive dynamic in this commercial rivalry, and provides a closer look at the mechanics of the LCA agreement. In detailing this case, the chapter provides some of the first evidence that full intervention has been debated on both sides of the Atlantic, making clear that the heated tone of this commercial rivalry owes to the fact that the states involved, rather than the firms, have been calling the shots, and that externalities, as opposed to votes, have long been the currency of strategic trade.

The Competing Explanation

Endogenous protection theory has much to say about this case. To be sure, the civil aircraft rivalry has long been viewed through these lenses, given the stock of highly skilled labor employed and the industry's legendary export prowess.[95] In working with the four independent variables that endogenous protection theory prefers, however, the story is not overly persuasive. Starting with the United States, direct employment peaked at 345,000 in 1991 and was estimated at 269,000 in 1996, placing it on par with the semiconductor industry. Only when these employment figures are amended to include military and space does the industry post the numbers endogenous protection theory might like (763,000 in 1996).[96] And like the semiconductor industry, roughly 40% of the aerospace industry's employment base casts a ballot on the Pacific coast, an advantage in that spatial proximity helps overcome the collective-action problem inherent in lobbying.[97] The industry is also spread across relatively few political districts, affording it a good number of voices in Congress, but not a large number. Finally, the score on the industrial concentration variable suggests Boeing (like Airbus) has a strong incentive to ask for subsidies, in that the rents at stake are not at risk of being competed away by would-be entrants. In light of all of this, where does endogenous protection theory go wrong?

Endogenous protection theory gets much of the demand-side story right, and yet this is *not* the same story the literature needs to tell. Boeing and McDonnell Douglas have often tried to rein this commercial rivalry back in, even if they have not always succeeded. In Boeing's case, for example, the concern has been that by lashing out at Airbus, Europe might close access to export markets in retaliation, and not just in Europe.[98] U.S. policymakers, though, have not sat idly by, moving unilaterally against Airbus on several occasions, filing against the German government under the General Agreement on Tariffs and Trade (GATT) to end an exchange-rate scheme involving Daimler-Benz's subsidiary, Deutsche Airbus, for example.[99] Across the board, the tone in Washington has been more heated than in Seattle or St. Louis. As chair of a panel examining the competitiveness of the U.S. civil aircraft industry, Jim Florio (D-New Jersey) complained that the private sector had been derelict in addressing Airbus's gains in market share. Echoing this sentiment, Bruce Smart, the Commerce Department's undersecretary for international trade, testified that "more yellow flags" were coming from industry than from the administration with respect to mounting a response to Airbus.[100] Indeed, arguing that Boeing and McDonnell Douglas had been slow on the draw, Sam Gibbons (D-Florida) went on to warn company representatives that "I have been attempting to get both of your companies to bring countervailing duty actions and, for reasons it will do no good to go into here, you have seen fit not to. *But my next escalation will be to require in these kinds of cases the U.S. Government to self-initiate the antisubsidy cases.*"[101] The government's lead role on the subsidies front has been no less apparent, both in terms of curbing public expenditures, as President Reagan did over the opposition of the AIA, or increasing them, as witnessed by the role of the Export-Import (EXIM) Bank through the early stages of this rivalry. Finally, the LCA agreement reveals that Washington has been anything but a neutral referee in this trade dispute. Boeing was keen to threaten Europe, for example, that if a subsidies agreement was not on the horizon, it would stand aside and let Washington do what it deemed necessary. And, at the time, one of the policy options being debated on Capitol Hill involved outspending Airbus "out of existence," as is discussed later. To the extent that threats of a trade war helped push negotiations on a subsidy ceiling forward, the government not only nudged this fight to the brink of a trade war, but also pulled it back again.

Things look much the same on the other side of the Atlantic. The European aerospace industry, for example, tallied direct employment, including military and space, of 360,746 in 1994, with France claiming 100,500 employees, Britain 119,353, Germany 67,965, and Spain 9,441.[102] Offsetting these small figures, of course, is the fact that this is an industry renowned for its exports. In 1993, for example, British aerospace firms led all domestic exporters, accounting for 9% of total exports of manufacturing goods and fully 4% of the country's manufacturing output more generally.[103] This has certainly given civil aircraft a voice in the policymaking process. Yet, even in Britain's case, presumably the "weakest" state in the consortium, the image of firms running roughshod over elected officials could not be further from the truth. Efforts to rationalize the civil aircraft industry, for example, have involved state-inspired "shotgun marriages" among some 20 design teams, resulting in two (Hawker Siddeley Aviation and the British Aircraft Corporation) and then just one (British Aerospace), the latter of which was nationalized in 1978.[104] Seldom at a loss to act on its own in this industry – the Plowden Report had concluded in 1965 that there was "no predestined place for an aircraft industry in Britain" – the state has guided its national champion on a schizophrenic path from Airbus to Boeing and back to Airbus, along the way revealing the importance of both the consumption and internalization variables.[105]

Even when we consider the geographic concentration and political dispersion of this employment, and factor in the concentration of the industry, the electoral clout wielded by Europe's aerospace industry remains a puzzle for endogenous protection theory, even if not for European officials. In an influential study, for example, the EC insists that "[t]he aerospace industry is a perfect example of a field with a maximum concentration of high-technology products in a wide, varied range of applications. For this reason *it is rightly regarded as being of strategic importance for industrial, commercial and technological reasons despite its relatively small size in economic terms.*"[106] Along these same lines, the coordinator for German aerospace affairs urges that "*[d]espite its limited size in terms of employees, sales, and gross value added*, a competent and capable aerospace industry is of great significance for the Federal Republic of Germany."[107] These conclusions, as the following pages make clear, are entirely representative. More importantly, they highlight that votes are *not* the motivation behind Europe's strategic-trade policies on behalf of the civil aircraft industry.

Background on the Civil Aircraft Rivalry

In 1967, France, Britain, and Germany agreed to develop the A300, two years prior to the Concorde's first flight test. The lessons of the Concorde project were twofold: first, it made it apparent that experience in military

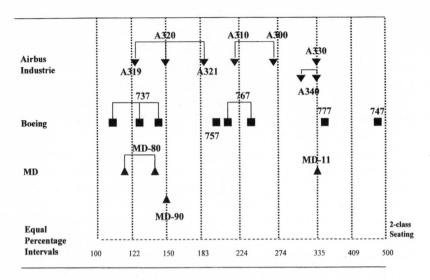

Figure 3.1. Competing product lines. *Source*: Airbus Industries.

aircraft did not necessarily lend itself to civil design, given the maintenance requirements of the airplane; and second, it revealed that a market
niche strategy was untenable for Europe, given that the novelty of the
airplane was vastly overshadowed by concern for the lack of scale and
scope efficiencies. To succeed, Airbus had to redress both problems. As
one British policymaker insisted, Airbus had to show that the "future
was not like the past."[108]

In the late 1960s, the landscape of the civil aircraft industry was not
overly conducive to entry. Boeing and McDonnell Douglas played key
roles in military and space projects of a size and scale simply not seen in
Europe.[109] Publicly dismissed in the United States as a costly symbol of
EC cooperation, Airbus soon garnered close attention from industry and
government officials. With the launch of the A300, Boeing set out to
lure European firms away from the Airbus consortium. Italy's Aeritalia,
for example, chose replacement work on the 707/727 over Airbus membership. France and Britain showed some interest in similar proposals,
but declined. Airbus committed to offer a family of aircraft in 1973 (see
Figure 3.1).

Europe had historically held 16% world market share in the civil
aircraft industry, and it was not clear that Airbus would surpass this
benchmark.[110] A 1986 study insisted that Airbus would gain no more

than 20% world market share, given the dominant position of the two giant U.S. aerospace contractors, both of which the study concluded had received considerable government assistance.[111] Subsidies for the design and development of the A300, estimated at 25–100% of costs, were slow to grab headlines in the United States.[112] With the A300 in service and the launch of the A310, Washington pegged Airbus's world market share at around 20%, but by this time, European spending was taking a toll on the fate of McDonnell Douglas. To get at this, two agreements helped usher in the 1980s: the first was the "Aircraft Agreement" signed under the auspices of the GATT, the second, the "Commonline Agreement," which more directly tackled export and credit subsidies.[113]

The two agreements soon proved ineffectual. Laura Tyson argues that this is because "[i]nternational rules can moderate trade conflict when the parties to the conflict can find common ground or mutual interest, but they cannot eliminate conflict when the interests of the parties are fundamentally antagonistic."[114] U.S. and EC policymakers could hardly have disagreed more, since there appeared little middle ground between a U.S. monopoly, on the one hand, and European subsidization of Airbus at McDonnell Douglas's expense, on the other. Yet there was common ground, as both sides made clear. The U.S.-EC rivalry in civil aircraft is best interpreted as a Beggar-Thy-Neighbor PD game, and not as a game of Deadlock.

The Cooperation Problem

By practicing full intervention, the United States and Europe hurt each other regardless of what the other does. This is the kind of high-technology trade war observers fear most. On the other hand, if they can limit subsidies, they can realize a Pareto-superior outcome. This requires that states not overly discount the future, and that they make provisions to cap and monitor each other's spending on the industry. The Beggar-Thy-Neighbor PD is illustrated in Figure 3.2.

U.S. Strategic Trade Policy

U.S. policymakers weighed the case for limited against full intervention. In presenting evidence that full intervention was even debated in the United States, this section offers a rare glimpse at Washington's strategic-trade calculus.

U.S.

	N	L	F
N	3,3	2,8	1,9
L	8,2	6,6	4,7
F	9,1	7,4	(5,5)

EC

Figure 3.2. U.S.-EC civil aircraft rivalry.

U.S. export and R&D subsidies were substantial – if indirect – through the early stages of this commercial rivalry. The EXIM had been especially active on behalf of civil aircraft, earning the nickname "Boeing's Bank" because 40% of its portfolio was invested in the aerospace industry. Between 1967 and 1977, for example, EXIM loaned $5.77 billion on sales of $12.8 billion of U.S. aircraft, and much of this in support of Boeing's exports.[115] U.S. firms also benefited from NASA and DoD outlays, although it is difficult to quantify exactly how much. One influential EC study estimates total direct and indirect subsidies for U.S. civil aircraft firms totaling over $22 billion between 1976 and 1991, a figure that the USTR demands is greatly in error.[116] Nonetheless, the OTA concedes that NASA and DoD programs significantly shaped the competitive landscape in civil aircraft, and even that Airbus would enjoy greater market share today were it not for EXIM.[117] Testifying before a Senate subcommittee, for example, an OTA representative explained that "unlike most manufacturing industries in the United States, commercial aircraft is an industry that has long enjoyed substantial Federal support in development and diffusion of technology. *It is no accident that it is a successful industry as a result.*"[118]

Airbus was all the rage on Capitol Hill by the end of the decade. Europe's unwavering support for the consortium, and McDonnell Douglas's slip in the rankings, begged for a response. Washington closely scrutinized evidence bearing on the consumption variable, given the view of Airbus as a "technological showcase," as well as evidence pertaining to the score on the internationalization variable, not least because of accusations that Airbus excluded U.S. firms from serving as suppliers. Many insisted that the only way to counter Airbus was to increase U.S. subsidies substantially. The AIA argued before a Senate subcommittee, for example, that "our competitors' use of government subsidized financing mechanisms . . . can only be countered by a strengthened Exim-bank."[119] Those representing industry were slightly more cautious about lobbying for a strengthened EXIM; Boeing and McDonnell Douglas both wanted offsetting support, but feared European retaliation.[120] Washington pursued a different option, negotiating a pact on subsidies and reducing EXIM funding by 12%, although things were just heating up.

Frustration with Airbus reached a new high with the release of a study prepared for the Department of Commerce. The study, known as the Gellman report, came to a dramatic conclusion:

At the prime private sector borrowing rate in each [Airbus] country, the value of committed net government support by 1989 had reached $26 billion. (This assumes that the AI member-companies were sufficiently creditworthy to have borrowed all the required aircraft development funds in private capital markets. The actual cost of capital for these firms would clearly have been higher given the riskiness of the investments. Thus the $26 billion estimate is conservative.)[121]

This figure outraged U.S. policymakers. Tensions over Airbus had been escalating, and it was clear that earlier agreements in civil aircraft had not limited Europe's spending on the consortium. Discussion in Washington also centered on an "Airbus Reflex," or what was seen as a willingness on the part of the four states (but especially France) to provide political inducements to win a sale. One notable example involved Indian Airlines: it was rumored that the sale was gained as a result of France's promise to lobby the World Bank on India's behalf, a military contract, and assistance in cleaning up the Ganges River.[122] The view on Capitol Hill was that, as one policymaker put it, "[t]here is no way that private companies can compete for long against determined efforts by governments who ignore market forces and spend taxpayer money to achieve non-economic goals." The statistics did little to ease this frustration. By one estimate, Airbus had cost U.S. firms $63 billion in exports, $25 billion in imports, and 1.4 million man-years of work(see Figures 3.3 and 3.4).[123] In concluding his testimony before a House

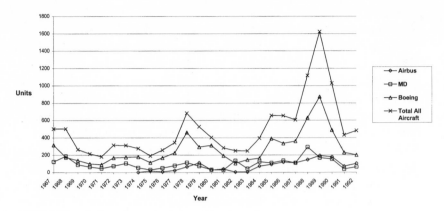

Figure 3.3. Large civil aircraft announced orders, 1967–1992. *Source*: Boeing 1992.

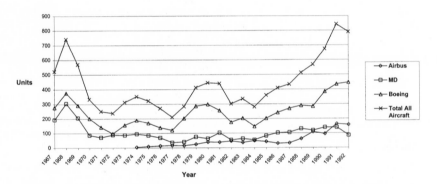

Figure 3.4. Large civil aircraft deliveries, 1967–1992. *Source*: Boeing 1992.

subcommittee, the Commerce Department's undersecretary for international trade offered this assessment: "We are not looking for a fight. But we are not willing to sacrifice the U.S. aerospace industry's well-earned preeminence *merely for the sake of an agreement.*"[124]

Nonetheless, an agreement is exactly what Washington pursued. This is not to say that full intervention had been ruled out. On the contrary, a more "predatory" stance had been considered. A study prepared for the Subcommittee on Technology and Competitiveness outlined five options for responding to Airbus, each calling for state support for American firms. As a final option, the study argued that "the Airbus consortium could be *outspent out of existence. All that would be necessary . . .*

would be for the U.S. Government to provide its commercial aircraft sector with the same manner of subsidy and other assistance provided to Airbus."[125] Voices favoring full intervention were loud, to say the least. Washington had been lashing out at Airbus for some time, and even at U.S. firms for not countering the "Airbus threat" with more zeal. With bilateral negotiations stalled during the early 1990s, Boeing piped up with a threat revealing the state's lead role in this commercial rivalry. Rather succinctly, Clarkson noted that "if the current negotiations are unsuccessful, *then we are prepared to back the Government in whatever action they deem is necessary to bring this problem to a resolution once and for all.*"[126] The "credibility" of this threat, in turn, hinged on Washington's contemplation of full intervention, and on Boeing's history of showing restraint in countering Airbus. Still, were it not for Washington's track record for acting unilaterally, the threat would have carried little sway. The LCA agreement was signed in due course.

EC Strategic-Trade Policy

EC policymakers, like their American counterparts, have weighed limited against full intervention. And like their American counterparts, they have been tempted by the lure of practicing full intervention.

In 1984, Margaret Thatcher pushed the launch of the A320 to the top of her agenda in talks with François Mitterrand and Helmut Kohl. Mitterrand's unwavering commitment to Airbus was representative of the three leaders, demanding that "the A320 will be built, and I am its number one salesman."[127] Washington responded by admonishing Europe to adhere to "free-trade" principles. The Reagan administration was fond of singling out the Airbus consortium as a symbol of all that was wrong in U.S.-EC trade relations. For their part, EC policymakers countered that free trade meant a Boeing monopoly and that, in any case, EXIM, NASA, and DoD support had already done much to distort the playing field. More specifically, an EC-commissioned study, written in the wake of the Gellman report, estimated that U.S. firms had been subsidized to the tune of $18–22.05 billion between 1976 and 1990 ($33.48–41.49 billion in 1991 dollars), a figure nearly identical to the one cited by the Gellman report.[128] This estimate hinged on assumptions that, for example, 90% of NASA R&D expenditures have direct implications for U.S. civil aircraft firms, as well as that 25–50% of DoD-funded R&D in aircraft similarly benefits commercial contractors, assumptions that the USTR vehemently rejected.[129] These "tit-for-tat" accusations were only part of the story. Airbus officials have long been quick to dismiss reports that the consortium's entry has yielded a net global welfare *loss*, as well as those studies purporting that the returns to Europe from investing in the consortium are meager, if not negative.[130] Criticizing the Gellman report, for example, one European study pointed to its failure to account for the "growing strength of ideas associated with the *Strategic Trade economic analysis*," which it argued "would undoubtedly demonstrate the more attractive *economic rates of return* on the investment in the Airbus programme."[131] Interestingly enough, the Gellman report was entirely aware of the currency of these ideas, concluding, for example, that the main concern with respect to Airbus was that greater competition jeopardized the linkage and spillover externalities that benefited wide sectors of the *American* economy.[132]

Emboldened by success, EC policymakers accused Washington not only of funding its civil aircraft industry, but also of politicizing sales. Citing cases involving China, Greece, India, Japan, Korea, Taiwan, and Thailand, EC officials charged that Airbus had lost firm orders because the United States had peddled political influence worldwide to sway deals favoring Boeing and McDonnell Douglas. A European report on this issue explains, for example, that "as Airbus' success grew at the expense of the American manufacturers, *the U.S. Government took an increasingly active role in promoting Boeing and McDonnell Douglas sales to foreign carriers*."[133] These charges made clear that Europe stood ready to fight it out with the United States, be it before the GATT, or by levying sanctions more directly. By the early 1990s, the two sides were poised on the brink of a trade war, and neither side looked ready to blink.

With the launch of the A330 and A340 in 1987, Airbus competed for every segment of the market except the 400+ seat segment, in which Boeing's 747 still enjoys a monopoly. Airbus, however, now boasted a family of five airplanes, and ousted McDonnell Douglas as the industry's number two, behind Boeing. This success prompted demands for *more*, not less, subsidization.[134] Germany is a case in point: subsidies for civil aircraft rose 63% between 1981 and the early 1990s, accounting for as much as 8.7% of all publicly funded R&D in 1988.[135] Aerospace, more generally, was the only industry in Europe to survive the 1980s drawing more than 50% of its R&D funding from government sources.[136] This fact was not lost on U.S. policymakers.

As Washington readied to file against Airbus under the GATT, Europe issued its own list of U.S. violations of the Subsidies Code, focusing the brunt of this attack on the level of indirect transfers routed through NASA and the DoD.[137] In a presentation made before the International Trade Commission, for example, Airbus officials argued that the biggest difference between government support for the civil aircraft industry in the United States and Europe is that U.S. support is indirect and offered with no expectation of repayment, whereas EC support is direct, efficient, and offered with the expectation of repayment.[138] By the early 1990s, Europe's tone had changed substantially. EC policymakers, no longer timid about confessing to having spent lavishly on the consortium, set their sights on the A3XX, a project that has ignited considerable passion on both sides of the Atlantic. If threats had worked to bring Europe back to the negotiating table, much the same could be said of the United States, prodded by fears of engaging Europe in a heated fight extending well into the future.

The LCA Agreement

Building on the GATT's Aircraft Agreement, the LCA agreement is, from head to toe, about limiting overspending and facilitating transparency. There are twelve transparency clauses under Article 8 requiring that information be exchanged on a "regular, systematic basis" and establishing minimum requirements for this exchange. The LCA agreement is rather bold in this respect, insisting that both sides reveal sensitive business data, much of which is hard to quantify. The staples include, for example, government funding for new launches, R&D outlays, indirect benefits of state-sponsored projects, repayment schedules on loans committed, industry and firm turnover, and nonproprietary project data. This is intended to help reveal overspending by defining "defection" under exceptional and not so exceptional circumstances. Aggregate data on spending and methods for quantifying direct and indirect supports are pillars of the text.

On the issue of direct support, the LCA agreement sets caps for new launches and any derivatives, and insists that there be a "reasonable expectation" of recoupment within the time frame established. Concern for overspending with respect to export credit financing is noted in Article 6, which binds the signatories to the terms of the Large Aircraft Sector Understanding of the OECD Understanding on Official Export Financing. On the issue of indirect support, the LCA agreement offers one of the first definitions brought to bear on this rivalry: Article 5.3 defines indirect benefits as cost reductions owing to any state-funded R&D, and sets out formulae for measuring and capping these benefits. Given the charge that U.S. contractors have benefited greatly from indirect supports administered by space and military agencies, this provision is as significant as it is contested.

These ceilings on supports provoked a distributional conflict along the way to signing this agreement. Indeed, the figures debated promised to advantage one or the other side, sparking a dispute along the Pareto frontier.[139] The United States wanted a low ceiling on all direct supports and preferred little discussion of indirect supports. In anticipation of the A3XX, this ceiling mattered a great deal, setting the tone for whether this project, and the Airbus consortium itself, would prove viable. Airbus's CEO, Jean Pierson, proposed a limit on direct support topping 45% on new programs in the event the United States made its indirect methods of support more transparent, urging that "[w]e want a more balanced redistribution of the world market in civil aircraft."[140] Indeed, Europe eyed NASA's new projects in sub- and supersonic aviation and demanded that indirect transfers be reined in. The 1985 Commonline Agreement had brought these positions to the fore some years earlier, although this time both sides were armed with new complaints, and worries. The deal struck reflects both U.S. and European concessions: the cap on direct support is more in keeping with U.S. demands (25%), whereas the formula for calculating indirect support reflects Europe's position. Yet the LCA agreement came under fire from both sides almost immediately. In an industry that exhibits externalities that both sides can consume and internalize, the incentive to outspend each other is sure to keep the United States and Europe on the brink of a trade war in civil aircraft.

CONCLUSION

The civil aircraft rivalry has long been presented as *the* textbook case of strategic-trade policy. The story is that, in their search for rents in this imperfectly competitive industry, firms demand, and governments supply, export and R&D subsidies, hoping to win market share at the expense of foreign competitors. This chapter argues that the states involved, rather than Boeing and Airbus, have been calling the shots in this commercial rivalry, and that externalities, rather than votes, are the currency of this fight. The evidence makes clear that the United States and Europe have spent lavishly on their national champions in civil aircraft, inspired to do so by the fact that national borders constrain the reach of the externalities at stake.

4

The Semiconductor Rivalry

Since the debut of the transistor in 1947, semiconductors have been at the heart of the electronics revolution. The many products and processes that have evolved alongside this industry span the high-technology "food chain," from equipment and materials upstream to computers downstream. Not surprisingly, policymakers have long identified success in the semiconductor industry as a necessary prerequisite for competing in high technology more generally.[1] The U.S.-Japan "chip" rivalry thus warrants close attention in theorizing about the calculus of strategic trade.

Much has been written about semiconductors, and Japan's inroads into the market for dynamic random access memories (DRAMs), in particular. The interest in DRAMs owes to the fact that these and other memory chips, such as static and video RAMs, serve as "drivers" of semiconductor technology more generally. Their simplicity enables vendors to gain experience, achieve scale and scope efficiencies, and compete for other segments of the industry. Market share in RAMs is thus a springboard into more complex devices, including a variety of logic chips. In this respect, Japan's success in the market for RAMs has been regarded as perhaps the greatest challenge to "American reliance on *laissez-faire* toward the commercialization of technology."[2]

Washington, however, has hardly left the American semiconductor industry to fend for itself. Government spending on R&D has contributed to nearly every development in this technology since the transistor first made its debut.[3] Through the 1960s, procurement by the National Aeronautics and Space Administration (NASA) and the Department of Defense accounted for most of the nation's semiconductor output (100%

until 1962), facilitating the jump made by U.S. firms from germanium to silicon in the first stage of this commercial rivalry.[4] In recent years, federally funded R&D has helped realize gains in the design and fabrication of successive generations of chips, most prominently of late through its support, with U.S. industry, of the Semiconductor Manufacturing Technology (Sematech) consortium.[5] In light of this track record, why is U.S. government support for the semiconductor industry so widely understated as a competitive factor? The answer is that Japan's semiconductor industry, too, has benefited from this helping hand.

Offered as a compelling example of "import protection as export promotion," the rise of Japan's semiconductor industry has received widespread attention.[6] Through the mid-1980s, tariffs and nontariff barriers protected the Japanese market from imports of chips. This protection helped the domestic semiconductor industry exploit "captive" demand and achieve the necessary production efficiencies to compete in export markets.[7] Even the pains of trade liberalization were eased by state-funded R&D programs. For example, the Very Large Scale Integration (VLSI) projects underwritten by Nippon Telephone and Telegraph (NTT) and the Ministry of International Trade and Industry (MITI) sought to help Japan's consumer electronics giants cope with imports in the absence of more formal impediments to trade. Yet, importantly, Japan's semiconductor industry has benefited as much from U.S. R&D – both public and private – as from these protectionist measures, or from consortia like the VLSI projects. Indeed, many observers suggest that protectionism and government spending on R&D would not have been especially useful, were it not for the leakage of U.S. technological know-how. This theme is taken up in the literature, but it is only half the story. Japan, too, has been concerned about the diffusion of technology resulting from its litany of R&D consortia, particularly on the eve of the VLSI period. By taking a closer look at the two-way diffusion of semiconductor technology, this chapter presents the U.S.-Japan rivalry in chips in a new light.

This chapter picks up the chip rivalry on the eve of the VLSI period, dating to the late 1970s. It argues that the United States and Japan can consume, but cannot internalize, the externalities exhibited by the chip industry. The linkages and spillovers at stake, to put it another way, are unconstrained by national borders. Given the scores on the independent variables, this book's theory interprets the U.S.-Japan chip rivalry as a Favor-Thy-Neighbor PD. Here, the expectation is that both sides would weigh limited intervention against nonintervention and lean toward *non-intervention* as a dominant strategy. Indeed, government support for the chip industry has long been debated precisely because of the international scope of the linkage and spillover externalities at stake. By free riding, however, states run the risk of going without a more optimal supply of externalities that they can consume. The challenge is thus to get both sides to practice limited intervention, which involves spending on an international public good. This chapter argues that the Semiconductor Trade Agreement (STA) has facilitated this outcome by setting out property rights, as market shares, in order to get the United States and Japan beyond the incentive to free-ride. In bringing this unconventional argument to life in the evidence, this chapter offers fresh insights into the U.S.-Japan semiconductor rivalry.

Endogenous protection theory underestimates the political influence of the semiconductor industry. To be sure, the electoral clout of U.S. chip vendors is difficult to reconcile with the industry's employment size, geographic concentration, political dispersion, or industrial concentration. This is true in the case of Japan as well, despite claims that vertical integration with downstream computer businesses gives these consumer electronics giants greater influence in shaping trade policy, strategic or otherwise. Like much of the literature, this chapter contends that the degree of vertical integration has, in any case, been exaggerated, and that Japan's chip firms see much the same competitive landscape as do their American rivals. Further, the level and timing of government subsidies do not mesh neatly with industry demands, as is clear on both sides of the Pacific. Finally, the success had in weaning industry of this support does not flow easily from this competing explanation. The book's theory bridges the gaps where endogenous protection theory falls short.

This chapter is in three sections. It begins by detailing the market imperfections that bring the semiconductor case within reach of strategic-trade theory. Then it sorts through the evidence concerning the score on the two independent variables. A final section evaluates the score on the dependent variable, contrasting the book's account of this commercial rivalry with the one put forward by endogenous protection theory.

THE ECONOMICS OF SEMICONDUCTORS

The semiconductor business is complex and costly. Entry barriers have been rising at a rate surpassed only by the gains in productivity realized with each generation of chips. Indeed, in light of the industry's steep learning curve, large economies of scale and scope, and high fixed costs of production, many observers regard semiconductors as an "ideal-typical candidate for strategic-trade policy."[8] These market imperfections are reviewed in turn.

Evidence that experience with *cumulative* output gives rise to efficiency gains in chip making is unmistakable.[9] Familiarity with new process and design technologies promises better yields (the percentage of nondefective chips per wafer) and lower costs. Yields of 10% are common in the first year of producing memories, for example, whereas yields of 80% are characteristic of the third year, given gains in expertise.[10] Cost reductions owing to better yields are dramatic: one U.S. study estimated that in the case of the 64K DRAM, an increase in yields from 35% to 45% would result in a 20% cost savings.[11] Cumulative experience also translates into cost reductions across devices within a generation. Indeed, the know-how required to produce the 64K and 256K DRAMs is not dissimilar, such that the slopes of these learning curves are somewhat interdependent.[12] In the late 1980s, for example, Japanese chip firms realized 20–30% greater yields in DRAMs than U.S. firms, to a large extent because of greater expertise dating back to the 64K.[13] This suggests that learning may be "path-dependent." Along these lines, one concern in the mid-1980s was that if U.S. vendors did not produce 256K DRAMs in any volume, future generations of these memories would be at a price disadvantage, if American vendors competed at all. It is, in short, rather difficult to overstate the importance of learning effects in this industry.

Evidence of scale economies in chip manufacturing is just as striking. The consensus in the industry is that for each doubling of *aggregate* output, the cost per bit of memory falls by 30%.[14] Thus, in tandem with learning effects, scale economies contribute greatly to the price competitiveness of firms. Continuing with the example of the 64K DRAM, unit prices fell from $28 in 1980 to less than $6 in 1982 as scale production increased.[15] This was not exceptional: the Commerce Department estimated that if U.S. firms held an additional 5% of the Japanese DRAM market, the gains would include a 4% cost savings and a 2.5% increase in the share held of the *domestic* DRAM market.[16] In that protection helped Japanese firms exploit these same scale efficiencies at the expense of U.S. vendors, "liberal trade" in semiconductors has long been a contentious issue in talks between the two countries.[17] As the Semiconductor Industry Association (SIA) testified before Congress in the mid-1980s, "[w]ithout domestic protection, we do not believe that Japanese targeting would be nearly as effective as it is – *in fact, it might not work at all.*"[18] Even after more formal restrictions had been lifted in Japan, informal barriers to trade in semiconductors sparked tension between the two states, primarily because they hold out the promise of facilitating economies of scale.

The interest in DRAMs traces to the central importance of economies of scope in this industry. Since more complex devices were, in this period, widely built using essentially the same facilities as larger volume chips (although not simultaneously), capital equipment and R&D had long been cross-subsidized by these technology drivers. And since DRAMs, on average, required less than a tenth the design engineering of a microprocessor, they were ideally suited to this role.[19] As U.S. firms exited the DRAM market in the mid-1980s, a key concern was thus that the cost of making more sophisticated semiconductors would rise, as rates of innovation fell. This "domino effect" was expected to be somewhat eased by the fact that U.S. firms still manufactured static RAMs (SRAMs), erasable programmable read-only memories (EPROMs), and other related products, although the concern was real enough.[20] The bottom line is that economies of scope matter a great deal in this industry, and in the late 1980s, Japan's gains in the DRAM market had put at risk U.S. economies of scope.

Finally, investment in equipment and R&D sets the semiconductor industry apart from most others. As a percentage of sales through the 1980s, outlays on equipment and R&D averaged 14% and 9.8% for U.S. firms and 20% and 15% for Japanese firms (today these shares are about 20% and 11% for U.S. firms).[21] In 1989, American firms invested $3.5 billion in equipment and $3 billion in R&D, and Japanese firms nearly *double* this.[22] In terms of equipment, the cost of a new fabrication facility (or "fab") has risen sharply with each generation of chips. For example, the cost of a 4M DRAM fab was double that of a 1M fab, which in turn cost approximately the same amount as a "clean room" for a 64M fab (annual operating costs roughly equal initial capitalization).[23] More recent estimates for new fabs range in excess of $1 billion for a single generation of chips, given that 20–80% of production equipment and process steps must be replaced.[24]

In terms of R&D, the constant upgrading of technology serves as a rather formidable entry barrier. Between 1960 and the early 1980s, for example, production processes for DRAM technology underwent 19 separate design changes, requiring sizable R&D outlays on the part of firms already incurring heavy losses.[25] To be sure, Texas Instruments (TI) invested more than $1 billion in DRAMs between 1986 and 1991 alone, and likely half of this just in R&D.[26] Outlays of this sort have long deterred would-be entrants from seeking to gain a foothold in semiconductors.

In light of these market imperfections, the semiconductor industry has been described as an ideal candidate for strategic trade. Yet the case for subsidies has not been clear-cut. The linkage and spillover externalities at issue reach beyond national borders, tempering the enthusiasm of U.S. and Japanese policymakers to help underwrite the exports and R&D of domestic firms in this quintessentially strategic industry. Framed in this light, the final section in this chapter contends that the U.S.-Japan chip rivalry has been anything but a typical case of "managed trade."[27]

THE INDEPENDENT VARIABLES

This section scores the consumption and internalization variables, seeking to show that, throughout the VLSI period, U.S. and Japanese policymakers have consistently concluded that the linkage and spillover externalities exhibited by the semiconductor industry can be consumed but not internalized. This assessment has been based on a careful reading of relations with the upstream semiconductor materials and equipment (SM&E) industry and the downstream computer industry. The score on the consumption variable may surprise few, and even the score on the internalization variable may be of little surprise to many. Yet, in telling the story about semiconductors, the literature neglects the incentive to free-ride that traces to this international diffusion of technology. In stressing the workings of the internalization variable, the book can thus hardly be accused of telling the same old story about DRAMs.

The Consumption Variable

In debating government policy toward the semiconductors industry, externalities have long enjoyed center stage. The dialogue on both sides of the Pacific has been revealing in this respect. In the United States, for example, the Congressional Budget Office (CBO), often critical of externalities arguments, concluded in no uncertain terms that "[t]he major federal interest in the semiconductor industry concerns *spillovers from research*, both in the industry itself and the economy in general."[28] In much this same spirit, Secretary of Commerce Malcolm Baldrige testified before a Senate hearing that semiconductors are "the building block of all of high technology. *They are tremendously the most important individual product I can imagine.*"[29] Likewise, the National Advisory Committee on Semiconductors (NACS) demanded that "a healthy semiconductor industry is imperative if the United States is to stay at the forefront of essential industries."[30] More to the point, one prominent expert testified before Congress that the semiconductor industry "touches almost anything we do."[31] These comments are entirely representative and would imply that there would be little question about subsidizing the semiconductor industry. Yet there has been considerable debate, the concern being that, to put a slightly different spin on this witness's expert testimony, the American semiconductor industry "touches almost anything" Japan does as well.

The language of externalities figures no less prominently in the statements of Japanese policymakers.[32] MITI's description of semiconductors as "industrial rice" taps the critical importance of this technology, an analogy not lost on U.S. observers.[33] Much like their counterparts in the United States, Japanese policymakers place considerable emphasis on the upstream linkage with the SM&E industry and downstream linkage with the computer industry. At first blush this is surprising, since vertical integration among semiconductor, SM&E, and computer divisions would seem to imply that the externalities at stake would be firm-specific as a matter of organizational design. Yet this view of Japan's chip industry is misleading. Upstream SM&E vendors have long been relatively autonomous from large chip firms, while downstream even the big four computer vendors buy only a small fraction of chips "in house," leading many to insist that vertical integration does not distinguish the Japanese from the American semiconductor industry.[34]

In evaluating the payoff to these linkage and spillover externalities, specific upstream and downstream activities have grabbed the attention of policymakers on both sides of the Pacific. The upstream SM&E industry supplies the basic inputs and processes used in the fabrication of chips, from purer chemicals and gases to design manufacturing equipment. The industry splits into wafer processing, testing, and assembly technologies, although the industry is best known for a few key staples. For example, the methods for etching circuit designs on silicon wafers, such as optical and X-ray lithography, account for one-quarter of the total equipment costs incurred by chip firms.[35] Photolithographic equipment, like steppers, also figure prominently in this respect. Because the health of the semiconductor industry is, to a very large extent, shaped by innovations upstream in the SM&E industry, this linkage externality figures prominently in the calculus of strategic trade, especially in light of the fact that many of these upstream technologies diffuse through the economy.[36] Miniaturization and purification processes are among the examples of technologies owing to SM&E R&D with applications in a wide variety of sectors. These and other examples will be examined more fully.

In scoring the consumption variable, U.S. and Japanese policymakers sought evidence that their SM&E industries were sufficiently competitive to start a fight over chips. The competitive landscape, in brief, has looked as follows: U.S. firms dominated this market in the late 1970s, lagged Japan in key sectors during the mid-1980s, and reclaimed market share by the early 1990s. In 1980, the ten largest SM&E firms (by sales) were American, and U.S. industry held 75% world market share, versus only four in 1989 and six in 1993, a year in which world market shares split 52–54% to 38% in favor of the United States, up from 45% in 1990.[37] Evidence of declining U.S. competitiveness in the SM&E industry was clear to all throughout the early 1980s: the Federal Interagency Task Force concluded that U.S. firms lagged Japan in 14 semiconductor processes and products, led in 6, but were losing ground in 5; the National Academy of Sciences insisted that Japan was ahead in 8 of 11 emerging semiconductor processes; while the Commerce Department pointed to a five-year Japanese lead employing CAD in the manufacture of semiconductor products more generally.[38] The SM&E industry, however, is no more homogeneous than the chip industry. Higher-value-added sectors were still dominated by U.S. firms, many of which were turning to specialty gases and software-intensive design tools, for example, as silicon wafer production moved offshore. Japanese purchases of U.S. firms, and MITI's VLSI program, certainly helped to mount a challenge in these sectors, but it was expected that the United States would retain this lead.[39] For example, of the estimated $4 billion spent by U.S. firms reoutfitting fabs in 1989, American SM&E vendors were expected to get 70% of this business.[40] Sounding out a confident voice, the NACS concluded that the United States was in the race upstream, and that "[a]dvances within the SM&E industry . . . spill over into almost *all aspects* of the American manufacturing base."[41] Once again, however, the question was whether this was strictly a *national* phenomenon.

The ascent of Japan's SM&E industry has received a great deal of attention, given its sizable gains in segments from silicon wafer production to packaging materials. Foreign direct investment (FDI) is widely cited as a crucial factor in this respect. The Commerce Department, for example, estimated that more than half of Japanese FDI in the American electronics industry during the 1980s was aimed at SM&E vendors.[42] Between 1987 and 1990 alone, fully 16 American SM&E firms were purchased by Japanese firms, sparking widespread concern among U.S. observers.[43] There is no denying that these acquisitions were helpful in reshaping the competitive landscape in sectors of the SM&E industry, but in reality they only served to reinforce Japan's score on the consumption variable. To be sure, Japan had long been dominant in many key sectors, such as lithography. Nikon and Canon, for instance, enjoyed considerable world market share in steppers (combining for 70% in 1990), an essential lithographic technology.[44] And Japan's imprint was clear in a host of other SM&E fields like optoelectronics, gallium arsenide circuitry, high-frequency transistors, and silicon-on-sapphire technologies, many of which derived from core competitive strengths in consumer electronics.[45] Similarly, projects including the Synchrotron Orbital Radiation Technology Center (SORTEC) and MITI's VLSI tapped a variety of domestic competencies in SM&E fields, such as optical electronics and electron beam technology, respectively.[46] Last, U.S. government restrictions on the sale of high-value-added SM&E firms prevented Japan from purchasing a foothold in a variety of cutting-edge technologies. This, in tandem with MITI's unwillingness to sponsor consortia without private-sector investment and a good deal of expertise, runs against the view that Japan created a capacity to consume this linkage externality.

Downstream, the computer industry is one of the most coveted in the global economy. Not surprisingly, the linkage externality between chips and computers feeds the view of semiconductors as being the "quintessentially strategic industry."[47] Chips are the heart of a computer: as "systems within a system," microprocessors and other logic chip sets, in combination with assorted RAMs, account for an ever greater percentage of the value of these machines (10% in the early 1980s versus 60% in the mid-1990s).[48] Given that the returns to chip R&D are largely realized at the systems level, the semiconductor industry tends to underinvest in R&D from the perspective of both the computer industry and the economy more generally.

In the eyes of U.S. policymakers, evidence concerning the consumption of this linkage externality has long been unambiguous. The CBO, for one, has been adamant that, given its ties to the computer industry, "the U.S. semiconductor industry may provide *as good a case as can be made* that the public benefits and spillovers resulting from . . . one industry justify federal financial support."[49] More succinctly than most, the Office of Technology Assessment (OTA) observed that "[w]hile there is a range of views about how important industrial and trade policies have been to some industries . . . *there is much less skepticism when it comes to the [U.S.] semiconductor industry, and still less for the computer industry*."[50] The two industries are inextricably coupled: the American computer industry accounts for roughly 60% of U.S. chip sales, almost *double* the percentage tallied by the Japanese computer industry.[51] An implication of this is that U.S. semiconductor vendors have specialized in higher-value-added microprocessors and digital signal processors, for example, boasting between three-quarters and 95% world market share in these devices through this period.[52] The dividends to this linkage externality have been striking: semiconductors cosponsor a social rate of return on computer R&D estimated at between 50% and 70%.[53]

In scoring the consumption variable the competitiveness of the American and Japanese computer industries has drawn close scrutiny. The United States held 70% world market share in personal computers (PCs) in 1987, with the private sector investing $8.5 billion in R&D.[54] The competitive landscape looked much the same in market segments ranging from workstations to supercomputers. Few doubted Washington's willingness to fight for this downstream linkage externality. With a greater number of functions integrated onto a single chip, semiconductor R&D has increasingly set the pace for advances in computer technology. As competition with Japan intensified through the mid-1980s, the American chip industry made this case in lobbying for government help. In justifying Washington's role in Sematech, for example, Intel's CEO, Robert Noyce, testified on behalf of the SIA that "[w]e feel [this] is well justified because the benefits will be far greater to the society than those that can be appropriated by the individual industrial sponsors."[55] Echoing this conclusion in the aftermath of the 1990 NACS report, International Business Machine's (IBM) John Armstrong discussed the logic behind Sematech with Al Gore (D-Tennessee), chair of the Subcommittee on Science, Space, and Technology:

Armstrong: [I]f there were to be a response from the [Bush] Administration on this recommendation . . . many of the members of Sematech would follow suit.
Gore: But not until then? As a practical matter it is not going to happen until the Government puts up its share?
Armstrong: I think that is right.[56]

It is hard to overstate the importance of this downstream linkage externality in Japan's calculus of strategic trade. As the SIA first testified in 1979, the semiconductor industry is the "bullseye of Japan's target industry for the future – the computer industry."[57] MITI has been unambiguous on this point, arguing since at least the early 1980s that computers are one of Japan's highest priorities.[58] In turn, the Japanese government played upon the nation's competitiveness in consumer electronics, pushing semiconductor "design-ins" as a springboard into computers.[59] This approach succeeded in establishing a foothold in the market for microcomputers, highlighting the extent to which the returns from chip R&D accrue downstream at the systems level.[60] Much the same is true with respect to gains in areas from vector-supercomputing to mainframes, though a lack of applications software has not helped exports on this front. In addition to concerns for chips as systems, returns to chip R&D are anticipated in the market for peripherals, especially in the area of floppy and hard disks. The Electronics Industries Association of Japan (EIAJ), for example, was of the view that the "second golden age of memory" would be marked by the replacement of these and other peripherals by various RAM chips.[61] Given Japan's dominant position in the market for peripherals, the country has long been poised to exploit this or any other "age" of memory.

In assessing Japan's score on the consumption variable, it is interesting to note that the computer industry is the nation's *second* largest end user of domestic chips, and a distant second at that (see Figure 4.1). Indeed, the Japanese semiconductor industry has grown up alongside the consumer electronics industry, weaned on calculators, watches, televisions, audio players, and other products using relatively simple discrete devices. Through work on a variety of more complex subsystems, consumer electronics giants like Fujitsu and Hitachi had some experience with higher-end application-specific chips, and thus were among the pillars of MITI's initiative to piece together several alliances to make

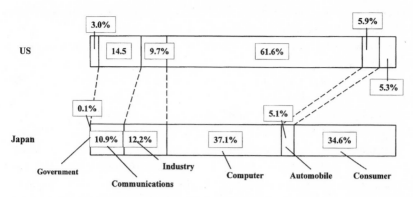

Figure 4.1. Semiconductor end use, 1994. Because figures are rounded, they may not add up to 100 percent. *Source*: Electronic Industries Association of Japan.

inroads into computers in the 1970s.[62] DRAMs were central in this respect, not only because the relative simplicity of their design helped firms to exploit scale and scope economies, but because these devices were used intensively in consumer electronics more broadly. Two milestones ushered in the VLSI period for Japan: Fujitsu outsold IBM in Japan in 1979, and the nation recorded its first trade surplus in computers in 1981.[63] Of course, these milestones turn attention to Japanese protectionism and government-industry consortia in computers.

First, tariffs and nontariff barriers restricted U.S. imports of computers during this period and drew domestic firms into the business, enticed by a captive market, as with chips. The Japanese Electronic Computer Company (JECC) sparked demand for computers through favorable leases, and insisted on Japanese inputs as a percentage of imported machines, estimated at 80–95% as late as 1985.[64] As efforts to liberalize semiconductor trade gained momentum, however, most formal barriers in the computer market were also reduced.[65] Much to their dismay, domestic firms were persuaded that MITI's VLSI project would offset pressures resulting from greater U.S. competition, easing their need for protectionism.[66] Promoting the linkage externality between chips and computers, rather than providing tariffs or nontariff barriers, was thus the mainstay of the government's strategy as this commercial rivalry heated up.

A second issue raised in discussions of Japan's computer industry concerns the role of consortia. Government-sponsored programs have received considerable attention, in part because programs like the Fifth

Generation Computer project (1979–91) are often seen as having been *un*successful.[67] Far from creating a capacity to consume, however, computer consortia built upon domestic competitiveness in chips and electronics, rather than setting out to "start from scratch." Business equipment, for example, was a key component part of projects ranging from the 3.75 Series Computer Development (1972–6) to the Fourth (1979–83) and Fifth Generation Computer programs, tapping synergies among electronics and higher value-added computer subsystems. Similarly, the Realtime Operating Nucleus project (TRON), distinguished for having pursued an architecture to rival IBM's Diskette Operating System (DOS), was also much more modest in its ambitions, tackling research on telecommunications and consumer electronics equipment, for example, in addition to semiconductor technology. The upshot of all this is that Japan did not create a capacity to consume this linkage externality through protectionism or computer consortia, but instead practiced the same brand of strategic trade as the United States through the VLSI period.

Competition over these externalities has been a key source of tension in U.S.-Japanese semiconductor trade. Policymakers on both sides of the Pacific insist that disputes in the industry are inevitable, not least because they place the same amount of weight on these externalities.[68] MITI's prediction that this commercial rivalry is likely to intensify traces to a similar logic.[69] Yet what is most interesting about the U.S.-Japan chip rivalry is that, far from being tempted to spend lavishly on their domestic firms, policymakers have, on the contrary, been motivated to free-ride on foreign subsidies to the industry, given the score on the internalization variable.

The Internalization Variable

By stressing the importance of the internalization variable, this chapter puts an entirely new spin on the U.S-Japan semiconductor rivalry. Much of the literature emphasizes the economics of the industry and finds semiconductors to be an ideal candidate for strategic trade. Yet the incentive for states to subsidize the industry has long been questioned because of the international diffusion of the externalities at issue. Indeed, convinced that spending on the chip industry amounts to investing in an international public good, U.S. and Japanese policymakers have been tempted to free-ride on each other's subsidies. This piece of the puzzle escapes much of the literature on chips, the result being that scholars

have greatly overstated the enthusiasm of policymakers for funding semiconductor R&D.

The domestic diffusion of technology has long figured prominently in
requests for the state to play an activist role in the semiconductor industry.[70] Intel's Noyce, on behalf of the SIA, offered Congress a telling
lesson in corporate strategy: "[i]n an industry with two equal competitors *the winning strategy is to have your competitor bear the expense of
creating the public good . . . and then appropriate that public good to
your own use as needed.*"[71] Noyce had a domestic competitor in mind,
but his strategy was already being played out on the international stage.
Indeed, this strategy would loom large in the debate over Sematech, but
with respect to foreign competitors. For example, in marked contrast to
the view that the consortium might not exhibit externalities for the
American economy, the CBO explained that "[t]he primary concern may
be, instead, that Sematech's results *would be disseminated too rapidly
and become readily available to foreign producers,* undermining the
purpose of the program."[72] Industry confirmed this assessment; Deputy
Commerce Secretary Thomas Murvin testified before a congressional
subcommittee that "Sematech's own advisory board . . . warned that *the
potential for international dissipation of its technology gains was very
real* and would have to be monitored."[73] Echoing this, NACS concluded
that "[s]harply higher costs for the development of new technology, and
the *quick, international diffusion of technical knowledge,* make it increasingly difficult for semiconductor firms to appropriate the benefits of
advanced technology research and development."[74] Far from making the
case for subsidies, these reports did much to undercut Washington's
resolve to fight.

U.S. policymakers have been as reluctant to invest in an international
public good as domestic firms. There is little shortage of evidence that
semiconductor technology diffuses beyond national borders. From fabrication equipment to the design of microprocessors, Japanese advances
have been greatly stimulated by U.S. R&D, both public and private.[75]
On the other hand, MITI's VLSI program, for example, benefited U.S.
technology, the results of which diffused through formal (i.e., patents)
as well as informal (i.e., scientific meetings) channels, much like at
home.[76] In debating strategic-trade policy, Washington has thus been as
attentive to Japan's score on the internalization variable as it has to its
own.

In mapping the landscape of the chip rivalry, Japanese policymakers have long held to the same conclusion as their American counterparts. The diffusion of chip technology on the domestic scene has often worried firms and has led to demands for an activist role on the part of the state more generally. Indeed, the government has struggled to coordinate a variety of consortia, given this leakage of know-how. The High Speed Computer project, for example, is argued to have succeeded not simply because of state funding per se, but because the government compensated members for the dissemination of knowledge that it helped foster.[77] This concern has been no less apparent at the international level. It is, of course, widely argued that Japan has enjoyed a free ride on U.S. R&D. And while MITI and other agencies concede that domestic semiconductor firms have benefited greatly from American technology, this is but half the story.[78] Even during the earliest phases of this commercial rivalry, Japanese advances in manufacturing technology have stimulated U.S. advances in fields that have been historically underfunded nationally.[79] Provisions under the STA to ensure U.S. access to Japanese patents, and vice versa, point to Japan's emergence as an important source of technological know-how.[80] Not that anyone thought this know-how could be internalized as a matter of policy; the CBO argued, for example, that the leakage of chip R&D beyond the borders of a nation was "inevitable, if less rapid, through the same media as domestic dissemination."[81] Rather, this clause in the STA made it clear that both sides recognized the implications of funding semiconductor R&D, and that cooperation in this industry required joint sponsorship of an international public good.

In scoring the internalization variable, several key linkage and technology externalities have figured prominently. These upstream-downstream effects are difficult to internalize where trade in inputs helps foreign firms at both the device and systems levels. From an upstream perspective, returns to SM&E R&D largely accrue at the component level, the upshot being that U.S. (Japanese) semiconductor vendors consume these benefits as readily as Japanese (U.S.) firms, given an equal opportunity to set specifications.[82] For example, it is estimated that between one-third and one-half of MITI's funds for VLSI were allocated for purchasing American production equipment, the benefits of which were realized primarily through trade by Japanese chip vendors downstream.[83] By arguing that VLSI succeeded *because* of these inputs, U.S. industry representatives lend support to this assessment.[84] This point is followed up momentarily.

The same dynamic is apparent downstream, where U.S. (Japanese) computer firms are poised to exploit Japanese (U.S.) semiconductor R&D, given that these returns are largely had at the systems level. Along these lines, the American computer industry has objected to policies smacking of "technonationalism," fearful that this downstream payoff might be jeopardized as a result, irrespective of the nationality of upstream firms. For example, the Computer Systems Policy Project (CSPP) demanded that the STA be tailored in such a way as not to curb relations with upstream Japanese chip firms, reflecting this trend. To be sure, as Washington prepared to sanction Japan for dumping chips in third markets, the list of "targeted" devices was written up to minimize the costs incurred by U.S. computer vendors, since the benefits of this linkage externality diffuse through trade.[85] Japan, too, has long conceded that imports of U.S. microprocessors (among other chips) enhance its exports and augment the social return to computer R&D at home. Indeed, with design-ins of U.S. semiconductors increasing sevenfold between 1986 and 1993 (or 32% annually), this pattern has been prolific through the VLSI period, especially since the signing of the STA.[86] As one MITI official put it, "[t]he division between Japanese-made or U.S.-made chips will become increasingly blurred if such cooperative affiliations increase."[87]

More dramatic still is the evidence bearing on spillovers. In terms of the materials and equipment industry, diffusion has been apparent everywhere. The SIA testified in 1981, for example, that Japan's VLSI project was realizing gains because of MITI's "systematic adaptation of American state-of-the-art products and processes."[88] Indeed, beyond the linkages shared through trade, the argument was that Japan benefited from the know-how exported with U.S. products. The other side of the coin, of course, was that U.S. vendors consumed spillovers owing to Japanese advances as well, as in steppers, packaging, and gallium arsenide circuitry, for example. Japanese advances in the area of manufacturing processes, in particular, have had a sizable influence on the U.S. semiconductor industry. Along these lines, Sematech expected to be dependent on Japanese submicron technology through its initial stages, improvements upon which have since diffused back to Japan.[89] More recently, Matsushita's technology for cutting to one-tenth the errors in etching circuit designs at the 0.25–0.35 micron level have inspired new initiatives at Intel, and this at less cost to the American semiconductor giant than would otherwise have been the case.[90]

In terms of chips, the speed with which imitations are offered is one of the most often cited indicators of diffusion. The pattern has been striking.[91] Memory and logic chips are both easily reverse engineered, the designs for which have been difficult to patent despite the Semiconductor Chip Protection Act (SCPA) in the United States and similar pieces of legislation abroad.[92] Japanese imitations of U.S. chips are well known: Nippon Electric Company (NEC), for example, announced its PD700 five months after Intel's 4004, and its 8080 right on the heels of Intel's 8-bit microprocessor. Even NEC's proprietary V-Series ("V" for "victory") microprocessors led Intel to file a lawsuit for what it claimed to be an infringement of its patented code.[93] Likewise, NTT announced a design for a 32-bit microprocessor within months of Bell Laboratories, Hewlett Packard, and Intel.[94] This was part of a bigger picture: the Japanese Technology Evaluation Center (JTEC) expected that Toshiba would enter production within a year of Intel, revealing the rate with which technology for the 80486 had diffused.[95] Identical concerns prompted Digital Equipment to schedule the release of the MicroVAXII computer chip set to coincide with the SCPA, hoping that patent protection might slow this rate of imitation.[96] Other examples include Fujitsu's bipolar PROMs and assorted high-end memories, which Japanese end users were encouraged to purchase from domestic suppliers.[97] More generally, the "avalanche" style with which Japanese firms have introduced substitute products is taken by U.S. observers in and out of government as evidence of the diffusion of semiconductor technology, both at home and abroad.[98] The problem, as Intel noted in the mid-1980s, is that a "family" of chips is costly to design (then roughly $80 million) but inexpensive to copy (then roughly $100,000 to make a photographic copy of the main chip, around which derivative chips are patterned).[99] This concern has not subsided: the Commerce Department warned in 1994, for example, that code infringements and the copying of chip designs will likely increase in the future, in light of both the maturation of the dominant complementary metal oxide semiconductor (CMOS) process technology and the widespread availability of CAD tools worldwide.[100]

Less familiar are the patent infringements filed by Japanese chip vendors against U.S. firms. Indeed, throughout the VLSI period the diffusion of semiconductor technology has increasingly been in both directions. NEC and Toshiba filed patent infringements against Texas Instruments

(TI), for example, for the design of its 256K DRAM, charging the firm had sought to reestablish itself in this segment of the memory market with an imitation of a Japanese chip.[101] Other examples of devices in which Japan was first to market include 1M CMOS SRAMs, 16M DRAMs, 4M EPROMs, and various "flash memories," niches of the market in which U.S. firms have had much to learn from Japan.[102] More generally, as licensees of American technology, Japanese firms have pushed products and processes forward in ways that have helped U.S. vendors, as in the case of Fujitsu's success with a reduced instruction set code (RISC) chip, patterned on Sun Microsystem's architecture.[103]

The inability on the part of the United States or Japan to internalize the externalities of the semiconductor industry sheds a great deal of light on this commercial rivalry, and the design of the STA. The next section examines how U.S. and Japanese policymakers have weighed the incentive to free-ride on each other's subsidies against the temptation to fight for their national champions in this quintessentially strategic industry.

THE DEPENDENT VARIABLE

Given the scores on the independent variables, the book interprets the U.S.-Japan chip rivalry as a Favor-Thy-Neighbor PD: both states can consume, but cannot internalize, the industry's externalities. Nonintervention is the dominant strategy; the incentive for each state is to free-ride on the other's spending on the industry. Yet if both states act on this incentive, they realize a collectively suboptimal supply of externalities, benefits that both can consume. With a sufficiently long "shadow of the future," these states may thus seek to remedy this problem of cooperation by establishing property rights, the purpose of which would be to get both states to invest in an international public good. The STA serves this function: the side agreement on market shares reached in 1986 and restated in 1991 set out a floor on subsidy practices. In particular, it committed both the United States and Japan to spend on their national champions despite the international reach of the externalities at stake. If this account of the U.S.-Japan chip rivalry is accurate, we should expect to see a reluctance on the part of both states to subsidize above this floor. In fact, this is precisely what the evidence bears out. As the STA's market shares came within reach in the early 1990s, Washington declared victory and cut Sematech's funding, while

MITI restructured its domestic industry and slashed spending as well. This section assesses the score on the dependent variable, probing the strategic-trade policies implemented by the United States and Japan.

The Competing Explanation

Endogenous protection theory speaks more directly to the domestic politics of the chip rivalry. Looking at employment size, geographic concentration, politicial dispersion, and industrial concentration, the theory explains that elected officials offer subsidies to a vocal semiconductor industry under siege from Japanese imports. There was certainly reason for concern on the part of the American chip industry: some 25,000 jobs were lost in 1985–6 alone, even if the fall in demand for chips traced as much to the business cycle as to Japanese competition.[104] In assessing the semiconductor industry's electoral clout, however, one cannot help but be struck by the fact that it fares poorly on the four variables endogenous protection theory favors. With an employment base of less than 250,000, nearly one-third of which casts a ballot in California, U.S. chip manufacturers boast relatively few votes, and enjoy narrow electoral representation.[105] The score on the industrial concentration variable does little to help this story: though more concentrated than during the first or second generation of chip technology, the American semiconductor industry is a heterogeneous one, comprising a number of specialty boutiques and large firms alike. Rents are thus more likely to be congested in this industry, dampening the incentive for firms to invest in lobbying.

Jockeying between the CSPP and the SIA would have led us to expect the STA to be a close call, at least in the view of endogenous protection theory. Washington was clear on its objectives, however, both before and after ratification, and not just in 1986. The most compelling part of this story, of course, concerns the postratification setting. Funding for Sematech was pegged to the STA's 20% market share arrangement and was terminated as this figure was reached in the early 1990s.[106] Shortly thereafter, Washington cut off support. As Sematech's CEO, Bill Spencer, explained it, "[o]ur supporters in Congress urged us to come forward with a new model that ended direct federal funding."[107]

Less provocative, but highly suggestive, is that Washington has seldom hesitated to act unilaterally in this commercial rivalry. Many observers point out that the Department of Commerce self-initiated an antidumping claim case against Japan in 256K DRAMs, although in fact other examples of the state's lead role abound. In negotiating the STA, for example, Washington led the way in saddling Japan with much of the burden for data gathering, as spelled out in the 1991 text. Rather than tracing back to any given demand on the part of industry, this effort owed instead to Washington's dismay with MITI, which insisted that the slow pace of U.S. gains in the Japanese marketplace reflected a lack of information on consumer needs and pricing. In short, the state has been anything but a neutral arbiter of demands for strategic-trade policy in the semiconductors industry.

While endogenous protection theory sheds light on protectionist policies across a wide variety of industries in Japan, it falls short in explaining strategic-trade policy toward the semiconductor industry. Employment figures compare favorably with those in the United States (225,778 in 1994), and the industry appears to be geographically concentrated with good political representation (441 facilities in 1994).[108] In terms of industrial concentration, four firms account for most of Japan's chip output, implying that each has a strong incentive to lobby representatives in government in pursuit of rents. Yet, far from catering to the demands of the nation's consumer electronics giants, the Japanese government has clearly set the policy agenda in this industry, determining which firms to include in state-sponsored projects, for example, and arranging "shotgun marriages" among chip vendors to consolidate the industry. This book explains the state's lead role in light of the fact that externalities, rather than votes, are the currency of strategic-trade policy.

Background on the Semiconductor Rivalry

On the eve of the VLSI period, the landscape of the semiconductor industry posed new challenges for the protagonists in this commercial rivalry. In the United States, first- and second-generation chip firms like General Electric, RCA, and Fairchild gave way to third-generation firms like Intel as the industry consolidated. In Japan, efforts to rationalize the domestic industry favored export-oriented vendors over small consumer electronics firms, few of which were likely to benefit from the consortia aimed at mounting an offensive in markets abroad. By the late 1970s, entry barriers and an unprecedented level of trade in chips forced policymakers on both sides of the Pacific to revisit questions about the role governments would play in this industry.

Having recorded its first trade deficit in semiconductors in 1978, the United States was pressed to confront serious doubts about the competitiveness of one of its high technology icons. The statistics were dramatic: in 1981, Japan held 70% of the 64K DRAM market, a product built by 5 U.S. firms (12 had built 16K DRAMs), only 2 of which had managed to achieve volume production.[109] National Semiconductor's Charles Spock told a congressional subcommittee that "what is disturbing about this challenge [from Japan] is that ultimately we won't be able to compete successfully unless markets are opened and *the effects of foreign industrial policies are dealt with.*"[110] Alan Lidow, testifying for the SIA, explained that industry did not want protectionism, but rather R&D subsidies, urging that "[o]ur industry is extremely sensitive to such incentives."[111] Indeed, the language of tariffs and nontariff barriers had given way to discussion of R&D subsidies by the mid-1980s, and not just in the United States.[112] Calls for Washington to respond had been mounting for some time. As Noyce urged an attentive congressional subcommittee, "[i]f measures cannot be found to counter the advantages of foreign producers afforded by targeting practices, *I see no alternative but to engage in similar activities ourselves as a last resort.*"[113]

Trade liberalization in chips had been initiated under the Nixon administration in the early 1970s, though Japanese barriers persisted until the mid-1980s. It was not at all clear that the removal of formal impediments would improve the standing of U.S. firms in the Japanese market. George Scalise, testifying on behalf of the SIA, was clear on this point: "I don't think the tariff barriers will have any significant impact on the trade balance at all."[114] Scalise had reason to be skeptical: Japan's lifting of restrictions on import license controls (1974) and on foreign direct investment (1976) had done little to help U.S. chip firms. The SIA noted in a petition pursuant to Section 301, for example, that, as of 1985, U.S. market share in Japan had held at roughly 10% through ten years of liberalization.[115] TI's experience became a rallying point: sales had remained constant from 1968 to 1988 despite four appreciations of the Yen *and* the repeal of Japan's 15% tariff on semiconductors.[116] LSI Logic boasted a similar record. CEO Wilfred Corrigan explained to Congress that his firm's hold on 5% of the Japanese market had held steady despite three appreciations of the Yen between 1986 and 1989. This, he quipped, was rather difficult to understand: "if our economists are correct and all the information is in the price, *we would have ex-*

pected to see a very significant change in market share in that time frame."[117]

Because the problem of market access had been coupled with Japanese dumping (i.e., exports were subsidized by charging a price premium at home), such accounts angered an increasingly frustrated Congress. As chair of the Subcommittee on Trade, for example, Sam Gibbons (D-Florida) put a popular spin on the market access problem: "I have come to the conclusion, you know, that it is no longer our responsibility to have to penetrate [the Japanese market]. *They have got to show us how to penetrate it.*"[118] The question of market access dominated bilateral trade talks through the 1980s.[119] Yet "numerical indicators" were sought in semiconductors, but not in industries ranging from software to pharmaceuticals, many of which were equally biased against U.S. imports.[120] The reason for this selective use of numerical targets speaks to the import of the internalization variable.

MITI's "counterliberalization" policies blended an element of import substitution with an emphasis on export promotion. First, domestic end users of chips were encouraged to buy Japanese over foreign products whenever substitutes were available. In certain cases the results were stark: imports of U.S. bipolar PROMs, for example, declined from $1.3 million to $0.2 million within six months of Fujitsu's release of a similar device.[121] Since these components were, at least in part, based on U.S. designs, Japanese end users put up little resistance to this, expecting quality on par with American products. In this way, the diffusion of semiconductor technology even helped facilitate import substitution in Japan.

Second, counterliberalization was intended to assist *export-oriented* chip vendors, a small subset of the Japanese semiconductor industry. Indeed, as *Nihon Keizai* reported in 1973, "MITI has decided it is *not* proper to apply its liberalization countermeasures to those enterprises which are turning out ICs only for incorporation into their own products."[122] This meant that small consumer electronics firms would find it difficult to retain in-house chip capabilities in competing with U.S. imports, a de facto rationalization of the industry aimed at doling out public and private R&D to firms pursuing global market share. Like their American rivals, Japanese chip firms thus entered the VLSI period dependent on trade. Like their American counterparts, Japanese policymakers were reluctant to fund their national champions, given the scope of the resulting externalities.

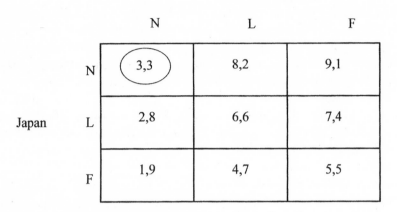

Figure 4.2. U.S.-Japan semiconductor rivalry.

The Cooperation Problem

This book's theory interprets the U.S.-Japan chip rivalry as a Favor-Thy-Neighbor PD: the United States and Japan can consume but cannot internalize the externalities at issue. The expectation is that both sides would thus weigh limited intervention against nonintervention; full intervention is dominated out because of the global diffusion of the resulting externalities. Limited intervention is tantamount to investing in an international public good; nonintervention, on the other hand, entails free riding on the other's subsidies. In this game, illustrated in Figure 4.2, nonintervention is the dominant strategy, yet if both states act on this incentive to free-ride, they forgo a more optimal level of linkage and spillover externalities. To get around this, these states must each spend on their national champions. Property rights are likely to play a role in facilitating this. If property rights can be assigned, ensuring at least some appropriable return on investment, then states may be more likely to spend, despite this international leakage of benefits. This chapter argues that the STA's market shares serve as property rights, the objective being to foster spending on this international public good. The rest of this section assesses the evidence in favor of this interpretation, and contrasts the book's argument with the one put forward by endogenous protection theory.

U.S. Strategic-Trade Policy

By 1985, the United States had all but exited the DRAM market, putting at risk U.S. world market share in logic chips as well, given the importance of memories as a driver of chip technology more generally. Those firms that remained in memories alleged that Japanese firms were pricing exports below cost, and filed an array of antidumping claims as a result. Hardly indifferent to what it viewed as a reversal of fortune in this "bedrock" industry, the Department of Commerce self-initiated a claim in 256K DRAMs, a decision that Secretary Baldrige would later explain was necessary because dumping had become "a standard business practice" in Japan's efforts to gain market share in high-technology industries.[123] These filings, coupled with the SIA's petition for 301 action, prodded the United States and Japan to strike a settlement. There were, of course, agreements already on the table: between 1979 and 1989 alone, 15 accords had been reached on trade in electronics, many bearing on trade in chips.[124] Yet, the 1986 STA was unique for several reasons. A five-year renewable pact mandated to cover third markets, the STA addressed issues of pricing, data collection, and a variety of mechanisms to enhance transparency.[125] It is best known, however, for its inclusion of a secret side letter, in which Japan pledged to help raise *foreign* market share to 20% of its domestic market, a figure that American observers had insisted would obtain under conditions where trade in chips was truly "free."[126] Though the agreement had been widely viewed as a quid pro quo for a U.S. promise not to sanction Japan, and as the first accord in high technology aimed at securing American competitiveness, rather than jobs per se, the STA is most usefully viewed as an effort to impose property rights on the diffusion of semiconductors externalities.[127]

Numerical targets had first been proposed in 1983 by the U.S.-Japan High Technology Working Group (HTWG) as a way to benchmark liberalization of the Japanese market.[128] In negotiations over the STA, MITI emerged as a staunch *proponent* of numerical targets, especially through the early stages of these talks. The STA's provision of 20% sparked a great deal of interest in managed trade, though rarely has it been examined with respect to how it served to guide government spending. There are some important reasons to do so.

Attention in Washington, having signed the STA, shifted to the Sematech proposal. In the debate that followed, iteration of the U.S.-Japan semiconductor rivalry, and the scope of the externalities at issue, figured prominently. Frank Squires, Sematech's chief administrative officer (CAO), told a congressional subcommittee that "[m]ost now understand that *this is a race that has no end*. The high risk/high reward inherent in this [U.S.-Japan] competition can and must be shared broadly between both Government and industry partnerships."[129] Noyce touted the externalities argument, insisting that "this project will offer significant benefits to the Nation as a whole," yet he and others expressed concerns about the international leakage of Sematech's R&D.[130] Washington grappled with the Sematech proposal, but hedged on the spending levels requested by the SIA, largely because the CBO and other agencies had argued that the scope of the resulting externalities helped to undermine the case for R&D subsidies more generally. The Commerce Department concluded that government outlays of $100 million annually for five years would constitute the "bare minimum necessary to enable the U.S. to reestablish manufacturing leadership by the early 1990s."[131] This, in fact, amounted to roughly 6% of total industry R&D, and 20% of federally funded R&D, and would be matched dollar for dollar by the consortium's membership.[132] Two points should be emphasized here. First, the legislation exempting Sematech from U.S. antitrust law *followed* the signing of the STA. This was no accident. Washington would not move on the Sematech proposal until the ink was dry on the STA or, more specifically, until the 20% arrangement was in place. This is because the clause made it easier for Washington to invest in an international public good, ensuring some appropriable return on investment. Second, this level of spending on Sematech was, as the Commerce Department noted, the "bare minimum necessary." Given the incentive to free-ride on Japan's subsidies to the industry, it would have been surprising if Washington had spent any more.

The STA's 20% benchmark proved elusive. Continued dumping and limited access to the Japanese market were cited as the reasons for this, leading the Reagan administration to levy $300 million in tariffs ($135 million for dumping, and $165 million for restricted market access). Coming six months after the signing of the STA, these sanctions did little to boost confidence in the agreement. With the expiration of the STA in 1991, moreover, foreign firms were still well short of 20% market share in Japan.[133] Rather than sanction Japan again, however, Washington sought to renew the STA.[134] This is not to imply that a more activist response had been ruled out. Indeed, such options were certainly inspired by a 1989 NACS report, which concluded that Asia was on the verge of dominating "the U.S. downstream electronics industry and ultimately the global electronics landscape."[135] Explaining that "there is a difference between potato chips and computer chips," Andrew Procassini, president of the SIA, testified before a concerned Congress that "trade policy is extremely important to our economic future and international competitiveness."[136] In a nod to the NACS report, Gore (D-Tennessee) framed the challenge this way: "[h]ere we have a key industry of the future on the ropes, an emergency situation with the industry leaders saying we need a government response as part of a larger national response, and there has been no public response at all from the Administration. What kind of signal does that send?"[137] The signal was clear, however. The temptation, all along, had been to free-ride, but with the STA up and running, Washington would fund in accordance with its property right, though no more than this. The Bush administration's stand in the STA negotiations was to put more emphasis on the 20% target, and ultimately it succeeded in positioning the provision within the text itself. The clause insists that the 20% target is not "a guarantee, a ceiling nor a floor," although negotiators assert that this was, indeed, a promise.[138] In part, this language was offered to ease domestic political tensions in Japan, pressures that in 1986 had led MITI to deny the existence of the side agreement itself. And in part it was offered to place more responsibility at the feet of U.S. industry to tailor devices more carefully to the needs of Japanese consumer electronics end users.

When the STA was renewed in 1991, foreign firms held roughly 14% of the Japanese market. This tally rose from 14.3% in the third quarter of 1991 to 14.4%, 14.6%, 16.0%, 15.9%, and 20.2% through the fourth quarter of 1992 (see Figure 4.3).[139] If the book's account of the chip rivalry is right – that is, that the STA set out property rights through market shares – then we should expect to see Washington back away from Sematech as this 20% figure came into view. In fact, this is precisely what we find. Washington reduced funding for Sematech in mid-1992, explaining that the consortium had brought the U.S. semiconductor industry back from the brink of ruin, and that the government's objectives had been met.[140] Thus, rather than build on success with more subsidies, Washington saw additional spending on Sematech as an unacceptable investment in an international public good. In contrast to the civil aircraft industry, in which success has led to more, rather than less,

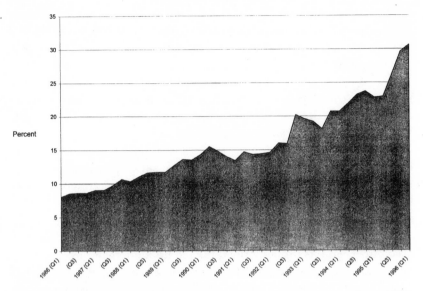

Figure 4.3. Foreign market share in Japan (by quarter). *Source*: Data from 1986-Q2 to 1991 are SIA estimates; 1991-Q3 to 1996 are from the U.S. trade representative.

spending on national champions, the fight over chips has unfolded as a race to the bottom. This makes sense where externalities diffuse internationally, as opposed to where they are constrained by national borders.

Japanese Strategic-Trade Policy

The Japanese semiconductor industry entered the 1980s reeling from the opening of its domestic market. Formal barriers to trade counted for little by the mid-1980s, and MITI backed off its countermeasures, favoring public-private consortia instead. Much has been made of NTT and MITI's projects, and for good reason. But there was a lot more to these projects than funding alone. In MITI's case, for example, administrative guidance meant providing market information, gauging technology trends, and seeding corporate alliances, efforts that were especially important in the wake of liberalization. The transfer of "high-risk R&D" to specific firms resulted in specialization, enticing reluctant collaborators to work together. In the case of NTT's R&D on the 64K and 256K DRAMs, recipients were selected on the basis of their core competencies and ability to contribute to other facets of the project.[141] MITI's VLSI project, organized around the manufacturing technologies for producing 1M DRAMs, involved industrial restructuring beyond just R&D spending. In brief, NTT and MITI ensured that Japan's semiconductor industry hit the VLSI period up and running.

The STA played out most interestingly in Japan. First, MITI reduced chip production by almost 30% through early 1987 to curb over-production and raise profitability.[142] MITI further encouraged firms to expand chip imports as per the STA.[143] Capital investments fell short of pre-STA levels, further reflecting MITI's goal of slashing public and private spending. As the *Japan Economic Journal* editorialized at the time, the STA "helped to virtually create a coordinated production control by chip makers that we have never seen before."[144] In fact, Japan was in a race to the bottom in terms of subsidizing its domestic chip industry. Anticipating the costs of competing in the Ultra Large Scale Integration (ULSI) period, MITI and NTT were eager for the United States to pick up more of this tab. Projects like SORTEC drew less state funding than might have been expected otherwise, in that Japan's supply of 16M DRAMs fell within the scope of the STA's mandate.[145] In addition, the 1991 renewal also sparked a reduction in Japanese DRAM production, just as in 1986. Small firms like Sanyo were encouraged to exit and large firms like Hitachi were encouraged to diversify beyond memory chips, prompting observers to point out that Japan's industry was consolidating again.[146] By the end of the 1980s, Japanese subsidies as a percentage of total R&D stood at 18%, on par with U.S. spending.[147] The success of the STA would solidify this trend within a few years. Limited intervention thus prevailed as the strategic-trade policy of choice on both sides of the Pacific.

The STA

In a secret side letter appended to the 1986 text, the STA set aside 20% market share in Japan for foreign firms, although predominantly of U.S. origin, since other competitors in the industry held only 0.2% of the Japanese market at the time. And because Japan's was the single largest market for chips, this provision was sure to influence world trade, an important, if partial, property right in the global economy. There is much debate about whether this was a promise or an aspiration. The book sides with the promise interpretation.[148] Article 2.10 of the 1991 text spells out the terms of this provision: "Japan recognizes that the U.S. semiconductor industry expects that the foreign market share will grow to more than 20 percent of the Japanese market by the end of 1992 and considers that this can be realized." Why is this a property right?

The first expectation is that in building the STA, states would contest the allocation of property rights, in this case set out by the 20% arrangement. In fact, this figure proved to be highly charged. The idea of setting out property rights as market shares had originally been proposed by the HTWG, though a figure had not been settled on.[149] Those involved in the negotiations looked for a figure that would reflect what foreign firms would hold if the Japanese market was truly "open." The SIA piped up with figures as high as 40% but Washington was hesitant, fearful that a bigger property right meant carrying more of the tab for funding an international public good. Interestingly, Japanese negotiators were not averse to a *higher* figure. MITI was a staunch supporter of numerical targets and representatives of the EIAJ had been at least as comfortable with a figure as high as 30%.[150] If the STA was *strictly* about market access, this would be quite puzzling, to say the least.

This is not to imply that extending a property right to foreign firms was an easy sell in Japan. Keeping the side letter secret at first was meant to shield MITI from having others clamor that a precedent had been set. When the terms of this provision were laid out in the 1991 text, care was taken to couch it in more palatable language. In contrast to the 1986 side letter, the 1991 text urges that this is not "a guarantee, a ceiling nor a floor." The 1986 side letter explains what this means: the expectation was that foreign vendors would reach 20% *if* trade was truly open *and* imported chips were designed and marketed with more attention to the needs of Japan's consumer electronics giants, rather than tailored to the American computer industry. To facilitate this, Article 2.7 explains that in evaluating any progress under the STA, attention should be paid to the 20% and other indicators, like the number of design-ins, which, in addition to increasing foreign sales, would also help to customize imported semiconductors to Japanese demand. This accords with the STA's stipulation that technology diffusion be fostered more generally (see Articles 1.4 and 3.12 [1986]), given the understanding that an international public good is at stake. Article 2.6, for example, calls for joint participation in seminars and in commercial applications while Articles 2.3–6 call for collaboration and "increased information exchange and mutual understanding" in the area of science and technology. Finally, Article 4 of the 1986 text puts this all into perspective, stipulating that foreign firms be guaranteed access to patents resulting from government-sponsored projects, a clear affirmation that the public benefits exhibited by this industry exceed the private gains conferred by any property rights.

The second expectation is that the subsidy floor set out by these property rights would guide spending on the industry. On this point there can be little doubt. The experience of Sematech is especially instructive. First, government matching funds were approved after the STA was signed, promising Washington an appropriable return on investment. To be sure, congressional testimony makes clear that the STA made all the difference in terms of getting Washington to subsidize Sematech, despite the concerns raised by the CBO and other agencies that the resulting technology would quickly diffuse abroad. Second, Washington stopped funding Sematech shortly after U.S. and foreign firms accounted for 20% market share in Japan.[151] In terms of confirming evidence, this is a "smoking gun." To wean Sematech at this point was highly provocative, particularly when compared with the case of civil aircraft, in which success generally led to more funding, not less.[152] Yet, Washington was unwilling to spend more, seeing this as overspending on an international public good. As noted earlier, the STA played out similarly in Japan, facilitating the rationalization of the industry, guiding the overall level of public spending on chips, and informing the way key consortia were organized and implemented in the semiconductor industry.

In 1996, U.S. and Japanese negotiators renewed the STA for the second time, although little was made of the property rights provision set out in 1986. With no expectation that foreign vendors would fall below 20%, both sides agreed to continue the exchange of data and enhance transparency more generally, declaring victory in light of their efforts to pay their fare share of this public good, but no more (see Figures 4.4–4.6).

CONCLUSION

The U.S.-Japan semiconductor rivalry has been the subject of considerable attention in the strategic-trade literature. Indeed, few industries seem as well suited to an analysis of this sort. However, much of the literature miscasts the cooperation problem feeding tensions in this industry. Pre-

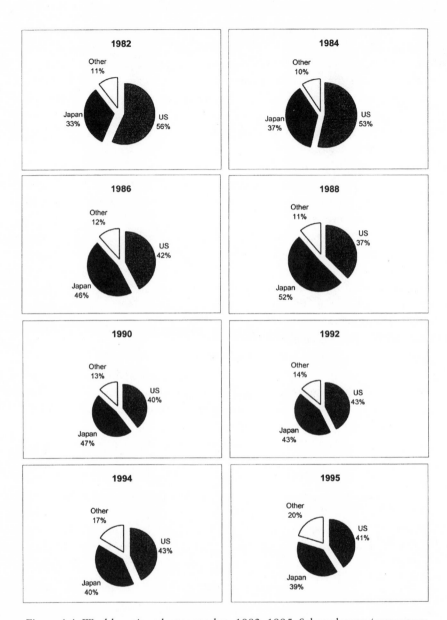

Figure 4.4. World semiconductor market, 1982–1995: Selected years (percentage share by country). *Source*: Semiconductor Industry Association.

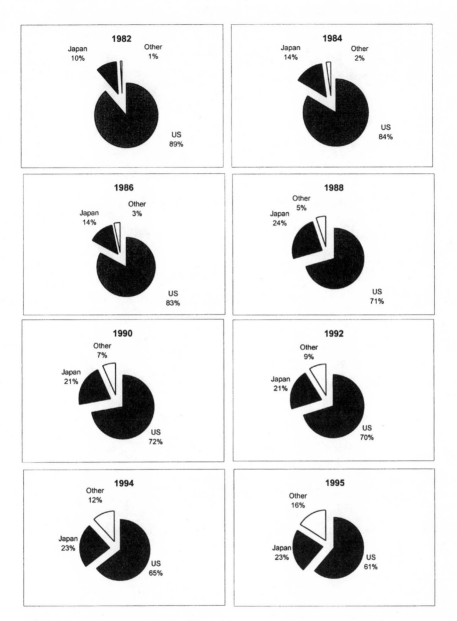

Figure 4.5. United States semiconductor market, 1982–1995: Selected years (percentage share by country). *Source*: Semiconductor Industry Association.

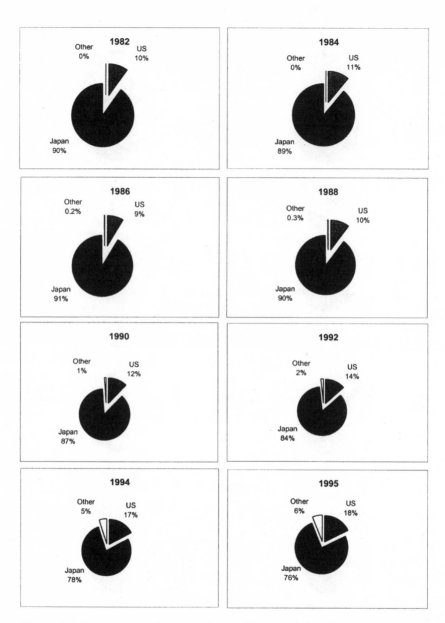

Figure 4.6. Japan semiconductor market, 1982–1995: Selected years (percentage share by country). *Source*: Semiconductor Industry Association.

sented with anything but another case of managed trade, the United States and Japan have been torn between subsidizing a critical high technology industry and free-riding on each other's investment in the international externalities that result. The implications of this argument escape much of the literature; far from hurting each other by spending too much on their national champions, the United States and Japan have risked hurting each other by spending too little. By focusing on the international diffusion of the externalities at stake in this commercial rivalry, the book can hardly be accused of recounting the same old story about DRAMs.

5

The High-Definition Television Rivalry

Few commercial rivalries have been as cloaked in controversy, or as misunderstood, as high-definition television (HDTV). In the United States, the debate over HDTV unfolded as a referendum on the principles of free trade and the government's role in the economy. In Japan, enthusiasm for the technology has been dampened by questions about the appeal of Hi-Vision television, highlighting concerns about the excesses of state activism on the part of this quintessentially activist state. Not surprisingly, HDTV is held up by critics as evidence that governments lack the wherewithal to practice strategic trade. This chapter raises a dissenting voice, explaining that HDTV has, instead, been a *success* story on both sides of the Pacific.

Japanese research on HDTV began in 1964, nurtured by the government through direct and indirect support. U.S. interest did not lag far behind; the debate over HDTV garnered widespread attention in the 1970s. As in Japan, Washington took up two questions: What is HDTV? And why does it matter? In answering the first question, policymakers saw an answer to the second. HDTV is basically a hybrid of television and computer technology, providing high-resolution images on par with 35-millimeter film. To display, process, and correct this large amount of information per picture frame – or what is roughly four times that offered by current color television technology – HDTV receivers use a lot of memory and logic chips. This requirement sheds considerable light on the question of why HDTV matters.

The fight over HDTV has been widely explained as a fight over semiconductors. This, of course, is misleading, given that digital displays, fiber optics, and related technologies are also at stake. Still, semiconductors have long enjoyed center stage in this commercial rivalry. Proponents on both sides of the Pacific reasoned that their country's market share in semiconductors would, in turn, depend on their country's market share in HDTV. This linkage externality has carried a lot of weight with U.S. and Japanese policymakers alike, and yet the verdicts they reached concerning what to do about HDTV could not have been more different. The reason is that consumer electronics serves to bridge HDTV with the semiconductor, display, and fiber optical industries, and only Japan has placed much stock in this bridge. For their part, U.S. policymakers have found it hard to see past the lack of an American presence in markets ranging from televisions to cameras and videocassette recorders (VCRs), the implication being that the externalities exhibited by HDTV were unlikely to be consumed at home. Indeed, this assessment prevented the United States from entering HDTV a decade earlier, revealing not only the centrality of the consumption variable, but the consistency with which U.S. strategic-trade policy in this industry has unfolded in line with the book's expectations.

This chapter presents the U.S.-Japan rivalry in HDTV as a Cautious Activist game. It argues that because the United States was absent or underrepresented in most consumer electronics markets, the linkage externalities at stake in this commercial rivalry could not be consumed. Washington therefore practiced nonintervention throughout the 1970s and 1980s. In contrast, Japan enjoyed considerable market share in consumer electronics, an industry that has long distinguished itself as that country's largest end user of chips, and affords it considerable leverage on displays, fiber optics, and related technologies. There was thus little doubt about Japan's score on the consumption variable, although the score on the internalization variable is a different story. Japanese policymakers were concerned about the future of HDTV, and America's place in it. First, U.S. logic chips would figure prominently on any HDTV motherboard, irrespective of who built these receivers. Second, given their fragility, HDTV receivers will be built in export markets, the largest of which is sure to be the United States. MITI and other agencies were thus fearful that, in setting up factories (and R&D facilities) in the United States, Japanese subsidies might eventually encourage local subcontracting, enticing American entry into HDTV, and quite possibly its reentry into consumer electronics more generally. As a variant of the "chain store paradox," Japan thus waged a limited fight for its national champions against a U.S. industry left to fend for itself.

Endogenous protection theory views this case in a somewhat similar light. The story it tells is that U.S. nonintervention traces to the television industry's lack of electoral clout, coupled with the wavering support of the semiconductor industry. On the Japanese side, endogenous protection theory explains the strategic-trade policy of limited intervention as owing to the political influence wielded by that country's consumer electronics giants. A closer look, however, reveals that these demand-side accounts fall short on both sides of the Pacific. In the United States, the attention policymakers afforded HDTV would have humbled an industry holding out many times the number of votes that Zenith and others could muster together. Additionally, the semiconductor industry was a staunch supporter of U.S. entry into HDTV, wavering only *after* it became clear that Washington would not fight for this industry. In Japan, endogenous protection theory greatly overstates the lead role of consumer electronics giants in prosecuting the battle over HDTV. Indeed, most of these firms were eager to delegate to government agencies on issues ranging from HDTV standards to product specifications. The book's theory fills in the gaps where endogenous protection theory falls short.

Two points of clarification. First and foremost, this chapter is about HDTV *products*, not about HDTV *standards*. It necessarily delves into the debate over standards in order to frame how the competition over the underlying technologies evolved. Still, the chapter focuses on concerns for world market share in HDTV receivers and related products, and not on the politics of HDTV standards per se. Second, the chapter frames HDTV as a bilateral commercial rivalry, given Europe's decision to "go it alone" on standards. Europe's decision on standards had a protectionist feel to it, but it also handicapped exports, not least because this standard was incompatible with the one U.S. and Japanese policymakers were converging on (or, for that matter, with either of the two current color television standards in the European Union). With Europe looking in, as opposed to abroad, the United States and Japan waged HDTV as a bilateral fight.[1]

After reviewing the economics of HDTV, the chapter scores the independent variables and then the dependent variable, contrasting the book's expectations with those of endogenous protection theory.

THE ECONOMICS OF HDTV

Entrants into the HDTV industry must grapple with a variety of market imperfections. Evidence of the industry's steep learning curve, sizable economies of scale and scope, and high fixed costs of production is widely apparent. Drawing on the manufacturing history of Japanese firms, and on estimates provided by U.S. industry, this section details each of these imperfections in turn.

Learning effects have been much anticipated in HDTV manufacturing but have seldom played out as expected. With *cumulative* output, most Japanese firms predicted that costs would fall dramatically, so much so that HDTV receivers might be competitive with large-screen color televisions on price. Sony had estimated, for example, that a 36-inch HDTV receiver would not be competitive with a color television until manufacturing costs fell to one-eighth the levels reached by the early 1990s.[2] The problem, though, was that few observers expected the long production runs that would be needed to achieve this. The American Electronics Association (AEA) insisted, for example, that small-screen receivers (i.e., less than 40 inches) would fall from roughly $3,000 to $2,500 only after 12 full years of manufacturing experience, and this assuming brisk demand. One obstacle along the way has been that consumers have been unwilling to pay a price premium for receivers less than 40 inches, although even in the case of 45-inch receivers, the AEA estimated that unit costs would fall $1,000 with a cumulative volume of 2 million units, from $4,000 to $3,000.[3] There are two hurdles to realizing sizable learning effects: (1) the popularity of competing formats (see subsequent discussion), which threatens long production runs, and (2) the lack of a "breakthrough" in display technology, which risks economies of scale and scope in this industry.

Economies of scale pertain to cost reductions realized as a result of gains in *aggregate* output. Inputs like semiconductors and displays are central in this regard, accounting for approximately 25% and 50% of the cost of a receiver, respectively.[4] The AEA estimated the cost of semiconductors at $1,520 per receiver with low volumes of 100,000 per year, falling as low as $62 per receiver with high volumes of 11 million per year.[5] This figure rested on the assumption that a breakthrough in large-scale integration (LSI) was in the near offing, making HDTV receivers more price-competitive with current color television technology. On the display front, observers remain less optimistic. One Japanese study insists, for example, that "[w]ith no technological leap-forward in sight in the near future, slow but steady efforts [in display technology] must be exerted for improvement in both the elemental and manufacturing technology domains."[6] Large-screen flat panels hold out promise in delivering picture quality but are particularly problematic in this respect. This technology has pushed forward in fits and starts but has not encouraged manufacturers to bet on further cost reductions with scale. Perhaps not surprisingly, most observers look to gains in semiconductor technology instead.

Economies of scope, by way of contrast, refer to the production efficiencies that result where costs can be amortized across a range of related products. Looking at HDTV, there is a variety of complementary products, such as videocassette recorders, laser discs, camcorders, studio cameras, and production equipment. Since these products build on related technologies, overhead costs and the like can be spread over different lines, the upshot being that a firm's competitiveness in any one of these fields depends on its being competitive in several fields. A widely cited study by the National Telecommunications and Information Administration (NTIA) insisted, for example, that some three-quarters of households owning an HDTV receiver would purchase a VCR, indicative of the potential to exploit scope economies in this industry.[7] Indeed, the HDTV market is expected to be many times the market for receivers alone. The AEA had estimated that related products would fetch $500 billion in U.S. sales within decades, far exceeding any estimates for the receiver market.[8] The problem with these estimates, and the many estimates for learning and scale economies based on them, is that competing television formats threaten to keep HDTV production runs short and thin.

In ascending order of picture quality, both improved-definition television (IDTV) and enhanced-definition television (EDTV) deliver better picture quality than current color television technology, and at a cheaper price than HDTV. These formats loomed large in the late 1980s. First, IDTV translates the American and Japanese standard – the National Television Systems Committee (NTSC) standard – into a digital signal and corrects for picture quality, much like a computer. EDTV goes further still, using digital technologies to enhance image resolution.[9] Early on, Japan offered two variants of its NTSC-compatible EDTV: EDTV-1, which retains the 4:3 aspect ratio (i.e., the screen's width to height) of NTSC TV; and EDTV-2, which instead boasts the same 16:9 aspect ratio that HDTV promises.[10] In estimating the size of the market for HDTV, it has often been assumed that EDTV is a complementary technology, giving customers an early and inexpensive taste of full digital HDTV. The merits of this assumption, however, are far from clear. Given the costs that HDTV will impose on consumers and broadcasters, one influential U.S. study insisted at the height of the debate over HDTV that "EDTV, with its small resolution improvement, is a distinct compromise."[11] Japan's umbrella Hi-Vision standard (see later discussion) has further encouraged firms to build compromise technologies in the scramble to bring receivers to market, and in the process risk production efficiencies.[12]

Finally, the high fixed cost of HDTV manufacturing is a significant barrier to entry. In the late 1980s, Zenith estimated that it would spend $21–30 million to upgrade its 14-inch flat tension mask picture tube facility in order to build larger high-resolution screens.[13] If Zenith was to compete in the more lucrative market for bigger flat-panel displays and the like, however, the cost would be considerably greater. In fact, Zenith representatives told Congress that such an investment was doubtful in the absence of state assistance. Fujitsu is expected to invest over $200 million building a production line for its plasma display panels, a technology that holds out considerable promise in manufacturing flat screens.[14] Given bottlenecks in reducing display costs, however, Fujitsu and other manufacturers of HDTV receivers will likely invest in an assortment of technologies, adding to the capital and R&D outlays required of those who compete. Perhaps not surprisingly, the Japanese Broadcasting Corporation (NHK) has played a lead role in allocating work shares among the nation's biggest consumer electronics giants, the aim being to ease redundancy and to foster a division of labor based on core business competencies.

These market imperfections help set up a story about strategic trade in HDTV, but tell us little about how this commercial rivalry might be expected to unfold. The chapter now scores the independent variables and then the dependent variable; but more concretely, and to the point, it challenges the literature's interpretation of the U.S.-Japan rivalry in HDTV, as well as the lessons for strategic trade that it draws from this case.

THE INDEPENDENT VARIABLES

This section assesses the scores on the consumption and internalization variables. The argument is that the consumer electronics industry provides the necessary bridge between HDTV and semiconductors, displays, fiber optics, and related technologies, and that, as a result, the debate over subsidizing HDTV has turned on the question of U.S. and Japanese competitiveness in consumer electronics. Echoing a verdict rendered a decade earlier, for example, U.S. policymakers concluded in the late 1980s that, because America had "lost" the consumer electronics industry, the linkage externalities at stake in HDTV could not be consumed. In contrast, Japanese policymakers were confident that HDTV would leverage a wide variety of upstream and downstream industries through consumer electronics. The score on the internalization variable, however, was a different matter. There were several concerns. First, U.S. market share in logic chips ensured some American participation in HDTV, even if every receiver was built in Japan. In fact, though, Japanese policymakers knew that few receivers would be built at home, given their size and fragility. Second, because the vast majority of HDTV receivers would be built in the United States, an effort more involved than just piecing together imported "knockdown kit" hardware, local subcontracting might create opportunities for U.S. firms to have a hand in manufacturing, casting doubt on Japan's prospects for fully internalizing the industry's externalities. Indeed, with consumer electronics experiencing its own digital revolution, the concern was that Japanese vendors might increasingly turn to U.S. computer and logic chip firms in overcoming bottlenecks in this technology, in which case Japan's subsidies might well be expected to pave the way for American entry into HDTV.

The Consumption Variable

The fight over HDTV has often been framed as a fight over semiconductors, and yet it has been much more than that. Indeed, digital displays, fiber optics, and a wide variety of related technologies positioned HDTV as being about more than just better television. In the United States, for example, proponents testified that, as Robert A. Roe, chair of the Committee on Science, Space, and Technology, explained it:

HDTV means more than just better pictures or larger displays or even a new generation of TVs in our living rooms, and it means more than the new jobs putting together cabinets and picture tubes. HDTV means new markets for the components of advanced television, such as *semiconductors, fiber optics, and flat screen displays*. These markets will bring with them new wealth for the United States and directly impact our national economy, international trade, competitiveness, and national security.[15]

Commerce Secretary Robert A. Mosbacher was no less enthusiastic, insisting that HDTV "involves serious questions regarding leadership in computers, imaging, and a broad range of related and underlying technologies."[16] Along these same lines, a study prepared by the NTIA argued that the objective in competing for HDTV was to exploit "advanced technology, which will quite likely be a significant driver of future innovation, and the source of new manufacturing and engineering spin-offs."[17] The AEA added some muscle to this forecast, estimating that "[n]ew market opportunities from [HDTV] technologies and their many spin off products are expected conservatively to total $20 billion by the year 2000."[18] The opportunity most of these proponents had in mind involved leveraging the upstream semiconductor industry. This, as it turned out, was a tough sell.

More straightforwardly than most, Craig Fields, director of the Defense Advanced Research Project Agency (DARPA), offered Congress the following rationale for funding HDTV:

[W]hatever companies are producing the semiconductors to go into high definition televisions will have a huge production volume. The net effect is that they will be in a tremendous competitive position for supplying semiconductors to all of the other products beyond HDTV, telecommunications, defense systems, automobiles, what have you. That is why [HDTV] is a very large issue. *If it weren't for that semiconductor* [sic] *spread to a lot of other products, I don't think [HDTV] would be getting the attention that it is now getting and which it certainly deserves.*[19]

Few in Washington were unimpressed by this logic. The linkage externality tying the fate of the semiconductor industry to HDTV was clear-cut. And proponents made a good case for why the government should step in. In no uncertain terms, for example, Intel's Robert Noyce, president of Sematech, explained that "we must have this industry established in America, or we will go broke."[20] Noyce's view was backed up by a highly influential and hotly debated AEA study that estimated that U.S. world market share in semiconductors would hold at 41% with 50% world market share in HDTV, but would fall to 20.5% with only 10% world market share in HDTV.[21] The AEA's president, Pat Hubbard, translated this for Congress: "We suggest that [the United States] must gain an industry in order to retain an industry."[22] There were several problems with this argument, all of which point to the centrality of the consumption variable.

The linkage externality between HDTV and semiconductors required a bridge through consumer electronics, an industry in which U.S. firms boasted a mere 5% world market share in 1989.[23] More telling still, consumer electronics accounted for as little as 5–6% of U.S. semiconductor output, and television a fraction of this.[24] Many observers were thus highly suspect of claims that HDTV would have a greater impact on the semiconductor industry than consumer electronics more generally. The estimates were not encouraging: one widely circulated report concluded that HDTV would account for a maximum of 1% of U.S. output in chips, prompting the Congressional Budget Office (CBO) to ask aloud how this total of $272 million in sales would make the difference between $62 billion (at 20% market share) and $124 billion (at 40% market share) in semiconductor revenue, and this assuming domestic HDTV vendors *only* bought American chips.[25] Proponents were quick to counter that a presence across a range of related HDTV products would bolster these numbers. In Japan, for example, VCRs alone accounted for 12% of that country's output in chips, and it was widely expected that HDTV VCRs would account for an even greater share.[26] Unlike Japan, however, the United States no longer manufactured VCRs or related products like laser discs and camera equipment.[27] Lacking a foothold in these products, HDTV seemed to promise little for the semiconductor industry. Assuming "all R&D is equally productive," the CBO went on to note, "most semiconductor engineering innovations are *more likely to come from the semiconductor R&D already in place* than from marginal HDTV R&D programs."[28] Things looked very different on the other side of the Pacific.

For more than three decades, Japanese policymakers have identified HDTV as an anchor for a variety of linkage externalities (see Figure 5.1). For example, NHK demanded that "[t]he application of Hi-Vision technology will extend far beyond broadcasting as it is combined in new ways with other video media."[29] The High Vision Broadcasting Research Committee estimated that investments in HDTV would have a "multiplier effect" of 2.2 by the year 2000, given complementary technologies.[30] Like their U.S. counterparts, Japanese policymakers have been especially interested in the linkage externality between HDTV and semiconductors. Unlike their American counterparts, however, Japanese policymakers have had reason to expect that HDTV might have a sizable impact on the domestic semiconductor industry. Through the late 1980s, consumer electronics tallied for between 30% and 40% of the country's output in semiconductors, by far the largest downstream end user.[31] Few in Washington were unimpressed by this; U.S. policymakers saw HDTV

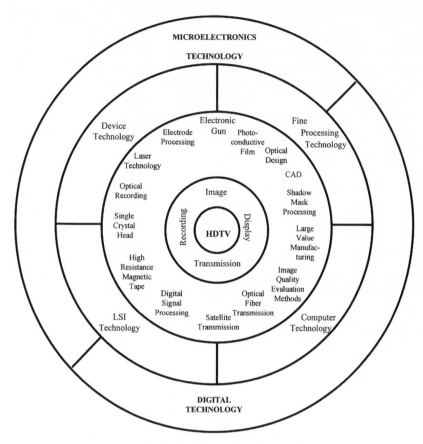

Figure 5.1. HDTV technologies. *Source*: Japanese Broadcast Association (NHK).

as mostly about memory chips, and in the late 1980s, Japan garnered all the attention in this market.

Assorted memories (i.e., dynamic, static, and video RAMs) figured prominently in the debate over HDTV, particularly in the late 1980s, when a U.S. exit from the DRAM market was a distinct possibility. Japan had an 85% world market share in 256 Kilobit (K) DRAMs in 1985 and a 95% world market share in 1 megabit (MB) DRAMs in 1988, for example.[32] Furthermore, Japanese firms specialized in DRAMs for consumer electronics applications in particular, providing a buffer against fluctuations in demand downstream in computers. Proponents in the United States argued that HDTV would give U.S. semiconductor firms a similar buffer. The Semiconductor Industry Association (SIA) argued, for example, that the 1986 trade deficit in consumer electronics had cost U.S. chip makers $284 million in lost sales and that world market share in HDTV would help ease this deficit, serving as a bulwark against the troughs in demand downstream in the computer industry.[33] Echoing this same logic, the National Advisory Committee on Semiconductors (NACS) called for the "Federal Government [to] encourage and purposefully support *market re-entry for the U.S. consumer electronics industry*."[34]

It was a leap to suggest that U.S. reentry into consumer electronics would help tilt the balance in favor of the semiconductor industry. The NTIA, long a vocal advocate of U.S. entry into HDTV, conceded that "the potential spillovers will be constrained only by *user preferences and production economics*."[35] The point was that if current consumption patterns in the chip industry persisted, subsidizing HDTV might just mean subsidizing the Japanese semiconductor industry, since by the late 1980s, few observers were bullish on America's outlook in memories.

In Japan, the expected payoff to the linkage externality between HDTV and chips was substantial. One estimate by the Electronic Industries Association of Japan (EIAJ) was that HDTV receivers would use at least 32 MB of DRAM, placing them on par with computer workstations of the day.[36] Figures concerning the market for HDTV and related products further convinced Japanese policymakers that even if DRAM usage per receiver declined over time (as was expected), this requirement would help to stimulate growth in semiconductor demand. In a report assessing the future downstream use of memories, the EIAJ was clear on this point: "HDTV is also highly expected as a product which promises to experience the *largest use of memory* among AV [audio visual] equipment."[37] Few in the United States thought this an exaggeration. Observers monitoring the semiconductor rivalry were only slightly relieved to learn that Japan's growth in memory output was, to a large extent, in anticipation of HDTV's likely demand for chips.[38] In turn, moreover, this linkage externality has generated spillovers upstream and downstream. Matsushita, for one, has produced a large-capacity high-speed 8MB VRAM for HDTV, using a novel surrounding capacitance memory cell technology developed for its 16MB DRAM prototype. Along these same lines, Toshiba's work on HDTV helped to produce a 1MB multiport DRAM with 10–500 times the image processing capacity of a standard DRAM, promising returns upstream in the memory market.[39]

These are exactly the type of synergies that the Ministry of International Trade and Industry (MITI) and others anticipated in scoring the consumption variable. They are also precisely the kind of synergies that have long been beyond the reach of U.S. industry.

Although semiconductors have enjoyed the spotlight in HDTV, display and fiber optic technologies have been no less central. AT&T Bell Laboratories' Solomon J. Buchsbaum testified before Congress that "[w]hat is at stake is image processing and the impact that that technological force will have on both telecommunications and computing."[40] To be sure, these industries stood out in mapping the HDTV "food chain," and yet observers in the United States have long thought it unlikely that R&D conducted by HDTV vendors would give the telecommunications or computing industries much of a boost. The Office of Technology Assessment (OTA) lent some weight to this argument, for example, urging that "HDTV developments are driving the state-of-the-art in several of these technologies more rapidly than are developments in computer or telecommunications systems," but did not say whether this return on investment merited state assistance for the industry.[41] For its part, the CBO was highly skeptical, insisting that "the ability of potential suppliers of semiconductors, flat-panel displays, and computers to compete in international markets would probably *not be determined* by the success or failure of the HDTV market."[42] The debate that ensued in Washington laid clear the centrality of the consumption variable.

Testifying on behalf of the Department of Commerce, Deputy Assistant Secretary Juan A. Benitz explained that, with respect to "the Congressional Budget Office report, I want to emphasize that we do not share its general pessimism about the promise of HDTV."[43] A joint AEA/House HDTV Caucus meeting also faulted the CBO for "concluding [that] there will be little downstream impact on non-consumer electronics," telecommunications and computers being foremost among these.[44] Proponents demanded that the scope of the inquiry be expanded to incorporate "high resolution systems" more generally, thus putting more emphasis on the imaging technologies used in medical and testing equipment. The CBO obliged, offering a second report. This, too, however, came to the same conclusion: issues of definitional latitude aside, the fact remained that the United States lagged Japan in television receivers, cathode-ray tubes (CRTs), and flat-screen displays, as well as in recording and storage equipment used in imaging technologies.[45] The numbers were daunting: Japan held 96% world market share in passive-matrix liquid-crystal displays (LCD) and monopolized the world market for active-matrix LCDs.[46] The same was true in flat-panel plasma display technology, the implication being that the United States was years behind in the design of large wall-mounted HDTV receivers.[47] And little was expected to change. More than a decade later, in fact, the Department of Defense (DoD), charged with overseeing HDTV, would concede that with 3% world market share in flat-panel displays, "*U.S. industry will continue to be of only marginal significance in the future.*"[48] These assessments did little to encourage U.S. policymakers, especially when interpreted against U.S. competitiveness in the television industry more generally. With Zenith in mind, for example, one witness argued before a House subcommittee that "[w]e have one domestic manufacturer left and they are not exactly cutting edge on this process."[49] Yet again, things looked different on the other side of the Pacific.

Japanese policymakers have had little reason to question whether linkage externalities between HDTV and a variety of imaging technologies could be consumed. The Ministry of Posts and Telecommunications (MPT) and other agencies have long viewed HDTV as a "technological driver" of telecommunications and computer equipment more widely.[50] This assessment reflects a number of factors. First, the process of building an LCD taps many of the same LSI manufacturing techniques used in manufacturing chips. An LCD is made up of millions of thin film transistors (TFTs) that are etched on a glass substrate and are responsible for the display's three primary-color pixels. In the late 1980s, Japan's lead in LSI manufacturing was obvious, especially to Sematech members.[51] While earlier technologies came from the semiconductor materials and equipment (SM&E) industry, second-generation production equipment is more specifically tailored to flat panels, tapping different upstream vendors, few of which are American.[52] Recent reports insist that this development is likely to push Japan even further into the lead in display technologies.[53] The linkages at stake are manifold: TFT deposition technology, with applications in optical recording and computing, stepper and masking technology for large-screen active-matrix displays, and semiconductor packaging and interconnect technologies, many of which fall within Japan's reach, again because of the bridge across consumer electronics.[54]

At the height of the U.S. debate over HDTV in the late 1980s, the ledger in fiber optics looked much the same. This was the technology proponents had in mind in tying HDTV to the telecommunications industry: variants of Japan's Hi-Vision standard entail sizable band-widths, and fiber optical cable (with the help of compression software) was expected to deliver HDTV "to the door." Yet Japan's lead in this field was unambiguous. The OTA, for example, identified shortfalls not only in U.S. production of fiber optics in relation to Japan, but in R&D as well, adding to a long list of benchmarks that pegged the United States years behind Japan in HDTV.[55] The Department of Commerce reached much the same conclusion. Long optimistic about this technology, officials stressed U.S. shortcomings in fiber optics in signaling a retreat from HDTV more generally.

U.S. proponents staged one final stand, revealing not only the importance of consumer electronics in scoring the consumption variable, but also Washington's unwillingness to reenter consumer electronics in order to *change* the score on the consumption variable. The idea of reentering consumer electronics was certainly popular with proponents and others unwilling to concede the fight over HDTV. Deputy Assistant Commerce Secretary Benitz, for example, warned members of Congress that, "[g]iven the impressive record of the Japanese in selecting promising technologies . . . it may *not be prudent* to underestimate the promise of HDTV."[56] It was a leap, though, to argue that the United States should reenter consumer electronics to win HDTV, which, in turn, would help stimulate consumer electronics and related industries upstream and downstream. The circularity of this logic served to confuse observers in and out of government. Illustrative of this, John Glenn, chair of the Committee on Governmental Affairs, found DARPA's Craig Fields unintentionally difficult as a witness:[57]

Glenn: Where does HDTV rank among these various technologies?
Fields: I consider HDTV within the context of the electronics industry as a whole. . . .
Glenn: You would put it number 1, then?
Fields: Well, I would put electronics number 1.

Fields clearly had more in mind than just consumer electronics, and yet the problem was that telecommunications, computers, and industrial electronics – the other three segments of the electronics industry – were seen to be competitive with or without HDTV. Against this backdrop, the argument that the United States would do well to "strike out on a new initiative today to revitalize the consumer electronics industry" by fighting for HDTV was simply not convincing.[58] MITI had estimated in 1988, for example, that of 40 high-technology electronics products,

Japan was equal to, or ahead of the United States in fully 90%.[59] Indeed, as Jeffrey Hart put it, "[t]o say that U.S. reentry into consumer electronics will be difficult is an understatement at best."[60] To be sure, the score on the consumption variable led the United States to (rationally) practice nonintervention for a second time in two decades.

The Internalization Variable

Two factors proved central in Japan's efforts to score the internalization variable: first, the nation's growing reliance on U.S. logic chips; and second, the incentive to build large-screen HDTV receivers in export markets, given their fragility. In light of these factors, Japanese policymakers concluded that many of the technology spillovers exhibited up and down the industrial linkages at stake in HDTV would be international in scope, promising substantial benefits for the United States in particular.[61] U.S. firms, for example, helped to design digital signal processors (DSPs) and decoder chips for Japanese HDTV vendors, affording them some access to many of the resulting technologies. This trend, moreover, was expected to accelerate, particularly if consumer electronics more fully embraced the digital revolution. Moreover, Japanese policymakers concluded that because the majority of HDTV receivers would be built in the United States, the risk of technology transfer in this industry was especially high. Indeed, it was argued that these spillovers might later encourage Washington to rethink its position on HDTV.

In scoring the internalization variable, U.S. world market share in logic chips weighed heavily on the minds of Japanese policymakers. Uncompressed HDTV signals carry over a billion bits of information per second, such that receivers use DSPs and other devices to convert, correct, and display this information, much like a computer. There was thus little doubt that American logic chip firms would have a say in the design of HDTV and related products. Texas Instruments (TI), for example, registered 60% of DSP sales worldwide in the late 1980s, reflecting the sizable lead the United States held in logic chips generally.[62] This lead was due to several factors (see Chapter 4), the most obvious being that U.S. firms had been pushed into higher-end architectures by the computer industry, while Japanese firms had specialized in memories and other less complex architectures, given the needs of the consumer electronics industry. To the extent that U.S. logic chips stood out on Japanese HDTV motherboards, particularly as "design-ins," some of the resulting spillovers were bound to reach American vendors, even if this linkage did not inspire Washington to fight for HDTV directly.

By 1989, U.S. chip vendors were designing DSPs specifically for HDTV, revealing the extent to which they might play a role in the industry. While U.S. memory manufacturers had long struggled to win access to the Japanese market, logic chip firms like LSI Logic, National Semiconductor, and TI were leading efforts to design successive generations of HDTV chips.[63] For example, second-generation LSI decoder chips for the Hi-Vision standard were developed by four U.S.-Japan consortia under the auspices of the HDTV Semiconductor Cooperation Committee.[64] Why, then, did Washington decide not to fight for HDTV on behalf of U.S. logic chip firms? This linkage externality was no less dependent on consumer electronics as a bridge, in this case provided by Japan. In terms of DSPs, for example, the devices at stake are highly tailored to HDTV and are not easily put to use in other applications. As a way of stimulating demand, HDTV promised a marginal boost for logic chip vendors in relation to their main lines of business with the computer industry. And clearly the move to digital technologies in consumer electronics resonated with U.S. proponents. Still, the competitive landscape in the late 1980s served to deter U.S. ambitions in HDTV.

The second part of the internalization story concerns the fact that large-screen HDTV receivers are extremely fragile and difficult to transport. This was the inescapable irony of HDTV: given a consumer preference for 40+-inch screens, nearly all receivers will be built in export markets, the largest being the United States. This meant that Japan's rival in this contest would also serve as host to its national champions. A report issued by the Electronics Industries Association (EIA) estimated, for example, that 92% of all receivers sold in the United States would also be assembled locally. More dramatic still, the report estimated that domestic content would account for as much as 85% of their value.[65] This figure was widely debated in light of trends in U.S. color television manufacturing, 87% of which is conducted by foreign firms.[66] One salient benchmark is that foreign firms do much of their value-added manufacturing in the United States, accounting for upward of 40% in the case of 20+-inch receivers.[67] Along with production facilities, Japanese firms also set up R&D facilities in the United States. Sony, for example, built an R&D facility in California, hinting that assembly might be more than a knockdown kit operation.[68] In partnering with Tektronix, Sony further signaled an interest in tapping local expertise in display technology.[69] By 1994, Hitachi, Matsushita, and Toshiba had also set up R&D facilities in the United States, with Thomson, Philips, Goldstar, and Samsung following in turn.[70] In scoring the internalization variable, it had long been MITI's fear that this trend would facilitate technology diffusion, potentially rolling back Japan's market share in an increasingly digital consumer electronics industry. Japan was thus in something of a bind and, as the book's theory predicts, fought for HDTV in a most unconventional way.

THE DEPENDENT VARIABLE

Given the scores on the independent variables, the book's theory interprets HDTV as a Cautious Activist game. Unable to consume the externalities at stake in this commercial rivalry, the prediction is that the United States would practice nonintervention in HDTV, whereas Japan, long able to consume but not internalize these externalities, would be expected to practice limited intervention in this industry. These predictions are intriguing for three reasons. First, they stand in sharp contrast to the criticism that externalities are invoked to justify any (and all) instances of strategic-trade policy. Externalities certainly figured prominently in decisions for strategic-trade policy on both sides of the Pacific, but did not hardwire the outcome. Second, and along these same lines, U.S. nonintervention was a strategic-trade policy *success*, not a failure of strategic-trade policy.[71] The score on the consumption variable in the late 1980s led U.S. policymakers to doubt the promise of HDTV with respect to semiconductors, displays, and fiber optics, much as it had a decade earlier. Third, the rather modest levels at which Japan opted to subsidize HDTV did not reflect doubts about the technology but rather owed to the score on the internalization variable. In backing up these points, this chapter presents the HDTV rivalry in an entirely new light.

The Competing Explanation

Endogenous protection theory taps the domestic political lobbying by industry. In this view, U.S. nonintervention traces to the lack of electoral clout wielded by Zenith, and to the semiconductor industry's change of heart as to whether the United States should enter HDTV. Similarly, Japan's activism on behalf of its national champions is explained as a reflection of the considerable electoral clout of that country's consumer electronics giants.

On closer inspection, endogenous protection theory fares poorly explaining both sides of this commercial rivalry. By any measure, the American television industry flexed little electoral muscle, yet HDTV was all the rage on Capitol Hill. Congress introduced nine HDTV bills between 1989 and 1990 alone, despite Zenith's lack of competitiveness and questions about its viability. This enthusiasm is difficult to reconcile with the industry's employment base, geographic concentration, political dispersion, or industrial concentration. Few observers were of the view that many jobs were at stake, and, in any case, foreign firms, which employed more Americans and actively lobbied against U.S intervention, had been all but ignored by U.S. policymakers. In fact, the AEA squared off with the EIA for this reason, leading Zenith to quit the EIA in defense of American "interests."[72]

The semiconductor industry adds a little flavor to this story. Surely the electoral clout of chip vendors would have counted for something in sizing up what to do about HDTV. Yet, for all the influence of the U.S. chip industry – electoral clout that is also hard to reconcile with the variables favored by endogenous protection theory – Washington held to the conclusion it had reached a decade earlier and continued its strategic-trade policy of nonintervention. In fact, only once it was clear that Washington was retreating from HDTV did the SIA back off. Illustrative of this, SIA president Noyce testified that, on the question of whether state spending on HDTV was necessary, "*I will say no*, as long as we can obtain participation in the business by other means."[73] This reversal on the part of the SIA, which had earlier argued that the United States had to win HDTV in order to retain world market share in semiconductors, was extraordinary. As Washington cut bait in HDTV, representatives of the chip industry turned their sights to renewing Sematech's funding.[74]

Endogenous protection theory would seem well suited to explaining Japanese strategic-trade policy in HDTV. It gets exceptional performance from the industrial concentration variable, leading us to expect that consumer electronics giants would lobby with vigor for assistance in HDTV. Japan's television industry has long been cartelized: Sanyo's entry in 1947 capped the number of manufacturers at seven.[75] Things have shaped up similarly in HDTV, with the top 7 firms holding 98%

of the active-matrix LCD market and the top 11 firms holding 87% of the passive-matrix LCD market.[76] The employment figures are more difficult to interpret: consumer electronics tallied 175,727 workers in 1994, yet because of vertical integration and offshore employment (the electronics industry tallied 1.2 million employees nationally and 647,000 abroad in 1994) these numbers are greatly understated. Geographic concentration and political dispersion are also hard to gauge precisely. In 1994, there were over 3,000 consumer electronics facilities across Japan and another 311 offshore.[77] This suggests a very highly concentrated industry prone to rent seeking, and one able to boast a lot of votes spread out geographically and politically. Yet, despite having its way with certain of these variables, the competing explanation comes up short in explaining Japanese strategic-trade policy in HDTV.

Background on the HDTV Rivalry

Japanese HDTV R&D gained momentum in anticipation of the 1964 Tokyo Olympics. Dissatisfied with the antiquated NTSC standard, government-industry consortia embarked on a wide range of efforts to push television technology forward and to enhance consumer awareness. Issues pertaining to both broadcast and transmission standards turned HDTV into an international contest shortly thereafter. The Comité Consultatif Internationale des Radio Communications (CCIR) agreed in 1974 to consider HDTV standards, a process in which U.S. and European input was needed. The positions taken by the United States and Europe, in turn, revealed a great deal about the way this commercial rivalry would unfold.

The NTSC standard, which traces its roots to the 1940s, had been adopted in Asia and North America, but not in Europe. To gain U.S. support for its Hi-Vision, Japan tailored a subset of its manifold Multiple Sub-Nyquiest Sampling Encoder, or MUSE standard, to be NTSC-compatible, including MUSE-6 and MUSE-9 (see Figure 5.2).[78] The economics of the industry, however, required access to as large a market as possible, including Europe, itself split up along two color television standards: Séquential Couleur à Mémoire (SECAM) in France, and Phased Alternation Lines (PAL) elsewhere. As the CCIR debated Japan's proposal, it became clear that a single HDTV standard would be difficult to negotiate. Europe was set on protecting its domestic television industry from Japanese imports, and its studios from Hollywood, and thus

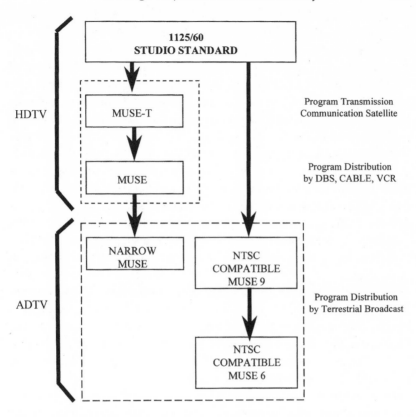

Figure 5.2. MUSE and ADTV structure. *Source*: Tech Search International.

opted for its own standard, called High Definition-Multiplexed Analog Component, or HD-MAC. This standard differed from MUSE both in its lines of resolution (1,250 versus 1,125) and fields per frame (50 versus 60), though its political and economic implications were more interesting still.[79]

One reason to choose a separate HDTV standard was to relieve pressure from Japanese imports, although this would at best offer temporary relief, since Japan promised to build a receiver capable of translating any standard.[80] Protectionist sentiment was high, though, as EC firms held on to 80% of Europe's market for color televisions, and no one wanted to make things easier for Japan by siding with the MUSE standard.[81] This decision put Europe's export opportunities at risk, since HD-MAC was never meant to be compatible with NTSC television, and was not even compatible with either SECAM or PAL for that matter, the upshot being that sales to Asia and North America would be costly, requiring decoder chips to negotiate these more widespread standards. This, together with Europe's poor standing in semiconductors, convinced the United States and Japan that HDTV was a bilateral fight. By 1992, HD-MAC was shelved by the European Research Coordination Agency (EUREKA-95), coinciding with a retreat on the part of Europe's national champions from HDTV more generally.[82]

The idea of going it alone on an HDTV standard was not lost on U.S. proponents. To be sure, the AEA asked Congress and the Federal Communications Commission (FCC) to adopt and license a proprietary standard, hoping that this would pave the way for U.S. entry into HDTV, or at least leverage concessions from Japan, including domestic content requirements.[83] Demands of this sort won little support from U.S. policymakers for two reasons. First, Brazil had played out this strategy in color television and lost. This stood out in the minds of many in Congress as a telling lesson. Second, going it alone on an HDTV standard risked U.S. sales abroad, and not just of receivers; if Europe wanted to *protect* its television industry, Washington wanted to *facilitate* sales of logic chips, even if the United States never competed for HDTV directly. With some distractions along the way – the National Broadcasting Company (NBC) championed a 1050/59.94 standard – the United States proved receptive to MUSE while at the same time lobbying for the more fully digital versions.[84] In 1996, the FCC sided with a modification of a digital television standard crafted by the Advanced Television Systems Committee (ATSC), a decision that falls short of a national standard (it is compatible with 18 formats) and leaves open a door for Japan to shape digital television by providing a few technological focal points.[85] This jockeying on standards has done much to influence the fight over HDTV, a fight that in the late 1980s was undeniably bilateral.

The Cooperation Problem

For U.S. policymakers, the decision variable was whether to practice limited intervention or nonintervention. In contrast, Japan's decision variable concerned whether to practice full intervention or limited intervention. If we turn to the Cautious Activist game, the equilibrium is U.S. nonintervention versus Japan's limited intervention, as in Figure 5.3.

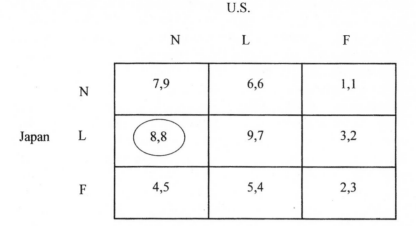

Figure 5.3. U.S.-Japan HDTV rivalry.

U.S. Strategic-Trade Policy. For the United States, limited intervention involved subsidizing a foothold in HDTV, whereas nonintervention involved conceding the industry to the market. Enthusiasm for the industry was widespread; between 1989 and 1990, Congress introduced nine HDTV bills covering measures ranging from tax incentives to support for an R&D consortium to be modeled on the experience of Sematech.[86] As Mel Levine (D-California) testified, HDTV had become "a symbol of America's willingness to compete in a tough new world in which foreign competitors successfully target every aspect of modern industrial technology."[87] However, HDTV proved not to be the industry in which to make this stand.

Proponents of limited intervention explained that, far from driving Japan from HDTV, modest subsidies would ensure a U.S. foothold in this industry. For example, Don Ritter (R-Pennsylvania) introduced the 1989 HDTV Competitiveness Act by noting that "[t]he rules of the HDTV game include strong government support and private sector cooperation."[88] Al Gore (D-Tennessee) pleaded the case for intervention in far more dramatic terms: "[w]hen it is obvious . . . that a particular industrial effort is critical to our economic future and that the patient is going to die if we do not intervene, then we have to have the intellectual courage to intervene. I believe this is the case with . . . HDTV."[89] In closing, Gore flagged to his colleagues that Commerce Secretary Mosbacher had not attended the session, and complained that this was evidence of the Bush administration's waning interest in HDTV. To borrow Gore's wording, the patient was already dead.

Proponents and critics agreed that Japan enjoyed the advantage of being first mover in HDTV. The House bipartisan HDTV caucus, for example, estimated that Japan enjoyed a ten-year lead in this industry.[90] Some in Congress demanded to know why HDTV had not been debated earlier. In truth, though, it had. In keeping with the book's argument, the General Accounting Office (GAO) reported that NASA, the DoD, and a variety of other agencies had been monitoring HDTV since the early 1970s, but that the data "on the potential impact of HDTV on the U.S. computer and semiconductor industry [*sic*], went unheeded because the U.S. consumer electronics industry . . . was in decline."[91] This little-known report makes it plainly clear that the United States could not consume the linkage externalities tying HDTV with the semiconductor, display, and fiber optics industries via consumer electronics, and that this calculation served to deter U.S. intervention twice in two decades, revealing the centrality of this variable.

Nonintervention entailed leaving the fate of HDTV to market forces. This was not an easy decision to reach. As one policymaker explained, the United States had to "recognize that the marketplace decision may not be the best decision for the American broadcast and cable industries, domestic manufacturers or consumers."[92] More forcefully still, one proponent argued that the United States had not risen "to greatness by surrendering major new markets and technologies to its competitors."[93] Others rallied around the theme that "the administration [was] missing the boat by seeing HDTV as simply better television," although in the end, this is precisely what HDTV meant for the United States.[94] Absent a presence in consumer electronics, the linkage externalities at stake were simply beyond reach.

When left to testify on its own behalf, HDTV made this point more convincingly than any critic. In a screening of HDTV arranged for the Committee on the Armed Services, for example, members were grudgingly informed that "the monitors were made in Japan, but the speakers came from Massachusetts."[95] This introduction revealed the extent to which the United States was unprepared to fight for HDTV. Against this backdrop, the AEA's request for some $1.3 billion in "launch" capital, including R&D grants, loans, and loan guarantees, was denied.[96] By late

1989 it was clear to observers in and out of government that nonintervention would prevail for the second time in two decades.[97]

Japanese Strategic-Trade Policy. For Japan, full intervention involved subsidizing at levels to drive (unsubsidized) U.S. firms from the industry, whereas limited intervention entailed subsidizing at lesser levels, given the concern that HDTV spillovers would diffuse beyond national borders. There is no doubt that the Japanese government has played a pivotal role in HDTV. The question, instead, is whether these efforts have been more in line with full or limited intervention. This chapter argues the latter, in light of the data on aggregate government spending and decisions made at the project level.

The main players on the government side include NHK, MITI, and MPT. Leaving its imprint on everything from standards to equipment and consumer awareness, the state can hardly be accused of keeping its distance from HDTV. NHK, for example, has long been active in transferring the fruits of its "high-risk" R&D to the private sector, particularly in semiconductors, displays, cameras, VTR, film-video exchange, and radio frequency band compression technologies, helping industry offset these costs.[98] NHK has also been active in allocating work among consumer electronics firms, giving Mitsubishi responsibility for the development and production of the 35-inch HDTV picture tube, for example, and organizing consortia to develop key technologies, including projects aimed at furthering developments in MUSE Decoder, the half-inch analog VTR, MUSE Decoder main circuitry LSI, peripheral LSI, and NTSC converter LSI technologies. NHK is also credited with the development of various MUSE transmission technologies, including the Hi-Vision two-thirds-inch High Grain Avalanche Rushing (HARP) camera and a 20-inch plasma display.[99] MITI and MPT's Key Technology Center (KTC) has sponsored consortia with the aim of pursuing research in the field of chip and display technologies, among others, and has actively promoted Hi-Vision research more generally.[100] Both agencies have done much to shape developments in HDTV. For example, MITI's Giant Technology Corporation (GTC), under the auspices of the KTC, launched a five-year $21 million project with the aim of designing technologies for a one-meter-square LCD, mask, exposure, printing, and liquid crystal and assembly. For its part, MPT invested $25 million over five years in its Advanced Image Technology Research Center, conducting R&D on image generation, transmission, and display technologies (MITI had a hand in certain of these technologies through its New Glass Forum project).[101] Finally, MITI and MPT have sought to build up interest in HDTV by giving the Japanese public a daily sampling of Hi-Vision broadcasts, and by leasing the necessary studio and production equipment to broadcasters.

Still, government subsidies as a percentage of total HDTV spending are more in line with limited than full intervention. Estimates range between $150 million and $500 million on total investments of $700 million to $1.3 billion through the late 1980s.[102] The OTA puts this at roughly 12% of spending on HDTV.[103] More telling still, certain projects have been subsidized at levels less than what industry had expected, not least because of the score on the internalization variable. MITI declined to ask for 100% state funding for its GTC project, for example, much to the surprise of those firms participating, and in lieu of the salience of the technology at stake. Public investment in consortia accounted for as much as 70% in certain cases – a sizable outlay by any standard – and yet it was expected that industry would be weaned from these government subsidies by 1995.[104] The idea was to launch a private-sector initiative with relatively modest funding, rather than fight out this commercial rivalry as the United States and Europe had waged civil aircraft, for example. And 1995 hardly proved an ideal time to withdraw this helping hand. Questions about a U.S. digital standard, for example, pushed NHK's schedule ahead several years, prodding vendors to rush to market. The evidence suggests, instead, that Japan set out to practice limited intervention and succeeded in its efforts. For a small outlay relative to what states have spent fighting for market share in other high-technology industries, no other country is likely to build HDTV receivers or capture the lion's share of the externalities that result. In contrast to much of the literature, HDTV has thus been a success story on both sides of the Pacific, though in very different ways.

CONCLUSION

The commercial rivalry in HDTV is widely misunderstood. Long regarded a failure of U.S. strategic-trade policy in particular, the case is, to the contrary, a ringing endorsement of the state's ability to discriminate among high-technology battles worth fighting, the lure of externalities notwithstanding. Absent a presence in consumer electronics, U.S. policymakers concluded twice over two decades that nonintervention was their best reply to Japan. Given the consistency of this strategic-trade calculus, it is difficult to see why observers chalk up HDTV as a failure of U.S. strategic-trade policy. The story is no less intriguing when told from Japan's perspective. With no apparent risk of U.S. retaliation, Japan might have been expected to fight for its national champions with abandon. Yet assistance to the nation's consumer electronics giants was reserved, prompting many observers to insist that Japan was unsure about the industry. This chapter challenges this interpretation. Japan's limited intervention made sense in light of the access U.S. firms had to certain key technologies and the greater access they are likely to have in the future, the irony being that this access will largely be underwritten by Japan.

6

Robotics, Superconductors, and Wheat

This book's theory offers new insights into the strategic-trade rivalries in civil aircraft, semiconductors, and high-definition television. These cases are important to get right, not only because the three industries are especially salient and widely interpreted through the lenses of the competing explanation, but because they provide sufficient variation on the book's independent variables, and thus put the theory through its paces. Still, it is useful to push the theory a bit further, taking a look at additional cases that it should be able to explain, and cases it should not be expected to explain. This chapter revisits the scope of the book's argument by offering a brief look at three additional cases: robotics, superconductors, and wheat. Robotics and superconductors are emerging high-technology industries offering a variety of traded products. The book's theory should thus shed light on how these commercial rivalries are taking shape. Wheat is beyond reach of the book's theory, but for reasons it can fully explain. Wheat is of interest to strategic-trade theorists because export subsidies are argued to have brought the United States and the European Community (EC) to the brink of a trade war.[1] If the book's theory is correct, however, the U.S.-EC wheat rivalry should bear little resemblance to the other cases in this study, since the factors privileging national interest considerations in high-technology trade are not at work in this case. As a result, a survey of the political economy of protection in wheat promises to be especially instructive in framing the scope of the book's theory.

ROBOTICS

Long the stuff of science fiction, robots are at the center of one of the most anticipated commercial rivalries in high technology. As a catalyst for developments in fields ranging from mechanical engineering to computing and artificial intelligence, robotics technology has garnered widespread interest on the part of the advanced industrial states.[2] Indeed, by all accounts, government spending on robotics R&D is on the rise, the expectation being that this industry will be among the foremost battlegrounds in building up the economy of tomorrow.[3]

While the language of robotics is esoteric, to say the least, the definition of a robot is not: "a reprogrammable, multifunctional machine designed to manipulate materials, parts, tools, or specialized devices, through variable programmed motions for the performance of a variety of tasks."[4] In coupling automation technology with specialized hardware and software, robots made the transition from the laboratory to the market in the early 1960s, finding a number of applications in manufacturing, most notably welding and painting in the auto industry, and materials handling in the electronics industry. The relatively simple manual manipulators and fixed-sequence robots that accounted for most of the industry's output in the 1970s gave way to more sophisticated robots by the 1980s, opening up applications in aerospace, for example.[5] Indeed, sparked by developments in task and motion control, sensors, and machine vision, robots capable of greater autonomy and dexterity have made their way to factory floors and into new fields like waste management and health care. Stocks of installed robots have risen sharply alongside these advances: between 1981 and 1996, the total number of robots in use in Japan increased from 21,000 to 399,629, and in the United States from 6,000 to 70,858.[6] Export sales, which had been negligible through the 1970s, have soared as well, Japan exporting roughly 20% of its output of $3.6 billion in 1990, the United States about 5–10% of shipments of $1 billion in 1996.[7] Interestingly, with the robotics industry more competitive than ever, state-sponsored R&D is leaving an increasingly sizable imprint on this commercial rivalry.

By the mid-1980s, robotics had emerged as one of the most salient entries on the lists of "critical technologies" put forward by the advanced industrial states, and yet this was very much a U.S.-Japan rivalry.[8] Japanese firms, which combined for more than half the world's total production of robots in 1987, built less sophisticated designs than their U.S. rivals, but nonetheless led in many of the underlying technologies (i.e., robotic arms) and tallied for most of the robotics patents filed, including two-thirds of those deemed "highly cited" through the 1980s.[9] U.S. firms, in contrast, held a lead in peripherals, software, and systems integration, building complex and costly robots for specialized applications (i.e., disposing of nuclear materials), often with imported Japanese actuators and manipulators. The ledger in robotics hardware, more generally, has long served to fuel debate over U.S. competitiveness in robotics – one witness hit on this concern in testifying before a House subcommittee in 1991 that "Japan practically owns that industry today" – although this is a misleading benchmark, in that robotics hardware per se is a relatively small part of this technology.[10] In explaining why, the importance of the internalization variable is brought to the fore.

The frontier of robotics technology is mapped out by "smart machines" and artificial intelligence, where recurrent neural networks and genetic algorithms drive motion control structures rooted in the biomechanics of insects, and where "tele-existence" means that a robot and operator can work together in real time to interpret and respond to unforeseen conditions.[11] More generally, artificial intelligence, together with advances in vision and nonvision sensors, actuators, manipulators, and related controls, holds out the promise of increasingly autonomous robots capable of learning about their surroundings, lending to a wide variety of uses, such as cleaning up hazardous sites, space exploration, and health care, for example. This "interface" between autonomous robots and operators, like the supporting infrastructure for robotics on the factory floor more generally, requires the integration of complex computer hardware and software as part of a larger system, shifting the focus to human-computer interaction technologies and intelligent complex adaptive systems more broadly.[12] The emphasis on robotics systems not only reveals the scope of the underlying technologies, but also sheds light on why this commercial rivalry is likely to be especially heated.

The book's theory interprets robotics as a Beggar-Thy-Neighbor PD: the United States and Japan (and, more recently, Europe) consume and internalize the externalities at stake. Studies of competitiveness upstream in industries from materials and machine tools to computer software and hardware bear out this score on the consumption variable. In materials and fabrication equipment, for example, the ledger is roughly balanced. Indeed, studies make clear that U.S., Japanese, and European vendors are competitive in ceramics, advanced fiber reinforcements, and other materials, although the United States and Europe lead in carbon composites, not least because of their presence in aerospace.[13] In the push to miniaturize robots – micro- and "mesoscopic" robotics are on the cutting edge of this technology – the demand for flexible, light-weight materials and the necessary fabrication equipment (including a variety of semiconductor materials and equipment technologies) is expected to increase dramatically, stimulating this linkage externality and the spill-over externalities that follow along. Not surprisingly, U.S., Japanese, and EC policymakers are adamant that their economies fully participate in the robotics industry.

In machine tools, U.S., Japanese, and European firms showcase different strengths, but raise few doubts about the score on the consumption variable. From mature technologies employed in metal cutting to computer-aided design and manufacturing (CAD/CAM) and related process automation equipment, the ledger in machine tools has long been roughly balanced. Indeed, while this industry is widely discussed as an example of declining U.S. competitiveness in manufacturing more generally, American strengths in CAD/CAM and in process automation R&D have been widely apparent, placing domestic vendors on the leading edge of "high-velocity" machine tools in the late 1980s, for example.[14] Japanese and European firms are world leaders in many machine tool technologies, Japan enjoying the lead in more mature equipment, and Europe in high-end niches of this market.[15] In Japan, machine tools and robotics are often discussed under the heading *mechatronics,* a term used to reflect the union between mechanical and electrical engineering in manufacturing equipment more broadly.[16] Computer software and hardware both figure centrally in this respect, especially when attention turns to robotics applications.

In computer software and hardware, U.S. and Japanese firms have long enjoyed a lead over their European rivals, though boasting different strengths. Still, policymakers on either side of the Pacific could not agree more about the score on the consumption variable (see Chapters 4–5). The U.S. lead in software, described by the Congressional Budget Office in 1987 as "almost insurmountable," has direct implications for the commercial rivalry in robotics.[17] To be sure, developments in robotics, as in logic chips and mainframes, hinge on advances in supporting software architectures and applications, technologies in which Japan has lagged the United States, impeding the forays of its national champions during the 1980s in vector-supercomputing and other advanced computing technologies relevant to robotics. This concern is especially true today, as robotics systems depend to a greater extent on advances in software to achieve more autonomy, dexterity, and interoperability.

In computer hardware, U.S. and Japanese firms compete on a more level playing field in a variety of technologies, ranging from workstations to supercomputers and peripherals (see Chapter 4). Advances in robotics tap many of these competitive strengths. Parallel supercomputing, for example, is a key to neural systems research in artificial intelligence, as well as a springboard for developments in information processing technologies that are likely to facilitate new robotics applications (including a variety of chip sets). "Plug-and-play" interfaces and open architectures for robotics controllers, in addition to peripherals, draw on a variety of computer hardware technologies, holding out the promise of opening new markets upstream and downstream. Indeed, robotics is widely viewed as a key to advanced computing more generally, the expectation being that the industry will anchor a variety of important linkage and spillover externalities, giving it pride of place in discussions about building up the economy of tomorrow.

Several studies of competitiveness in the robotics industry, more specifically, touch on each of these assessments, speaking to the score on the consumption variable. In a report for the Commerce Department in 1985, for example, the Japanese Technology Evaluation Center (JTEC) contrasted American and Japanese strengths in nine mechatronics fields: flexible manufacturing systems, vision systems, nonvision systems, assembly/inspection systems, intelligent mechanisms, software, assorted standards, manipulators, and precision mechanisms. The report concluded that the United States was far ahead in software, that Japan held a sizable lead in the development and implementation of assembly/inspection systems, and that the two sides were roughly on par across these other technologies.[18] In a study commissioned in 1996 focused on human-computer interaction technologies more broadly, JTEC painted much the same picture, observing a U.S. lead in robotics research, but concluding that the two countries enjoy rough parity in robotics technology overall.[19] Beyond industrial robotics, the same view is echoed in a report on space robotics, pointing to a balanced ledger in the most sophisticated of these technologies.[20] Finally, a 1996 report by the Office of Science and Technology Policy notes that European robotics technology is on par with that found in the United States and Japan.[21] These studies shed light on the score on the consumption variable, and help to explain why robotics is among the most anticipated commercial rivalries in high technology. Nonetheless, the score on the consumption variable is but half the story.

The expectation that the commercial rivalry in robotics will increasingly heat up traces to the score on the internalization variable. Like a commercial airplane, robotics systems are more than the sum of their parts, systems integration being a key to competitiveness, and a barrier to the industry's linkage and spillover externalities reaching beyond national borders. Indeed, robotics shares much in common with civil aircraft in this respect: trade in inputs (like robotic arms) accounts for a small percentage of the value of a system, the integration of which is the staple of this industry. As a study by the Office of Technology Assessment explains, for example, corporate strategy with respect to robotics hardware is akin to the logic behind giving away free razors to sell blades, the goal being to "lock-in" customers for follow-on sales of more value-added products and services like customized software, programming controls, and systems integration. The study concludes that "[an] emphasis on service or on integrating robots into complex systems would *argue against a strong import presence* (in the traditional sense), because close relations with customers and retaining a local presence are important aspects of service provision and applications planning."[22] Indeed, national biases in subcontracting have long been noted in the case of Japan, but also in the United States and Europe, particularly with respect to higher-value-added products, and especially services.[23] These national biases not only obstruct foreign access to the relevant linkage externalities, but to the spillover externalities that follow in their wake. The complexity of integrating robotics systems, more generally, keeps know-how from diffusing beyond borders, offering insights into Japan's "stepwise" approach to developing this technology, versus the larger leaps taken by U.S. and European firms. In brief, few charges of free riding have been leveled in robotics, the concern, instead, being that gains and losses may be path-dependent in this industry.

Moving on to the dependent variable, the book's theory predicts a race to the top over subsidy levels, since, in a Beggar-Thy-Neighbor PD, states have incentive to practice full intervention on behalf of their national champions. This, of course, puts them at risk of a collectively suboptimal trade war, fear of which may motivate both sides to negotiate an agreement limiting subsidy levels. There is, as yet, no such agreement, though there is no question that state spending on robotics R&D is rising sharply, calling increased attention to this commercial rivalry.

In the United States, government support for robotics R&D has come from a variety of agencies, including the Departments of Defense (DoD), Commerce (DoC), Energy (DoE), and Agriculture (DoA), the National Aeronautics and Space Administration (NASA), and the National Science Foundation (NSF). Process automation technologies have long been funded under the auspices of the DoD's Manufacturing Technology (ManTech) program (budgeted at $200 million in 1984), robotics among them. Similarly, the DoC and NASA have been active in robotics technology, Commerce's National Institute for Standards and Technology (NIST) taking a lead on many commercial fronts, NASA in the field of space robotics.[24] NASA, however, has also played a key role in industrial robotics, conducting R&D in advanced welding, for example, and spending over half its $5.9 million budget in 1984 on robotics and artificial intelligence more generally.[25] In turn, DoD expenditures have helped to realize returns in the field of space robotics, as in the case of the Strategic Computing Initiative, which inspired the Autonomous Land Vehicle program and pushed forward NASA's R&D in "tele-operated" robots.[26] NSF grants have also seeded cutting-edge robotics R&D on a limited budget, allocating $2.6 million in grants and $830,000 in other R&D efforts in 1987, for example.[27] It is estimated that total federal funding for automation technologies (including robotics) amounted to $80 million in 1984.[28]

Over the past decade, U.S. spending on robotics has surged and, by most accounts, will increase dramatically in the future. In 1996, the federal government helped to underwrite 819 nonclassified projects in the field of robotics technology, bringing together industry, universities, and national laboratories on research in machine vision systems, remote telepresence robots, modular autonomous robotic systems, intelligent resistance welding, and parallel hardware and machine learning, for example. Although sizable gaps in the data make it impossible to calculate total U.S. spending, data for 494 of the projects reported (60%) reveal a commitment of $122.5 million, while data for 341 of the projects reported (42%) add up to a fiscal year commitment of $41.3 million, or over half of the investment in all process automation technologies combined in 1984.[29] In 1997, there were 596 nonclassified projects in robotics sponsored by the federal government, data for 349 of which (59%) point to a commitment of $108 million, and for 99 of which

(17%) point to a fiscal year commitment of $14.2 million.[30] More generally, DoD, DoC, and NSF officials point out that spending on robotics is increasing markedly. The NSF, for example, which spent $3.2 million on robotics in 1987, allocated more than twice this amount a decade later.[31] Funding for specialized applications, such as space robotics, is reported to be generous and more readily available than in Japan.[32] This comparison with Japan is, of course, important, in that both the level and timing of increases in U.S. funding for robotics R&D have been influenced by foreign subsidy programs.

In Japan, the Ministry of International Trade and Industry (MITI) has taken the lead in sponsoring robotics R&D since the 1970s. The range of Japanese projects with a hand in robotics speaks not only to the country's commitment to this industry, but to the breadth of the underlying technologies. MITI's Advanced Robot Technology program, started in 1984, is among the more salient projects in this field, the aim of which has been to build a robot for each of three applications: (1) nuclear power plants, (2) subsea, and (3) disaster and fire fighting. This program, in turn, resulted in the formation of the Advanced Robot Technology Research Association, a consortium of 18 firms and two national laboratories focused on robotics hardware more generally.[33] Autonomous robots have been the focus of a number of MITI-funded programs, including the Juvanescent Pioneering Technology for Robots, or so-called Jupiter program ($83 million over eight years), the Intelligent Manufacturing Systems project as part of the Industrial Science and Technology Frontier Program, and the Intelligent Robotics program under the auspices of the Fifth Generation Computer project. MITI's Robotics in Extreme Environments project (¥7.7 billion over four years) and its Micromachine Technology project (¥12 billion over seven years) have also done much to further advances in this field.[34] Finally, R&D in software and artificial intelligence for robotics has been cross-subsidized by other, well-funded programs, such as the Next Generation Application Software project, the Real World Computing project, and the Exploratory Research for Advanced Technology program.[35] Although it is difficult to gauge aggregate government spending on robotics in Japan, figures at the project level, coupled with initiatives in space and other fields (a program on "human friendly network robotics" is slated to begin in 1999), suggest at least as great a funding commitment as in the United States, leading many observers to predict a race to the top over subsidies, one that promises to involve Europe as well.[36]

SUPERCONDUCTORS

Few emerging industries hold out as much commercial promise as super-conductors. If current applications of this technology are any indication, superconductivity will leverage a variety of old markets and stimulate new ones. Not surprisingly, the industry has drawn considerable attention from a number of advanced industrial states, many of which regard establishing a foothold in superconductivity as a key to their future economic growth and competitiveness.

Superconductors exhibit zero resistance to the flow of electricity when cooled below a critical temperature, and expel a magnetic field.[37] These properties make superconducting materials ideal for commercial applications in electric energy and storage, transportation, propulsion, industrial and medical equipment, and electronics. Since the 1970s, so-called low-temperature superconductors (LTS), with critical temperatures close to absolute zero, have found a number of downstream uses, notably in magnetic resonance imaging (MRI) equipment. Yet the complexity and high cost of cooling LTS materials has served to slow the rate at which this technology has been commercialized more generally. In 1986, the discovery of high-temperature superconductors (HTS) changed the landscape of the industry. With critical temperatures above 77° Kelvin, HTS materials can be cooled with liquid nitrogen, as opposed to liquid helium, thereby greatly reducing the complexity and cost of refrigeration systems. Families of materials with even higher critical temperatures have fueled interest in HTS technologies, and have raised expectations that materials that are superconducting at room temperature may be close at hand, materials that would truly revolutionize the industry.

The challenge of commercializing HTS, however, has been formidable. Most telling, in this respect, is that there is no theory of HTS with which to predict the limits on critical temperatures, critical current densities, and critical magnetic fields of these materials. In addition, HTS materials are highly sensitive to impurities, brittle, and difficult to work with. Not surprisingly, fabrication techniques used in manufacturing HTS coils and wires for power applications, for example, are highly costly. The investment in R&D needed to bring HTS to market has thus raised several concerns on the part of industry. First, it is widely expected that profits may well be a decade away, though U.S. and Japanese firms offer different timelines. Second, it is generally agreed that the benefits to this R&D diffuse to competitors at home and abroad, undermining the incentive to spend on R&D. As one key witness explained to a House subcommittee, "for any given company, for any given industry, the amount of benefit that they can capture personally may not be large enough to justify for them the kind of expenditure that's needed."[38] In fact, however, industry has never had to shoulder this cost by itself.

Dating back to some of the earliest research on, and prototyping of, LTS technologies, government subsidies have helped underwrite the commercialization of superconductivity in the United States and Japan. Indeed, in the wake of the discovery of HTS, this was all but a two-country race.[39] Externalities have drawn states into this commercial rivalry; the linkages and spillovers at stake reach widely throughout the economy, tapping industries upstream and downstream. Indeed, from materials and equipment to power applications, state-funded R&D projects have helped industry to design, prototype, and manufacture devices and systems. National laboratories, as well as the public-private consortia funded on both sides of the Pacific, have realized results in the marketplace, stimulating trade in LTS and HTS technologies. Industry, however, has hardly had its way paid, incurring roughly half the total investment in R&D in fields ranging from magnets and thin-films to systems that depend on these technologies. This "cost-sharing" model has long informed the design of public-private consortia in both countries, as well as projects funded by new entrants like Germany. Given that the United States and Japan agree that this commercial rivalry will heat up considerably and expect a $45 billion market by 2010, state funding for R&D on either side of the Pacific has struck many observers as not being up to the task. Why this approach to nurturing one of the most highly anticipated emerging industries?

The book's theory interprets superconductivity as a Favor-Thy-Neighbor PD: both the United States and Japan consume, but cannot internalize, the externalities at stake. First, assessments of U.S. and Japanese competitiveness upstream and downstream bears out the score on the consumption variable. Upstream, the ledger in materials and equipment is roughly balanced. Japanese leads in specific ceramics and manufacturing processes were evident through the late 1980s, although U.S. firms led in high-end niches and reasserted a wider market presence by the early 1990s. U.S. and Japanese (as well as German) firms exhibit particular strengths in certain ceramics and fabrication techniques, yet both clearly enjoy a robust presence upstream. Downstream, U.S. and Japanese competitiveness in electric energy and storage, transportation, propulsion, industrial and medical equipment, and electronics reveals why these states pay such close attention to superconductivity. In power applications, for example, U.S., Japanese, and European firms are among the world leaders. When HTS was discovered in 1986, U.S. firms had been losing ground to Japan and Europe in electric generators for years – in part because of foreign-trade barriers and a sharp fall in domestic demand – but continued to dominate other sectors of the industry, such as turbine generators.[40] A recent study of power applications suggests that trends in the development of HTS technologies, and industry's willingness to carry much of the tab for this R&D, can readily be traced to the competitiveness of U.S. and Japanese firms.[41]

In transportation and propulsion technologies, the United States and Japan anticipate a number of downstream applications, from railroad systems to naval technologies. One of the most familiar uses of LTS involves Japan's magnetically levitated (MagLev) train system. HTS may serve to popularize this technology, which is also being pursued by the Europeans, but not by the United States, which in 1975 ended its MagLev train program. Japan is thus well positioned to exploit developments in this industry, not least because of its greater experience with LTS. Naval applications, including ship propulsion, resonate with the United States and Japan, both of which have a long history of subsidizing related R&D on behalf of the maritime industry.[42] A highly contested and increasingly crowded market, shipbuilding technology has evolved rapidly over time, the expectation being that superconductivity may shake up this industry again, pushing the United States and Japan to the forefront of this commercial rivalry.[43]

In industrial and medical equipment, HTS is expected to serve as the underpinning for highly advanced sensors and magnetic diagnostic technologies, for example. Devices for gauging small magnetic fields and electromagnetic radiation emissions are among the key downstream applications envisioned for HTS. Similarly, HTS is expected to benefit MRI equipment and make possible other biomagnetic sensors with which to replace electrodes, for example.[44] U.S. and Japanese firms are among the primary suppliers of industrial and medical equipment worldwide. Indeed, industry investment in LTS R&D to date reflects considerable confidence in these downstream applications, as well as the competitiveness of U.S. and Japanese firms.

In electronics, superconductivity is expected to offer downstream applications ranging from smaller, more efficient computer chips to communications equipment that accesses unused frequencies of the electro-magnetic spectrum.[45] Both the United States and Japan enjoy a robust presence downstream in the computer and communications industries (see Chapters 3–5), and are well positioned to exploit the related link-ages and spillovers that HTS promises. Electronics applications, how-ever, are proving to be elusive, in part because of questions about the commercial promise of key underlying technologies – such as Josephson Junctions for computing – and in part because of industry's greater familiarity with cheap substitutes. Prototypes of HTS electronics appli-cations have been as impressive as they have been expensive, notably in the field of computing. Practical, near-term applications, such as hybrid chips using both superconductor and semiconductor materials, are widely anticipated, but are not the main emphasis of public or private research, least of all in the United States. HTS may also find important applications in communications, particularly in aerospace, an industry that, in the United States, may also provide sufficient demand to help inspire investment in these technologies, as in the case of computer-aided design and manufacturing equipment, for example.

A strong presence across the relevant upstream and downstream in-dustries affords the United States and Japan considerable opportunity to consume the linkages and spillovers exhibited by superconductivity. The score on the internalization variable is another story. U.S. and Japanese gains in commercializing LTS technologies reveal the extent to which product and process know-how diffuses beyond national borders in this industry. Indeed, from trade in fabrication equipment to the participa-tion by foreign firms in public-private consortia, numerous channels facilitate technology diffusion. In response to the "technonationalist" policies proposed in the wake of the discovery of HTS, for example, a report by the Office of Technology Assessment demanded that such efforts would achieve little and, moreover, that "measures seeking an equitable two-way flow [of HTS technologies] with countries such as Japan have much more to recommend them."[46] Similarly, a recent study commissioned by the National Science Foundation reports that Japanese managers placed considerable emphasis on "the importance of a strong U.S. program even to the Japanese," revealing the crucial role technology diffusion plays in superconductivity.[47]

Turning to the dependent variable, the book's theory predicts a race to the bottom over subsidy levels, since in a Favor-Thy-Neighbor PD, states have incentive to free-ride on the investments others make in their national champions. However, since nonintervention is collectively sub-optimal, states may instead pursue an agreement, setting out floors on the contributions each side makes to the provision of what amounts to an international public good. These expectations are largely borne out by the evidence, despite the infancy of this technology. U.S. and Japanese subsidies have been starkly modest, yet supplemented by each other's R&D programs, the benefits of which readily escape national borders. This diffusion is bolstered, moreover, by the U.S.-Japan Agreement on Cooperation in Science and Technology, an agreement that has done much to internationalize HTS programs more generally.

In the United States, HTS was all the rage in Congress within months of its discovery. Of the dozen bills introduced, many championed public-private consortia to help leverage a modest federal budget for superconductivity. In 1987, total spending on LTS and HTS amounted to $85.8 million, reaching a high of $358 million in 1992 but declining to $141 million (estimate) in 1997.[48] The DoD and DoE have taken the lead in spearheading U.S. efforts, although the DoD originally received a larger share of the federal budget (almost half), spending on the Strategic Defense Initiative and dual-use technologies.[49] The DoE has long taken the lion's share of the federal LTS budget, given its focus on commercial applications, and since 1996 has boasted a larger share of the federal HTS budget than the DoD. In 1988, the DoE inaugurated the Superconductivity Program for Electric Systems (SPES) to facilitate the development of wire and systems technology, and in 1993 started the Superconductivity Partnership Initiative (SPI) to sponsor R&D on power components, sharing costs with industry. In the case of SPI proposals, industry has carried nearly 50% of the cost of designing and developing power applications. Total SPES funding, which amounted to $3.9 million in 1988, reached $19 million in 1996, or less than half the total of $50 million invested by industry and government sources.[50] More interestingly still, in this respect, is that the DoE has long courted Japan's participation in projects such as the Superconducting Supercollider, invitations that have been eagerly reciprocated by Japan.

In Japan, the discovery of HTS inspired widespread interest on the part of industry and government alike. Japanese firms are more committed to LTS than their U.S. rivals, and expect that HTS will complement these efforts in the long run. The government, too, has a history of being bullish on superconductivity, identifying the commercialization of HTS as a national priority. Programs under the auspices of MITI and the

Science and Technology Agency (STA) have set the pace for a wide variety of HTS applications, as have programs funded by the Ministry of Education (MOE) and the Ministry of Transportation (MOT). One of MITI's most prized ventures is its International Superconductivity Technology Center (ISTEC), a consortium that charges its members – including foreign firms – a fee to participate in materials R&D and other related efforts. MITI's Engineering Research Association for Superconductive Generation Equipment and Materials program, or "Super-GM," is credited with having placed Japan in the lead in superconducting windings for power generators.[51] The Science and Technology Agency's Multi-Core Project in Superconductivity, the MOE's program in high-temperature oxide superconductors, and MOT's Magnetic Levitation program, also receive high marks from observers in Japan and the United States.[52] Like the DoE's SPI, these programs typically involve cost-sharing arrangements with industry, often transferring more than 50% of the cost to the private sector. Like U.S. programs more generally, Japanese programs operate with modest budgets. In 1990, MITI funding for ISTEC was reported to be $6.8 million, but in 1996 was estimated at $3 million. The Science and Technology Agency's Super-GM program boasted funding of $29 million in 1996, though this figure includes substantial investments in LTS as well. The MOT's MagLev program receives significant funding, but more so because of the high cost of the land and construction that Japanese train systems entail. Funding for Japanese superconductivity is thus modest (total spending on power applications in 1996 was $90 million, versus $50 million in the United States), but clearly long term.[53] Total Japanese spending on superconductivity in 1994 reached $174 million, a figure that is roughly on par with current U.S. spending.[54] Yet what is most interesting about Japan's programs is the extent to which foreign firms have been invited to participate as risk-sharing partners.

The book's theory suggests that states might cooperate in a Favor-Thy-Neighbor PD by negotiating an agreement on subsidy floors, thereby escaping the collectively suboptimal outcome that results when states free-ride. The U.S.-Japan Agreement on Cooperation in Science and Technology does not establish formal subsidy floors, like the Semiconductor Trade Agreement, but it does facilitate technology sharing in superconductivity by bringing government, industry, and universities from both countries together in a number of R&D projects ranging from ceramics and refrigeration to organic superconductors and fabrication technologies. Much like the Semiconductor Trade Agreement, the Agreement on Cooperation in Science and Technology increases transparency with respect to publicly funded R&D; unlike the Semiconductor Trade Agreement, these specific projects are a more direct way of sharing R&D costs, somewhat akin to the goals of the DoE's Superconducting Supercollider or MITI's ISTEC programs. In general, industry collaborations and workshops are common in superconductivity; the Fifth International Superconductivity Industry Summit in 1996 reported that joint projects in a variety of fields were gaining popularity, citing proposals by ISTEC, the Consortium of European Companies (CONECTUS), and the Council on Superconductivity for American Competitiveness (CSAC).[55] This, coupled with the maturation of HTS technologies – and the resulting cuts in basic science funding – may put increasing pressure on the United States and Japan to reduce overall R&D budgets, a trend already in evidence on both sides of the Pacific. As a means of leveraging national contributions to an international public good, however, the U.S.-Japan Agreement on Cooperation in Science and Technology is very much designed in the spirit of the Semiconductor Trade Agreement, and is certain to guide the way this commercial rivalry unfolds in the future.

WHEAT

In 1985, blaming a strong dollar and European subsidy practices for declining sales of wheat, the United States initiated the Export Enhancement Program (EEP).[56] Billed as a way to boost prices, offset EC subsidies, and force Europe to the GATT bargaining table, the EEP has often been interpreted through the lenses of strategic-trade theory. On closer inspection, however, this case shares little in common with any of the other cases in this study. Most notably, the EEP was the product of interest group politics, a concession that the Reagan administration exchanged for the votes of three wheat-state representatives on the budget. Moreover, despite arguments about the program's value as a bargaining chip, the level of subsidies under the EEP, much like wheat subsidies under Europe's Common Agricultural Policy (CAP), has been much more responsive to budget constraints at home and price volatility than to export subsidy programs abroad. In examining the design and implementation of the EEP, the case of wheat thus helps put the book's theoretical scope into clear perspective.

Export subsidies have historically played a limited role in U.S. farm trade, although by the mid-1980s, the idea of a subsidy program was very much in vogue in Congress.[57] To be sure, stocks of wheat held by the government's Commodity Credit Corporation (CCC) had risen sharply, encouraging those demanding an "in-kind" subsidy program that would help U.S. farmers and empty CCC silos. The Reagan administration, though opposed to the proposals making their way through Congress, needed help passing its 1985 budget – not least because of cuts to farm supports more generally – and swapped the EEP for the votes of Mark Andrews (R-North Dakota), Edward Zorinsky (D-Nebraska), and Robert Dole (R-Kansas), key representatives of the main wheat-producing states.[58] Well shy of an across-the-board export subsidy program, the EEP was to promote U.S. wheat sales by adding a set amount of CCC stocks to sweeten deals with importing countries targeted by the program. The EEP was also meant to be "budget neutral" in that emptying CCC silos was argued to cost the taxpayers nothing, the expectation being that the program was thus unlikely to spark political opposition. Indeed, proponents advertised the EEP as a fiscally sound way not only to assist U.S. farmers but also to bring pressure on Europe's subsidy program.

The design and implementation of the EEP, however, raise questions about the aim of the program. First, EEP subsidies are primarily transfers to foreign consumers and their governments, not to U.S. farmers. As a result, wheat producers and agribusiness interests have long been opposed to the EEP, frustrated as well by the program's list of designated importers.[59] Second, the "additionality" criterion to which the EEP has been held – that is, that CCC stocks must necessarily serve as a catalyst for additional exports, not substitute for them – has largely gone unfulfilled. To be sure, observers argue that nearly all of the exports covered under the EEP would have shipped in the program's absence.[60] Third, the EEP's value as a bargaining chip has also been vastly overstated. Outspent by the EC by a margin of as much as 10 to 1, the EEP has exerted little direct pressure on Europe's subsidy program, spending for which has been far more responsive to budget constraints under the CAP and the price of wheat on world markets.[61] Finally, the EEP does nothing to offset EC credit financing, a key issue for most countries targeted by the program, like Egypt, where access to credit is often more important than the price of wheat per se.[62] In sum, the EEP has curried little favor with many of the constituents it was intended to benefit and has done little to force Europe's hand on subsidies. Why has the EEP been so ad

hoc in its design and implementation, in contrast to the subsidy programs in the high-technology industries reviewed in this book?

In explaining why the "rational unitary actor" assumption is useful
in theorizing about the state's strategic trade calculus, Chapter 2 provides two justifications. First, correcting for market failures is among the
most important of the state's functions, and on this front, concern for
aggregate welfare prevails over distributional politics. In the high-
technology cases, the undersupply of externalities – that is, market failure – uniquely positions the state to design and implement export and
R&D programs to help not only national champions but also upstream
and downstream industries, the aim being to leverage economic growth
and competitiveness more generally. In this regard, the politics of distrib-
uting gains from trade protectionism takes a back seat to aggregate
welfare, or, to put it a different way, the programs in high technology
have been in keeping with the "national interest." In wheat, by way of
contrast, the problem is price volatility, not market failure. This brings
wheat within reach of interest group politics and puts it beyond reach of
the book. Here, votes are the currency of trade protectionism, as is most
clearly evidenced by the EEP. The ad hoc design and implementation of
the program owes to divisions between different farm constituents,
within Congress, and between lawmakers and the executive. For example, it is not clear that American farmers would necessarily have focused
on exports as a way to improve their financial health in the mid-1980s,
lending to the argument that the EEP was offered to fill the void left by
cuts in farm supports, rather than to change the landscape of the commercial rivalry in wheat.[63] Even if exports were indeed the answer, EC
subsidies could hardly be blamed for all of the problems besieging U.S.
farmers, since competition from nonsubsidizing wheat export countries
like Canada has long been fierce. The EEP has thus been ill-suited to
solving a largely misdiagnosed problem, a program pulled in a variety of
directions by farm and agribusiness groups vying for a larger share of
the gains from trade protectionism. Absent any concern on the part of
the state to correct problems of market failure, the book concedes the
case of wheat to endogenous protection theory.

Second, the market imperfections characteristic of high-technology
industries help bring the risk of foreign retaliation more sharply into
focus, since firms and the states that subsidize them compete directly
with each other, rather than against world prices. This is important in
that the risk of foreign retaliation serves to condition strategic-trade
policy in a way that points up the utility of treating the state as if it were

a rational unitary actor. To be sure, the risk of foreign retaliation – in trade or security – privileges state efforts on behalf of a national constituency. The more clear-cut the source of these retaliatory threats – that is, the fewer the number of foreign firms and states competing for the industry – the greater will be the state's latitude in this respect. The book's high-technology cases bear this out, but not the case of wheat, a highly competitive industry by any measure. Despite the EEP's billing as a bargaining chip to trade away with the EC, for example, the landscape of the commercial rivalry in wheat is far more complicated. Indeed, competition from the nonsubsidizing wheat export countries, notably Argentina, Australia, and Canada, adds to the equation. Interestingly, the EEP has long been a source of tension in trade relations with these and other members of the Cairns Group, at times to Washington's surprise, as when the Australians made the program the lead item for talks with the Bush administration in 1991.[64] Given that the Cairns Group has been vocal in its opposition to Europe's subsidy program, the irony of the EEP is that it has alienated would-be allies by opening up the United States to similar charges. This is not to imply that spending on the EEP has been unresponsive to the demands of the Cairns Group, for in fact U.S. trade negotiators have been sensitive to the policy stand of these countries, looking to win their favor in advance of the Uruguay Round in particular. Rather, what is most telling about EEP spending is that it has been far more responsive to domestic budget constraints and the volatility of wheat prices on world markets than to foreign subsidy programs. Indeed, the subsidy caps set out by the Congressional Budget Office have been stricter and more influential than subsidy caps under GATT, although since 1985 this has presented few problems, since the EEP has lain dormant amid soaring wheat prices.[65] In a market that is far more perfectly than imperfectly competitive, this is not surprising, in that firms compete against world prices, rather than directly with each other. Accordingly, the book once again concedes the case of wheat to endogenous protection theory, which offers far greater insights into the political economy of the EEP.

CONCLUSION

This chapter revisits the scope of the book's argument by providing for a brief look at robotics, superconductors, and wheat. Robotics and superconductors are among the most widely anticipated commercial rivalries in high technology, the contours of which should be within reach of the book's theory. Indeed, the evidence from both cases bears out the argument: robotics is shaping up as a Beggar-Thy-Neighbor PD, super-conductivity as a Favor-Thy-Neighbor PD. Wheat, on the other hand, is beyond reach of the argument, but for reasons the book fully anticipates. Despite the central role of export subsidies, and talk of strategic trade in wheat more generally, the U.S.-EC wheat rivalry shares little in common with the other cases in this study, since the factors privileging national interest considerations in high-technology trade are not at work here. This chapter thus highlights that, while the book's theory speaks to a small subset of commercial rivalries in the global economy, it performs well across a wide variety of cases it should be expected to explain, offering new insights into strategic trade in high technology.

7

·━○━━·

Conclusion

The theory and practice of strategic-trade policy present us with a puzzle. On the side of theory, states are argued to have a strong incentive to fight for their national champions in high-technology industries, but are seldom expected to follow through, given the threat of foreign retaliation. In practice, however, states *do* fight for their national champions in certain high-technology industries, and at times go unchallenged. Moreover, when states do fight, they sometimes cooperate with each other to ease trade tensions, even though the risk of foreign retaliation did not deter them from intervening in the first place. Why this gap between theory and practice? The book provides answers to this puzzle by elaborating the strategic-trade calculus of states. This chapter takes up some of the more salient implications of the argument, considers the book's limitations, and draws out several policy prescriptions.

IMPLICATIONS OF THE STUDY

This book argues that externalities inform the state's strategic trade calculus. It argues, more specifically, that states subsidize the exports and (or) R&D of national champions in those industries exhibiting externalities that the domestic economy is primed to make use of, given a presence upstream and downstream. The level at which these national champions are subsidized depends, in turn, on whether the resulting externalities diffuse beyond national borders, and whether foreign trade rivals are primed to make use of these benefits as well. This argument hits squarely on two themes in the strategic-trade literature: the role of the state, which is important in theorizing about foreign economic policy more generally; and the import of externalities, which figure centrally in the literatures on endogenous growth and economic geography (among others) as well.

More broadly, the book insists that strategic-trade policy gives rise to a *multiplicity* of cooperation problems among states. Indeed, in contrast to the literature, it argues that the Prisoner's Dilemma (PD) game is neither the only, nor even necessarily the most useful, model for studying strategic-trade policy. With two dichotomous independent variables, and three simplifying assumptions, the book predicts the contours of five different rivalries in high technology. The book thus taps a debate about a constraints- versus a preference-based approach to thinking about problems of cooperation among states, and offers some insights into questions of institutional design as well. This chapter takes up these themes in turn.

The State of the State in Strategic-Trade Theory

The literature on strategic trade seldom envisions the state as being anything other than a bank, opening its purse in exchange for the votes of influential industries. Industries, no doubt, wield influence over policymakers, but votes are not the currency of strategic-trade policy.

The need for a supply-side theory of strategic trade is borne out in the cases detailed in this book, not just because the demands of firms rarely map neatly on to policy outcomes, but because the electoral clout of these industries is hard to reconcile with the scores on the variables endogenous protection theory favors. Taking the second part first, consider civil aircraft in the United States and Europe, an influential industry to be sure, but hardly because it boasts a lot of votes. On the contrary, employment figures on either side of the Atlantic could hardly excite those seeking returns at the ballot box. From one angle, the geographic concentration and political dispersion of the industry gives it electoral muscle, and no one would deny that the industrial concentration variable plays out better in this than in almost any other industry. Still, few observers argue that the civil aircraft industry gets attention for these reasons, least of all the governments involved. As the coordinator for German Aerospace Affairs explains, "*[d]espite its limited size in terms of employees, sales, and gross value added,* a competent and capable aerospace industry is of great significance for the Federal Republic of

Germany."[1] The point is *not* to deny that lobbying by this industry makes a difference, but rather that this industry gets heard in the policymaking process because it resonates for reasons having to do with the externalities it promises for related sectors of the economy.

Taking the first part second, the gap between what firms demand of the state, and what the state gives them, makes clear the need for a supply-side theory. This is true in that the states involved have often resisted industry demands, provided more or less subsidization than industry asked for, and even influenced *what* industry asked for. The case of HDTV provides for a taste of something not widely discussed in the literature: a state conceding an industry to a foreign rival, despite vocal opposition from firms and upstream suppliers. In contrast, efforts on behalf of the civil aircraft industry have often greatly exceeded the demands of firms, leaving these national champions uneasy about the heated tone of this commercial rivalry. Finally, industry has often anticipated state preferences in framing its demands. Take Japan's semiconductor firms, which lobbied for MITI's and NTT's Very Large Scale Integration (VLSI) projects only after it became clear that, in the wake of trade liberalization, these were the only items on the menu, much to their dismay. In bridging this gap between industry demands and strategic-trade policy outcomes, a closer look at the supply side is an important first step.

Finally, the literature on foreign economic policy is as much in need of a supply-side corrective as strategic-trade theory. The "strong state/ weak state" taxonomy has certainly given way to more blended analyses, and yet progress has largely been on only one of two fronts, with the rediscovery of the demand side in studies of strong states like France and Japan. This book encourages the rediscovery of the supply side in analyses of weak states like Britain and the United States, and not just for the sake of building better theory. To be sure, Britain's maneuvering in civil aircraft, whereby the government forced shotgun marriages among competing design teams, had much the same feel to it as MITI's efforts in semiconductors. The image of firms running roughshod over a porous Congress is also off the mark in explaining U.S. nonintervention in high-definition television (HDTV), or in explaining why this industry received as much political attention as it did. This suggests the need to embrace a supply-side perspective, not only in studies of strong states, and not just in the study of strategic-trade policy.

Externalities and the Calculus of Strategic Trade

Externalities have long been invoked as a *deus ex machina*, accounting for any and all unexplained variance in strategic-trade policy outcomes. This is unfortunate, since externalities clearly matter and, in the view of many scholars and policymakers, matter more than rents.

The book's argument about externalities builds from two independent variables. First, the intuition behind the consumption variable is that not all economies are equally primed to make use of the externalities for which states fight. Industries upstream and downstream are required not only to anchor the linkage externalities at stake, which are particularly salient in increasing-returns competition, but to exploit spillover externalities as well, which tend to diffuse among suppliers and end users, given their complementary R&D. Second, the intuition behind the internalization variable is that these externalities may be national or international in scope, trapping states either in a race to the top over subsidies or a race to the bottom, respectively. In matching up how rival states fare on the two independent variables, and making three simplifying assumptions, the book anticipates the contours of five different commercial rivalries, and the cooperation problems these give rise to. The argument is thus more nuanced than most accounts in this literature, predicting not only *which* externality-exhibiting industries a state is likely to fight for, but *how much* a state is likely to invest in waging this fight. The argument is also more empirically testable than most other accounts of externalities in the literature, since by placing emphasis on linkage externalities, there is a more overt paper trail to follow.

Externalities receive considerable attention beyond the literature on strategic trade. To be sure, linkages and spillovers figure prominently in theories of endogenous growth, and theories of economic geography. The book's independent variables have implications for both literatures. First, upstream-downstream linkages are a key part of the Silicon Valley effects that draw the attention of scholars looking to explain why certain industries cluster in a given region, for example.[2] Students of economic development also conjecture about the importance of externalities. Even those who would urge governments to let the market "play its hand" are nonetheless willing to prescribe an interventionist role where cutting-edge externality-exhibiting industries are at stake.[3] Industrial policy analysts follow suit.[4] The consumption variable begs a closer look at the industries that anchor these linkages. Upstream-downstream effects are more likely to pay dividends where firms on either side of these linkages are independently engaged in similar R&D. The trend is clear: recipient firms do not ride entirely for free, simply reverse-engineering what they see at zero cost to themselves. Rather, industries upstream and downstream must necessarily be primed to adopt, assimilate, and employ the product, process, and management skills at stake, and they are more likely to invest independently in complementary R&D if they themselves are also competitive. This gets at much of the criticism that states cannot "pick winners," since in evaluating the score on the consumption variable, states let the market pick their winners for them.

The internalization variable informs decisions about the level of subsidies needed, and the prospects for exploiting a "second mover" advantage. First, the level of subsidies that a state grants its national champions depends on whether the externalities at stake leak out beyond national borders, and on whether a foreign rival is able to consume these external benefits as well. This variable helps make sense of the variety of strategic-trade policies that states practice, and the counterintuitive dynamics witnessed in industries like HDTV, where the scope of the resulting externalities curtailed Japan's enthusiasm to fight for its national champions, against U.S. firms left to fend for themselves. This variable also speaks to the logic of the second-mover advantage. Analyses of economic growth and development often suggest that the global diffusion of technology is making it easier for late starters to catch up in cutting-edge industries. Yet, as civil aircraft makes clear, this global diffusion of technology is not apparent across the board. Indeed, Japan has been unable to catch up in this industry despite decades of subcontracting to Boeing and others, for example, sidelining the quintessentially activist state in this commercial rivalry. At least in certain high-technology industries, the message is thus that being late sometimes means not competing at all. The internalization variable sheds light on when this is likely to be the case.

Cooperation Problems among States

The debate over absolute and relative gains drove an artificial wedge between students of international political economy and students of security, as well as between neoliberals and realists. If we caricature both sides of this debate, the argument has been that absolute gains are the stuff of international political economy, neoliberalism, and cooperation, and that relative gains are the stuff of security, realism, and conflict. Few hold firmly to these views; recent scholarship cites a multiplicity of cooperation problems, not only across but within issue areas.[5] The book follows suit but traces this variation to the constraints of different strategic interactions, rather than to changes in state preferences per se.

This tack is suggested by Robert Powell who argues that, in debating absolute versus relative gains, international relations students "should focus less attention on anarchy and much more attention on characterizing the strategic settings in which the units interact."[6] Along these lines, the book assumes egoistic states and yet finds behavior consistent with concerns for "keeping up with the Joneses." The U.S.-Japan rivalry in HDTV stands out in this regard. Interpreted in Chapter 5 as a Cautious Activist game, the constraints of this strategic interaction made Japan's limited intervention in HDTV seem like "predation on the cheap" when viewed against U.S. nonintervention. To the extent that this is what we mean by relative gains seeking, it owes to the constraints of this commercial rivalry, rather than to a change in Japan's motivational concern with respect to foreign economic policy per se.[7]

LIMITATIONS OF THE STUDY

The limitations of the book's theory should also be spelled out. First, the puzzle traces to a model of strategic trade that assumes competition over output (Cournot) versus price (Bertrand). This means that the policy instrument of choice is a subsidy rather than a tax, though the bigger picture is that it skews the view of the cooperation problem that results. More specifically, a subsidy is a beggar-thy-neighbor policy where competition centers on output, whereas a tax is a favor-thy-neighbor policy where competition centers on price, because it raises foreign as well as domestic profits.[8] The debate about whether the Cournot or the Bertrand assumption is more useful is long-standing and legion.[9] Still, the Cournot assumption is particularly well suited to the cases in this book, given a wealth of evidence that output is the primary decision variable, feeding concern for scale economies and the like. For this reason, the assumption, with all its attendant theoretical baggage, is nonetheless useful.

Second, the book assumes perfect information, in that states know each other's scores on the independent variables. Recent research reveals, not surprisingly, that low and high levels of uncertainty greatly complicate almost any story told about strategic trade, from the willingness of policymakers to act, to the policy instrument of choice.[10] Still, the iteration of the commercial rivalries examined in this book does a lot to ease this uncertainty, even if not entirely.[11] The evidence largely brings this out as well, notwithstanding the spotlight on externalities. While some degree of uncertainty will no doubt loom in any commercial rivalry, assuming perfect information is a reasonable luxury, at least in taking a first cut at the puzzle of strategic trade.

Third, and perhaps most obvious, by treating the state as a rational unitary actor, the book gives little attention to the domestic politics of strategic trade. Factors ranging from proportional representation versus "winner-take-all" electoral systems, to the makeup of state institutions and the role of ideas, are likely to matter in comparing Japanese, European, and U.S. policymaking processes.[12] Chapters 2 and 6 insist that the rational unitary actor assumption is useful in theorizing about strategic trade in high technology, where concern for market failure (i.e., the undersupply of externalities) and the risk of foreign retaliation privilege state actions on behalf of a national constituency, even if this assumption is less useful in theorizing about broader trends in protectionism or industrial policy. Moreover, by setting up endogenous protection theory as the competing explanation, the book hardly turns a blind eye to the domestic politics of strategic trade. Ultimately, the evidence must convince the reader.

Finally, the case studies involve only a few advanced industrial states. One question is thus whether the theory can speak to the efforts of developing states to establish a footing in high technology. The evidence suggests it can. For example, Korea and Taiwan have sought a presence in civil aircraft, offering the same arguments heard on either side of the Atlantic with respect to the Boeing-Airbus rivalry. Nothing about the book's argument is specific to the advanced industrial states, save that these economies tend to be much more diversified across capital-intensive industries, and thus especially likely to score favorably on the consumption variable. A sampling of the strategic-trade policies of the developing states would nonetheless shed light on the robustness of the book's theory.

POLICY PRESCRIPTIONS

The book is likely to frustrate critics and proponents of strategic trade alike, though for very different reasons.

Proponents are likely to demand that different scores on the independent variables are within reach of policy. In other words, if the market hands down an unfavorable verdict on a state's capacity to consume and internalize externalities, then the verdict can simply be changed by implementing the appropriate industrial policy. While it is surely tempting to make endogenous what the book's theory takes as exogenous, this would be a mistake. First, industrial policy is also likely to take cues from the consumption variable: returns to investing in nontraded infrastructure should be assessed in a similar light, even if, absent the threat of foreign retaliation, industrial policy is far less constrained. Second, the internalization variable will also draw fire from proponents who see tighter restrictions on National Aeronautics and Space Administration or Department of Defense R&D as a way to encourage greater subsidies for national champions. This prescription is unwarranted. Access to NASA has not changed the competitive landscape in civil aircraft, nor did Sematech's policy on the participation of foreign firms sway the consortium's own advisory board on the question of whether Japan would benefit from its R&D. The same is true in superconductivity, where technonationalist policies have held little sway with policymakers, given the many channels through which this technology is prone to diffuse. The book urges caution on the part of policymakers before setting out to change the scores on the independent variables. Of course, this policy prescription is sure to frustrate proponents of strategic trade.

Critics are likely to counter that states lack the information necessary to make strategic-trade policy and that, in any case, technology diffuses so readily beyond national borders that it makes little sense to get worked up about foreign R&D subsidies.[13] The book goes to great lengths to argue that states let the market pick their winners for them, particularly with respect to the score on the consumption variable. The evidence reveals, moreover, that states do not take the externalities argument on faith alone. Studies looking into the score on the consumption variable kept the United States out of HDTV through the 1970s and 1980s, and have kept Japan on the sidelines of civil aircraft. As for sending along a "note of thanks," free riding is not always a viable option, as European Community (EC) studies are quick to note in the case of civil aircraft. Second mover advantage may be more common today than in the past, but it does not hold true across the board, and not in many of the most treasured high-technology industries, like aerospace. Thus, while recommending that policymakers be cautious in setting out to change the scores on the independent variables, the book also insists that they should not ignore the scores on these variables, either entrusting the fate of domestic industries to foreign technologies where diffusion is minimal, or carrying too much of the tab for subsidizing domestic industries where diffusion is widespread. If this comes as little surprise to some, it is nonetheless sure to frustrate critics of strategic trade.

This book has sought to shed light on the theory and practice of strategic trade, and on the problems of cooperation that these commercial rivalries give rise to. It will be useful to the extent that it inspires political scientists and economists, equipped with a few new theoretical insights and renewed curiosity, to take a closer look at the tensions arising over strategic trade.

Notes

1. Introduction

1 U.S. Senate, *Trade Agreements Compliance Act*, Hearing before the Subcommittee on International Trade of the Committee on Finance, 101st Congress, 2nd Session, July 13, 1990, p. 30. Testimony of Andrew A. Procassini.

2 U.S. House of Representatives, *High Definition Television*, Hearing before the Subcommittee on Research and Development and the Subcommittee on Investigations of the Committee on Armed Services, 101st Congress, 1st Session, May 10, 1989, p. 66. Testimony of Pat Hubbard.

3 U.S. Senate, *Department of Defense Authorization for Appropriations for Fiscal Years 1990 and 1991*, Hearings before the Committee on Armed Services, 101st Congress, 1st Session, March 17; May 11, 16, 17, 31; June 2, 1989, p. 10. Testimony of Mel Levine (D-California).

4 The strategic-trade literature generally takes "high technology" to mean R&D intensity, which serves as an entry barrier and thus conveys information about the degree to which an industry is imperfectly competitive. Other characteristics further distinguish high-technology industries, as is discussed more fully in Chapter 2.

5 This logic obtains where this supplier also competes under conditions of increasing returns to scale.

6 James Brander and Barbara J. Spencer, "Export Subsidies and International Market Share Rivalry," *Journal of International Economics* 18 (1985): 83–100.

7 This is to say that the United States and Europe have shied away from subsidizing a market presence in the HDTV and semiconductor industries, respectively, not that they have invested zero resources. See Chapters 5 and 4, respectively.

8 See, for example, Gene M. Grossman and Elhanan Helpman, "Trade Wars and Trade Talks," *Journal of Political Economy* 103.4 (1995): 675–708; and John A. C. Conybeare, *Trade Wars: The Theory and Practice of International Commercial Rivalry* (New York: Columbia University Press, 1987).

9 Harry G. Johnson, *International Trade and Economic Growth: Studies in Pure Theory* (Cambridge, MA: Harvard University Press, 1967). See also Joanne Gowa and Edward D. Mansfield, "Power Politics and International

Trade," *American Political Science Review* 87.2 (1993): 408–20; and Conybeare, *Trade Wars*.

10 Joanne Gowa, "Rational Hegemons, Excludable Goods, and Small Groups: An Epitaph for Hegemonic Stability Theory?" *World Politics* 41.3 (1989): 307–24; and David A. Lake, *Power, Protection and Free Trade: International Sources of U.S. Commercial Strategy, 1887–1939* (Ithaca, NY: Cornell University Press, 1988).

11 David A. Lake, "Leadership, Hegemony, and the International Economy: Naked Emperor or Tattered Monarch with Potential," *International Studies Quarterly* 37.4 (1993): 473.

12 Market power in the optimal tariff context implies that a state is a sufficiently large purchaser that it faces a less than perfectly elastic foreign supply curve. This means that the price of imports does not increase by the full amount of the tariff, part of the cost being passed on to foreign trade rivals. Market structure in the strategic-trade context raises questions about barriers to entry and exit and sources of increasing returns to scale. This is discussed more fully in Chapter 2.

13 Paul R. Krugman, "Introduction," in Krugman and Alasdair Smith (eds.), *Empirical Studies of Strategic Trade Policy* (Chicago: University of Chicago Press, 1994), p. 1–9; J. David Richardson, *Sizing-Up U.S. Export Disincentives* (Washington, DC: Institute for International Economics, 1993); Laura D'Andrea Tyson, *Who's Bashing Whom? Trade Conflict in High-technology industries* (Washington, DC: Institute for International Economics, 1992); Cynthia A. Beltz, *High-Tech Maneuvers: Industrial Policy Lessons of HDTV* (Washington, DC: American Enterprise Institute, 1991); Michael E. Porter, *The Competitive Advantage of Nations* (New York: Free Press, 1990); Robert Wade, *Governing the Market: Economic Theory and the Role of Government in East Asian Industrialization* (Princeton: Princeton University Press, 1990); Jeffrey A. Hart, "Strategic Impacts of High Definition Television for U.S. Manufacturing" (Ann Arbor, MI: National Center for Manufacturing Sciences, 1989); Jeffrey A. Hart and Laura D'Andrea Tyson, "Responding to the Challenge of HDTV," *California Management Review* 31.4 (1989): 132–45; Daniel I. Okimoto, *Between MITI and the Market: Japanese Industrial Policy for High Technology* (Stanford: Stanford University Press, 1989); and Hugh Patrick, "Japanese High Technology Policy in Comparative Context," Columbia University Graduate School of Business, Center on Japanese Economy and Business Working Paper No. 1 (New York, 1986).

14 Robert Ford and Win Swyker, "Industrial Subsidies in the OECD Economies," *OECD Economic Studies* 15 (1990): 37–81; and Gene M. Grossman, "Promoting New Industrial Activities: A Survey of Recent Arguments and Evidence," *OECD Economic Studies* 11 (1988): 87–125.

15 See, for example, Beltz, *High-Tech Maneuvers*.

16 Avinash Dixit, "How Should the United States Respond to Other Countries' Trade Policies," in Robert M. Stern (ed.), *U.S. Trade Policies in a Changing World Economy* (Cambridge, MA: MIT Press, 1987), p. 246.

17 See, for example, John Mark Hansen, *Gaining Access: Congress and the Farm Lobby, 1919–1981* (Chicago: University of Chicago Press, 1991); Cheryl Schoenhardt-Bailey, "Lessons in Lobbying for Free Trade in 19th Century Britain: To Concentrate or Not," *American Political Science Review* 85.1 (1991): 37–58; and Vinod K. Aggarwal, Robert O. Keohane, and David B. Yoffie, "The Dynamics of Negotiated Protectionism," *American Political Science Review* 81.2 (1987): 345–66.

18 See, for example, Gene M. Grossman and Elhanan Helpman, "Protection for Sale," *American Economic Review* 84.4 (1994): 833–50; Arye L. Hillman, "Protection, Politics, and Market Structure," in Elhanan Helpman and Assaf Razin (eds.), *International Trade and Trade Policy* (Cambridge, MA: MIT Press, 1991), pp. 118–40; Stephen P. Magee, William A. Brock, and Leslie Young, *Black Hole Tariffs and Endogenous Policy Theory: Political Economy in General Equilibrium* (Cambridge: Cambridge University Press, 1989); and Marc L. Busch and Eric Reinhardt,"Industrial Location and Protection: The Political and Economic Geography of U.S. Nontariff Barriers," *American Journal of Political Science* (forthcoming).

19 Europe, in this case, being a shorthand for the four Airbus states, including Britain, France, Germany, and Spain.

2. The Argument

1 Paul R. Krugman, "Introduction," in Krugman and Alastair Smith (eds.), *Empirical Studies of Strategic Trade Policy* (Chicago: University of Chicago Press, 1994), pp. 1–9.

2 For a review of the literature, see Klaus Stegemann, "Policy Rivalry among Industrial States: What Can We Learn from Models of Strategic Trade Policy?" *International Organization* 43.1 (1989): 73–100.

3 James A. Brander and Barbara J. Spencer, "Export Subsidies and International Market Share Rivalry," *Journal of International Economics* 18 (1985): 83–100.

4 Gottfried Haberler, "Strategic Trade Policy and the New International Economics: A Critical Analysis," in Ronald W. Jones and Anne D. Krueger (eds.), *The Political Economy of International Trade: Essays in Honor of Robert E. Baldwin* (Cambridge, MA: Blackwell, 1990), pp. 25–30; J. David Richardson, "The Political Economy of Strategic Trade Policy," *International Organization* 44.1 (1990): 107–35; Jagdish Bhagwati, *Protectionism* (Cambridge, MA: MIT Press, 1988); and Gene M. Grossman and J. David Richardson, "Strategic Trade Policy: A Survey of Issues and Early Analysis," Princeton University Special Papers in International Economics No. 15 (Princeton, 1985).

5 James A. Brander, "Rationales for Strategic Trade and Industrial Policy," in Paul R. Krugman (ed.), *Strategic Trade Policy and the New International Economics* (Cambridge, MA: MIT Press, 1986), p. 44. Emphasis added.

6 See, for example, Bruno van Pottelsberghe de la Potterie, "Inter-Industry Technological Spillovers and the Rate of Return on R&D," MITI Discus-

sion Paper No. 96-DOF-23 (Tokyo, 1996); Paul M. Romer, "The Origins of Endogenous Growth," *Journal of Economic Perspectives* 8.1 (1994): 3–22; and Paul R. Krugman, "Strategic Sectors and International Competition," in Robert M. Stern (ed.), *U.S. Trade Policies in a Changing World Economy* (Cambridge, MA: MIT Press, 1987), pp. 207–32.

7   The social rate of return is the private rate of return plus the interindustry marginal cost reductions owing to these technology spillovers. See, for example, Jeffrey I. Bernstein and M. Ishaq Nadiri, "Interindustry R&D Spillovers, Rates of Return, and Production in High-Tech Industries," *American Economic Review* 78.2 (1988): 429.

8   See Chapter 5.

9   In the case studies, the state, as a rational unitary actor, is operationalized as the executive. This accords with studies that link the rational unitary state assumption to executive politics more generally, as where, for example, the executive monopolizes information or holds the same preferences as the legislature. The book speaks of states as rational unitary actors, rather than invoking the language of executive politics, because of its focus on international, not domestic politics, the latter being the focus of the competing explanation. For a discussion of rational unitary states and executive politics, see Helen V. Milner, *Interests, Institutions, and Information: Domestic Politics and International Relations* (Princeton: Princeton University Press, 1997), pp. 11–12. For a more general discussion of the utility maximization assumption, see Jeffry A. Frieden, *Debt, Development, and Democracy: Modern Political Economy and Latin America, 1965–1985* (Princeton: Princeton University Press, 1991), pp. 17–19.

10   Jean Tirole, "The Internal Organization of Government," *Oxford Economic Papers* 46 (1994): 1–29.

11   Wesley M. Cohen and Richard C. Levin, "Empirical Studies of Innovation and Market Share," in Richard Schmalensee and Robert D. Willig (eds.), *Handbook of Industrial Organization*, Vol. 2 (Amsterdam: North Holland, 1989), pp. 1059–1107.

12   Geoffrey Carliner, "Industrial Policies for Emerging Industries," in Krugman, *Strategic Trade Policy and the New International Economics*, p. 156.

13   Lewis M. Branscomb, "The National Technology Policy Debate," in Branscomb (ed.), *Empowering Technology: Implementing a U.S. Strategy* (Cambridge, MA: MIT Press, 1993), pp. 1–35; Organisation for Economic Cooperation and Development, *Technology and the Economy: The Key Relationship* (Paris: OECD, 1992); and Eric von Hippel, *The Sources of Innovation* (New York: Oxford University Press, 1988).

14   Fabian Fecher and Sergio Perelman, "Productivity Growth and Technical Efficiency in OECD Industrial Activities," in Richard E. Caves (ed.), *Industrial Efficiency in Six Nations* (Cambridge, MA: MIT Press, 1992), pp. 459–88; Edwin Mansfield, "Appropriating the Returns from Investments in R&D Capital," in Karel Cool, Damien J. Neven, and Ingo Walter (eds.), *European Industrial Restructuring in the 1990s*, pp. 331–56 (New York: New York University Press, 1992); F. M. Scherer, *International High-*

Technology Competition (Cambridge, MA: Harvard University Press, 1992); Richard J. Caballero and Richard K. Lyons, "External Effects and Europe's Integration," in L. Alan Winters and Anthony Venables (eds.), *European Integration: Trade and Industry* (Cambridge: Cambridge University Press, 1991), pp. 34–51; Cohen and Levin, "Empirical Studies of Innovation and Market Share"; Jeffrey I. Bernstein, "Costs of Production, Intra- and Interindustry R&D Spillovers: Canadian Evidence," *Canadian Journal of Economics* 21.2 (1988): 324–47; Bernstein and Nadiri, "Interindustry R&D Spillovers, Rates of Return, and Production in High-Tech Industries"; and Martin B. Zimmerman, "Learning Effects and the Commercialization of New Energy Technologies: The Case of Nuclear Power," *Bell Journal of Economics* 13.2 (1982): 297–310.

15 Organisation for Economic Co-operation and Development, *Technology and Industrial Performance* (Paris: OECD, 1996), p. 19.

16 Annelee Saxenian, *Regional Advantage: Culture and Competition in Silicon Valley and Route 128* (Cambridge, MA: Harvard University Press, 1994).

17 Charles Monck (ed.), *Science Parks – Their Contribution to Economic Growth* (Proceedings of the U.K. Science Park Association's annual conference, December 1985); and U.S. Senate, *Space Benefits – The Secondary Application of Aerospace Technology in Other Sectors of the Economy*, prepared for the Committee on Aeronautical and Space Sciences, April 16, 1975.

18 U.S. House of Representatives, *The Role of Basic Research in Economic Competitiveness*, Hearing before the Subcommittee on Science of the Committee on Science, Space, and Technology, 102nd Congress, 1st Session, June 20, 1991, p. 63. Emphasis added.

19 See, for example, David T. Coe, Elhanan Helpman, and Alexander W. Hoffmaister, "North-South R&D Spillovers," Centre for Economic Policy Research Discussion Paper No. 1133 (London, 1995); and David T. Coe and Elhanan Helpman, "International R&D Spillovers," Centre for Economic Policy Research Discussion Paper No. 840 (London, 1993).

20 Antonio Ciccone and Robert E. Hall, "Productivity and the Density of Economic Activity," *American Economic Review* 86.1 (1996): 54–70; Romer, "The Origins of Endogenous Growth"; Gene M. Grossman and Elhanan Helpman, "Endogenous Innovation in the Theory of Growth," *Journal of Economic Perspectives* 8.1 (1994): 23–44; C. Fred Bergsten and Marcus Noland, *Reconcilable Differences? United States–Japan Economic Conflict* (Washington, DC: International Institute for Economics, 1993); Paul R. Krugman, "Technology-Intensive Goods," in Michael Finder and Andrej Olechowski (eds.), *The Uruguay Round: A Handbook for the Multilateral Trade Negotiations* (Washington, DC: World Bank, 1987), pp. 1–9; and Edwin Mansfield, "How Rapidly Does New Industrial Technology Leak Out?" *Journal of Industrial Economics* 34.2 (1985): 217–23.

21 Avinash Dixit, "How Should the United States Respond to Other Countries' Trade Policies?" in Stern, *U.S. Trade Policies in a Changing World Economy*, pp. 245–82.

22 Congressional Budget Office, "Federal Financial Support for High-Technology Industries" (Washington, DC: Government Printing Office, 1985), p. x. Emphasis added. See also Science and Technology Agency, "White Paper on Science and Technology 1988 (Summary): Towards the Establishment of a New Creative Research Environment" (Tokyo: Science and Technology Agency, 1988), p. 11.

23 Office of Technology Assessment, "Competing Economies: America, Europe, and the Pacific Rim," OTA-ITE-498 (Washington, DC: GPO, 1991); and David C. Mowery, *Alliance Politics and Economics: Multinational Joint Ventures in Commercial Aircraft* (Cambridge, MA: Ballinger, 1987).

24 See Frank R. Lichtenberg, "R&D Investment and International Productivity Differences," National Bureau of Economic Research Working Paper No. 4161 (Cambridge, MA, 1992).

25 Douglas A. Irwin and Peter J. Klenow, "Learning-By-Doing Spillovers in the Semiconductor Industry," *Journal of Political Economy* 102.6 (1994): 1200–27.

26 See Sylvia Ostry and Richard R. Nelson, *Techno-Nationalism and Techno-Globalism: Conflict and Cooperation* (Washington, DC: Brookings, 1995).

27 Hae-Sin Hwang and Craig T. Schulma, "Strategic Non-Intervention and the Choice of Trade Policy for International Oligopoly," *Journal of International Economics* 34 (1993): 74–93.

28 See Robert O. Keohane, *After Hegemony: Cooperation and Discord in the World Political Economy* (Princeton: Princeton University Press, 1984).

29 Stephen D. Krasner, "Global Communications and National Power: Life on the Pareto Frontier," *World Politics* 43.3 (1991): 336–66; and Jack Knight, *Institutions and Social Conflict* (Cambridge: Cambridge University Press, 1992).

30 Dixit, "How Should the United States Respond to Other Countries' Trade Policies?"

31 Laura D'Andrea Tyson, *Who's Bashing Whom? Trade Conflict in High-Technology Industries* (Washington, DC: Institute for International Economics, 1992).

32 See Organisation for Economic Co-operation and Development, *Technology and Industrial Performance*, p. 37.

33 See, for example, Wendy L. Hansen and Kee Ok Park, "Nation-State and Pluralistic Decision Making in Trade Policy: The Case of the International Trade Administration," *International Studies Quarterly* 39.2 (1995): 181–212; Edward D. Mansfield and Marc L. Busch, "The Political Economy of Nontariff Barriers: A Cross-National Analysis"; *International Organization* 49.4 (1995): 723–49; Daniel Trefler, "Trade Liberalization and the Theory of Endogenous Protection: An Econometric Study of U.S. Import Policy," *Journal of Political Economy* 101.1 (1993): 138–60; John A. C. Conybeare, "Voting for Protection: An Electoral Model of Tariff Policy," *International Organization* 45.1 (1991): 57–82; Stephen P. Magee, William A. Brock, and Leslie Young, *Black Hole Tariffs and Endogenous Policy Theory: Political Economy in General Equilibrium* (Cambridge: Cambridge University

Press, 1989); and Marc L. Busch and Eric Reinhardt,"Industrial Location and Protection: The Political and Economic Geography of U.S. Nontariff Barriers," *American Journal of Political Science* (forthcoming).

34 Robert M. Uriu, *Troubled Industries: Confronting Economic Change in Japan* (Ithaca, NY: Cornell University Press, 1996); Ayre L. Hillman, "Protection, Politics, and Market Structure," in Elhanan Helpman and Assaf Razin (eds.), *International Trade and Trade Policy* (Cambridge, MA: MIT Press, 1991), pp. 118–40; Vinod K. Aggarwal, Robert O. Keohane, and David B. Yoffie, "The Dynamics of Negotiated Protectionism," *American Political Science Review* 81.2 (1987): 345–66; and Richard E. Caves, "Economic Models of Political Choice: Canada's Tariff Structure," *Canadian Journal of Economics* 9.2 (1977): 278–300.

35 Helen V. Milner, *Resisting Protectionism: Global Industries and the Politics of International Trade* (Princeton: Princeton University Press, 1988).

36 Paul R. Krugman, *Rethinking International Trade* (Cambridge, MA: MIT Press, 1991); and Helen V. Milner and David B. Yoffie, "Between Free Trade and Protectionism: Strategic Trade Policy and a Theory of Corporate Trade Demands," *International Organization* 43.2 (1989): 239–71.

3. The Civil Aircraft Rivalry

1 See, for example, Richard Pomfret, "The New Trade Theories, Rent Snatching and Jet Aircraft," *World Economy* 14.3 (1991): 269–77; Gernot Klepper, Robert W. Crandall, and Didier Laussel, "Entry into the Market for Large Transport Aircraft," *European Economic Review* 34.4 (1990): 775–803; and Richard Baldwin and Paul R. Krugman, "Industrial Policy and International Competition in Wide-Bodied Jet Aircraft," in Robert E. Baldwin (ed.), *Trade Policy Issues and Empirical Analysis* (Chicago: University of Chicago Press, 1988), pp. 45–71.

2 Office of Technology Assessment, "Competing Economies: America, Europe, and the Pacific Rim," OTA-ITE-498 (Washington, DC: GPO, 1991), p. 342.

3 Martin B. Lieberman, "The Learning Curve and Pricing in the Chemical Processing Industries," *Rand Journal of Economics* 15.2 (1984): 214.

4 Gernot Klepper, "Industrial Policy in the Transport Aircraft Industry," in Paul R. Krugman and Alasdair Smith (eds.), *Empirical Studies of Strategic Trade Policy* (Chicago: University of Chicago Press, 1994), p. 104. The 80% figure was provided by Airbus North America in a 1996 interview with Jonathan Schofield, chairman and CEO.

5 Daniel Todd and Jamie Simpson, *The World Aircraft Industry* (London: Croom Helm, 1986), p. 113.

6 "Deutsche Airbus to Begin Joining Wing of First A321 This Week," *Aviation Week and Space Technology*, July 13, 1992, p. 23.

7 David B. Yoffie, "Collision Course in Commercial Aircraft: Boeing-Airbus-McDonnell Douglas 1991 (A)," Harvard Business School Case No. 9-391-109 (Cambridge, MA, 1991), p. 3; and U.S. Department of Commerce, *A*

Competitive Assessment of the U.S. Civil Aircraft Industry (Boulder, CO: Westview Press, 1986), pp. 3–4. Others are skeptical of benchmarks of this sort. See John Newhouse, *The Sporty Game: The High-Risk Competitive Business of Making and Selling Commercial Airlines* (New York: Knopf, 1982), p. 4.

8   Airbus Industrie North America explains, for example, that the typical break-even point is more in keeping with 350–400 airplanes today.

9   David C. Mowery and Nathan Rosenberg, *Technology and the Pursuit of Economic Growth* (Cambridge: Cambridge University Press, 1989), p. 173.

10 David C. Mowery, *Alliance Politics and Economics: Multinational Joint Ventures in Commercial Aircraft* (Cambridge, MA: Ballinger, 1987), p. 71.

11 U.S. House of Representatives, *Major Issues in United States European Community Trade*, staff report prepared for the use of the Subcommittee on Oversight and Investigations of the Committee on Energy and Commerce, July 1987, p. 10.

12 Oral Statement of Lawrence W. Clarkson, Corporate Vice President for Planning and International Development, The Boeing Company, before the House Committee on Public Works and Transportation, Subcommittee on Aviation, February 24, 1993, p. 3. Testimony courtesy of the Boeing Company.

13 Interview with Schofield and Alan Boyd, former CEO of Airbus North America.

14 Baldwin and Krugman, "Industrial Policy and International Competition in Wide-Bodied Jet Aircraft."

15 Boeing Commercial Airplane Group, *Current Market Outlook: World Market Demand and Airplane Supply Requirements, 1992* (Seattle: Boeing, 1992), p. 2.3; and Vicki L. Golich, "From Competition to Collaboration: The Challenge of Commercial-Class Aircraft Manufacturing," *International Organization* 46.4 (1992): 908. See also "ANA Dumps Airbus, Opts for Boeing Jets," *Japan Economic Journal,* January 4 and 11, 1986, p. 1; and "The Big Six: A Survey of the World's Aircraft Industry," *Economist,* June 1, 1985, p. 59.

16 Commission of the European Communities, "Demand Prospects for Civil Transport Aircraft" (Brussels: Commission of the European Communities, 1975), p. 15.

17 U.S. House of Representatives, *Competitiveness of U.S. Commercial Aircraft Industry*, Hearing before the Subcommittee on Commerce, Consumer Protection, and Competitiveness of the Committee on Energy and Commerce, 100th Congress, 1st Session, June 23, 1987, p. 34.

18 Only 19 Concorde airplanes were ever built.

19 Derivative airplanes extend the range (i.e., Boeing's 777-200ER) or seating capacity (i.e., Airbus's A340-300) of a base model.

20 See, for example, "Aerospatiale Wary of Superjumbo Project," *Financial Times,* March 3, 1994, p. 4.

21 Todd and Simpson, *The World Aircraft Industry*, p. 3; National Academy of Engineering, *The Competitive Status of the U.S. Civil Aviation Manufac-*

turing Industry: A Study of the Influences of Technology in Determining International Industrial Competitive Advantage (Washington, DC: National Academy Press, 1985), p. 19.

22 Interview with Schofield.

23 Testimony of Lawrence W. Clarkson, Corporate Vice President for Planning and International Development, The Boeing Company, before the Senate Finance Committee, June 2, 1992, p. 2. Testimony courtesy of the Boeing Company.

24 Aerospace Industries Association, "Does the United States Support Its Commercial Transport Manufacturers like Europe Supports Airbus?" (Washington, DC: AIA, 1985), pp. 4–5.

25 Malcolm S. Salter, "Airbus Versus Boeing (A): Turbulent Skies," Harvard Business School Case No. 9-386-193 (Cambridge, MA, 1987), p. 3.

26 U.S. Department of Commerce, *A Competitive Assessment of the U.S. Civil Aircraft Industry*, p. 25. Emphasis added.

27 U.S. House of Representatives, *Competitiveness of U.S. Commercial Aircraft Industry*, p. 24.

28 Quoted in Office of Technology Assessment, "Government Support of the Large Commercial Aircraft Industries of Japan, Europe, and the United States" (Washington, DC: OTA Contractor Report, 1991), p. 9. Emphasis added.

29 Gellman Research Associates, "An Economic and Financial Review of Airbus Industrie," report prepared for the U.S. Department of Commerce, International Trade Administration (Washington, DC, 1990), p. 5–5.

30 Desmond Hickie, "Airbus Industrie: A Case Study in European High Technology Cooperation," in Ulrich Hilpert (ed.), *State Policies and Techno-Industrial Innovation* (New York: Routledge, 1991), pp. 193, 211.

31 Commission of the European Communities, "A Competitive European Aeronautical Industry" (Brussels: Commission of the European Communities, 1990), p. 9.

32 Keith Hayward, *International Collaboration in Civil Aerospace* (New York: St. Martin's, 1986), p. 166.

33 Quoted in Mark A. Lorell, "Multinational Development of Large Aircraft: The European Experience," Rand Corporation Document R-2596-DR&E (Santa Monica, 1980), p. 58.

34 Ian McIntyre, *Dogfight: The Transatlantic Battle over Airbus* (Westport, CT: Praeger, 1992), p. 190. See also Bundesministerium für Wirtschaft, "Die Konkurrenzsituation der deutschen Luft-und Raumfahrt im internationalen Vergleich" (Bonn: Bundesministerium für Wirtschaft, 1988), p. 22.

35 European Commission, "The Aeronautics Task Force: Interim Report" (Brussels: EC Directorate-General III/D Industry, 1995), p. 1.

36 Quoted in Congressional Research Service, "Airbus Industrie: An Economic and Trade Perspective," report prepared for the Subcommittee on Technology and Competitiveness, transmitted to the Committee on Science, Space, and Technology, 102nd Congress, 2nd Session, March 1992, p. 4.

37 "Come Fly with Me," *National Journal*, March 31, 1990, p. 77; U.S. Department of Commerce, *A Competitive Assessment of the U.S. Civil Aircraft Industry*, pp. 77–94; and U.S. House of Representatives, *Industrial Policy*, Hearings before the Subcommittee on Economic Stabilization of the Committee on Banking, Finance, and Urban Affairs, 98th Congress, 2nd Session, July 13, 14, 18, and 26, 1983, p. 699.

38 U.S. House of Representatives, *U.S. International Trade Performance and Outlook: Competitive Position in the Automotive, Aerospace, and Chemical and Pharmaceutical Sectors*, Hearings before the Subcommittee on Trade of the Committee on Ways and Means, 102nd Congress, 2nd Session, March 11, 23, 30, 31, and April 7, 1992, p. 448.

39 Aerospace Industries Association, "National Benefits of Aerospace Exports" (Washington, DC: AIA, 1983), pp. 12–14.

40 U.S. House of Representatives, *Europe and the United States: Competition and Cooperation in the 1990s*, study papers submitted to the Subcommittee on International Economic Policy and Trade and the Subcommittee on Europe and the Middle East of the Committee on Foreign Affairs (Washington, DC: GPO, 1992), p. 215.

41 F. M. Sherer, *International High-Technology Competition* (Cambridge, MA: Harvard University Press, 1992), p. 135. The significance of this distinction is that manufacturing industries perform 97% of all industrial R&D in the United States.

42 Congressional Research Service, "Airbus Industrie: An Economic and Trade Perspective," pp. 47–51.

43 Aerospace Industries Association, "Technology Diffusion – The Movement of Technology between Aerospace and Other Industries" (Washington, DC: AIA, 1985), p. 22.

44 B. Bowonder and S. V. Ramana Rao, "Creating and Sustaining Competitiveness – An Analysis of the World Civil Aircraft Industry," *World Competition: Law and Economics Review* 16.4 (1993): 12; "Composites: Reaching New Heights in Aerospace," *Production*, August 1987, p. 56; and U.S. Department of Commerce, *A Competitive Assessment of the U.S. Civil Aircraft Industry*, p. 87.

45 U.S. Department of Commerce, *1994 U.S. Industrial Outlook* (Washington, DC: ITA, 1994), pp. 17-7, 17-9.

46 "Flying High with Advanced Materials," *Purchasing*, July 20, 1989, pp. 100B14–100B16.

47 "Advanced Polymer Composite Makers Look toward Infrastructure Markets," *Chemical and Engineering News*, March 25, 1996, p. 12.

48 U.S. House of Representatives, *U.S. International Trade Performance and Outlook: Competitive Position in the Automotive, Aerospace, and Chemical and Pharmaceutical Sectors*, Hearings before the Subcommittee on Trade of the Committee on Ways and Means, p. 461; and Aerospace Industries Association, "Technology Diffusion – The Movement of Technology between Aerospace and Other industries," p. 7.

49 U.S. Department of Commerce, *1994 U.S. Industrial Outlook*, p. 27-13.

50 National Academy of Engineering, *The Competitive Status of the U.S. Civil Aviation Manufacturing Industry*, p. 108.

51 Congressional Budget Office, "The Benefits and Risks of Federal Funding for Sematech" (Washington, DC: GPO, 1987), p. 17.

52 "Aerospatiale Strives to Keep Stability in CAD/CAM Hardware, Software," *Aviation Week and Space Technology*, June 22, 1992, pp. 55–6.

53 "Parallel Processing Gains in Supercomputer Market," *Aviation Week and Space Technology*, June 22, 1992, pp. 62–4.

54 "Digital, Other Firms Focus on Aerospace CASE Needs," *Aviation Week and Space Technology*, June 22, 1992, pp. 61–2.

55 See, for example, Aerospace Industries Association, "Maintaining Technological Leadership: The Critical Role of IR&D/B&P" (Washington, DC: AIA, 1989), pp. 7–8.

56 This taxonomy was provided by John Potter of Boeing Avionics.

57 National Aeronautics and Space Administration, "Spinoff 1994" (Washington, DC: GPO, 1995).

58 U.S. Department of Commerce, *1994 U.S. Industrial Outlook*, p. 31-4.

59 "Quest for Ever More Power," *Financial Times*, September 2, 1994, p. 3, aerospace supplement.

60 U.S. Department of Commerce, *1989 U.S. Industrial Outlook* (Washington, DC: ITA, 1989), p. 35-8.

61 U.S. International Trade Commission, "Global Competitiveness of U.S. Advanced-Technology Manufacturing Industries: Large Civil Aircraft" (Washington, DC: ITC, 1993), p. 2-8.

62 National Academy of Engineering, *The Competitive Status of the U.S. Civil Aviation Manufacturing Industry*. A more recent, but similar assessment, is offered in U.S. Department of Commerce, *1992 U.S. Industrial Outlook* (Washington, DC: ITA, 1992), pp. 21-3, 21-4.

63 U.S. Department of Commerce, *A Competitive Assessment of the U.S. Civil Aircraft Industry*, p. 87.

64 See, for example, Walter A. McDougall, "Space-Age Europe: Gaullism, Euro-Gaullism, and the American Dilemma," *Technology and Culture* 26.2 (1985): 179–203; and Michiel Schwarz, "European Policies on Space Science and Technology 1960–1978," *Research Policy* 8 (1979): 204–43.

65 Lorell, "Multinational Development of Large Aircraft: The European Experience," p. 70.

66 Airbus Industrie, "The Airbus Industrie Production System" (Washington, DC: Airbus Industrie North America); and Airbus Industrie "An Introduction to Airbus Industrie" (Washington, DC: Airbus Industrie North America, 1992), p. 12. See also British Aerospace, "Annual Report 1994" (Farnborough: British Aerospace, 1994), p. 23.

67 "Component and Avionics Firms' Support Keeps French Aircraft Companies Strong," *Aviation Week and Space Technology*, May 11, 1992, pp. 51–2.

68 See, for example, Andrew Moravcsik, "Armaments among Allies: European Weapons Collaboration, 1975–1985," in Peter B. Evans, Harold K. Jacob-

son, and Robert D. Putnam (eds.), *Double-Edged Diplomacy: International Bargaining and Domestic Politics* (Berkeley: University of California Press, 1993), p. 139; and M. Y. Yoshino, "Global Competition in a Salient Industry: The Case of Civil Aircraft," in Michael E. Porter (ed.), *Competition in Global Industries* (Boston: Harvard Business School Press, 1986), p. 519.

69 Matthew Lynn, *Birds of Prey: The War between Boeing and Airbus* (London: Heinemann, 1995), p. 205.

70 U.S. House of Representatives, *Proposed Joint Development of the FSX Fighter with Japan,* Hearings before the Subcommittee of the Committee on Banking, Finance, and Urban Affairs, 101st Congress, 1st Session, April 15 and May 5, 1989, pp. 239–42. On Japan's civil aircraft industry, see David B. Friedman and Richard J. Samuels, "How to Succeed without Really Flying: The Japanese Aircraft Industry and Japan's Technology Ideology," in Jeffrey A. Frankel and Miles Kahler (eds.), *Regionalism and Rivalry: Japan and the United States in Pacific Asia* (Chicago: University of Chicago Press, 1993); and Long-Term Credit Bank of Japan, "The Japanese Aircraft Industry: Entering a Period of Progress Spurred by International Joint Development," LTCB Research Special Issue on Japan's High-Technology Industries No. 6 (Tokyo, 1986).

71 U.S. Department of Commerce, *1994 U.S. Industrial Outlook,* p. 20–3. Emphasis added.

72 U.S. House of Representatives, *Proposed Joint Development of the FSX Fighter with Japan,* Hearings before the Subcommittee of the Committee on Banking, Finance, and Urban Affairs, p. 230.

73 Wesley M. Cohen and Richard C. Levin, "Empirical Studies of Innovation and Market Structure," in Richard Schmalensee and Robert Willig (eds.), *Handbook of Industrial Organization* (Amsterdam: North-Holland, 1989), 2:1093.

74 United States Securities and Exchange Commission, *FORM 10-K: The Boeing Company* (Washington, DC: December 31, 1991), p. 3. Emphasis added.

75 Adrian Kendry, Peter Duffield, and John Butler, "The Economic and Industrial Importance of the Airbus Partnership" (Bristol: Centre for Social and Economic Research, 1995), p. 14.

76 Office of Technology Assessment, "Competing Economies," p. 347.

77 Office of Technology Assessment, "Government Support of the Large Commercial Aircraft Industries of Japan, Europe, and the United States," p. 84.

78 Ibid., p. 85.

79 Aerospace Industries Association, "Technology Diffusion – The Movement of Technology between Aerospace and Other Industries," p. 28.

80 I am most grateful to Professor Linda Sprague, School of Industrial and Manufacturing Science, Cranfield University, for sharing with me her expertise on the process of manufacturing civil aircraft.

81 Aerospace Industries Association, "The Importance of Aerospace to the Nation's Economy" (Washington, DC: AIA, 1992), p. 6.

82 Wilbur Smith Associates, "The Economic Impact of Civil Aviation on the

U.S. Economy: Update '91" (Columbia, SC: Prepared for Martin Marietta Corporation, 1993), p. 12.

83 Oral Statement of Lawrence W. Clarkson, Corporate Vice President for Planning and International Development, The Boeing Company, before the House Committee on Public Works and Transportation, Subcommittee on Aviation, p. 2; Mowery, *Alliance Politics and Economics*, p. 132; Aerospace Industries Association, "The Importance of Aerospace to the Nation's Economy," p. 6; Boeing Commercial Airplane Group, "European Targeting of the Commercial Aircraft Industry – Why Is Boeing Concerned?" (Seattle: Boeing, 1991), p. 4; Malcolm S. Salter, "Airbus versus Boeing (B): The Storm Intensifies," Harvard Business School Case No. 9-388-145 (Cambridge, MA, 1988), p. 3; and U.S. Department of Commerce, *1985 Industrial Outlook* (Washington, DC: ITA, 1985), p. 37-7. The quotation is from U.S. Department of Commerce, *1989 U.S. Industrial Outlook*, p. 35-10. See also Airbus Industrie, "U.S. Content in Airbus Industrie Aircraft" (Washington, DC: Airbus Industrie North America, 1992).

84 Randy Barber and Robert E. Scott, "Jobs on the Wing: Trading Away the Future of the U.S. Aerospace Industry" (Washington, DC: Economic Policy Institute, 1995), pp. 5–6; and Mowery, *Alliance Politics and Economics*, p. 54.

85 Jacques S. Gansler, *The Defense Industry* (Cambridge, MA: MIT Press, 1980), p. 43.

86 Yoffie, "Collision Course in Commercial Aircraft: Boeing-Airbus-McDonnell Douglas 1991 (A)," p. 8; Yoshino, "Global Competition in a Salient Industry: The Case of Civil Aircraft," p. 519; and "Which Airlines, Which Continent," *Economist*, April 22, 1978, p. 88.

87 Hayward, *International Collaboration in Civil Aerospace*, p. 99.

88 Quoted in Aerospace Industries Association, "U.S. Aerospace Technology Development: Stepping Up the Pace" (Washington, DC: AIA, 1989), p. 3.

89 Quoted in Office of Technology Assessment, "Government Support of the Large Commercial Aircraft Industries of Japan, Europe, and the United States," p. 11. Emphasis added.

90 Klepper, "Industrial Policy in the Transport Aircraft Industry," p. 111.

91 U.S. House of Representatives, *Competitiveness of the U.S. Commercial Aircraft Industry*, Hearing before the Subcommittee on Commerce, Consumer Protection and Competitiveness of the Committee on Energy and Commerce, p. 3. Emphasis added.

92 U.S. House of Representatives, *U.S. International Trade Performance and Outlook: Competitive Position in the Automotive, Aerospace, and Chemical and Pharmaceutical Sectors*, Hearings before the Subcommittee on Trade of the Committee on Ways and Means, p. 454.

93 U.S. House of Representatives, *Proposed Joint Development of the FSX Fighter with Japan*, Hearings before the Subcommittee of the Committee on Banking, Finance, and Urban Affairs, pp. 239–42; and Long-Term Credit

Bank of Japan, "The Japanese Aircraft Industry: Entering a Period of Progress Spurred by International Joint Development."

94   Aerospace Industries Association, "Tools of the Trade: Why Offsets, Outsourcing, and Joint Ventures Are Crucial to U.S. Aerospace" (Washington, DC: AIA, 1996), p. 3.

95   Boeing Commercial Airplane Group, "European Targeting of the Commercial Aircraft Industry – Why Is Boeing Concerned?" p. 4.

96   Aerospace Industries Association, "1995 Year-End Review and Forecast" (Washington, DC: AIA, 1995), table 9.

97   Aerospace Industries Association, "The Importance of Aerospace to the Nation's Economy," p. 5.

98   "Zoom! Airbus Comes on Strong," *Business Week*, April 22, 1991, p. 50.

99   United States Trade Commission, "Operation of the Trade Agreements Program 41st Report" (Washington, DC: GPO, 1989), p. 97; Office of the United States Trade Representative, "1992 Trade Policy Agenda and 1991 Annual Report of the President of the United States on the Trade Agreements Program" (Washington, DC: GPO, 1992), p. 51; and Office of the United States Trade Representative, "1992 National Trade Estimate Report on Foreign Trade Barriers" (Washington, DC: GPO, 1992), p. 83.

100 U.S. House of Representatives, *Competitiveness of U.S. Commercial Aircraft Industry*, Hearing before the Subcommittee on Commerce, Consumer Protection, and Competitiveness of the Committee on Energy and Commerce, p. 31.

101 U.S. House of Representatives, *U.S. International Trade Performance and Outlook: Competitive Position in the Automotive, Aerospace, and Chemical and Pharmaceutical Sectors*, Hearings before the Subcommittee on Trade of the Committee on Ways and Means, p. 461. Emphasis added.

102 European Commission, "The European Aerospace Industry: Trading Position and Figures 1996" (Brussels: European Commission, 1996), pp. 13-224, 13-229. Of these totals, "space" accounts for 8,700 French workers, 5,003 German workers, 875 British workers and 548 Spanish workers.

103 Kendry et al., "The Economic and Industrial Importance of the Airbus Partnership," p. 47.

104 Hickie, "Airbus Industrie: A Case Study in European High Technology Cooperation," pp. 195–6.

105 Keith Hayward, *The British Aircraft Industry* (Manchester: Manchester University Press, 1989), p. 206; Richard R. Nelson, *High-Technology Policies: A Five Nation Comparison* (Washington, DC: American Enterprise Institute, 1984), p. 55; and Newhouse, *The Sporty Game*, p. 124.

106 Commission of the European Communities, "A Competitive European Aeronautical Industry," p. 3.

107 Bendesministerium für Wirtschaft, "Report by the Coordinator for German Aerospace Affairs in 1996" (Bonn: Federal Ministry of Economics, 1996), p. 5.

108 Hayward, *International Collaboration in Civil Aerospace*, p. 61.

109 U.S. House of Representatives, *International Science and Technology and Foreign Policy*, Hearings before the Subcommittee on International Science Cooperation of the Committee on Science, Space, and Technology, 101st Congress, 2nd Session, April 4, 26, 1990, p. 5.
110 Council on Competitiveness, *Roadmap for Results: Trade Policy, Technology and American Competitiveness* (Washington, DC: Council on Competitiveness, 1993), p. 94.
111 U.S. International Trade Commission, "Global Competitiveness of U.S. Advanced Technology Manufacturing Industries: Large Civil Aircraft," p. 7-1; and U.S. Department of Commerce, *A Competitive Assessment of the U.S. Civil Aircraft Industry*, p. 109.
112 Hayward, *International Collaboration in Civil Aerospace*, p. 163.
113 The Commonline Agreement was a bilateral accord binding export credit agencies to 1977 financing levels. It was replaced in 1985 by the Large Aircraft Sector Understanding and attached to the OECD Arrangement on Official Export Credit Financing.
114 Laura D'Andrea Tyson, *Who's Bashing Whom? Trade Conflict in High-Technology Industries* (Washington, DC: Institute for International Economics, 1992), p. 200. Emphasis added.
115 Office of Technology Assessment, "Government Support of the Large Commercial Aircraft Industries of Japan, Europe, and the United States," p. 98.
116 Arnold and Porter, "U.S. Government Support of the U.S. Commercial Aircraft Industry" (Washington, DC: Prepared for the Commission of European Communities, 1991). See also United States Trade Representative, "U.S. Government Response to the EC-Commissioned Report 'U.S. Government Support of the U.S. Commercial Aircraft Industry' " (Washington, DC: USTR, 1992).
117 Office of Technology Assessment, "Government Support of the Large Commercial Aircraft Industries of Japan, Europe, and the United States," p. 30. See also U.S. House of Representatives, *The Future of the U.S. Space Program*, Hearing before the Subcommittee on Space and Science Applications of the Committee on Science, Space, and Technology, 101st Congress, 2nd Session, July 23, 1990, p. 5.
118 U.S. Senate, *Technology Policy and Competitiveness: The Federal Government's Role*, Hearing before the Subcommittee on Government Information and Regulation of the Committee on Governmental Affairs, 102nd Congress, 2nd Session, March 12, 1992, p. 3. Testimony of Julie Fox Gorte. Emphasis added.
119 U.S. Senate, *Export-Import Bank Amendments of 1983*, Hearings before the Subcommittee on International Finance and Monetary Policy of the Committee on Banking, Housing, and Urban Affairs, 98th Congress, 1st Session, March 22 and 24, 1983, p. 154.
120 Helen V. Milner and David B. Yoffie, "Between Free Trade and Protectionism: Strategic Trade Policy and a Theory of Corporate Trade Demands," *International Organization* 43.2 (1989): 239–71.

121   Gellman Research Associates, "An Economic and Financial Review of Airbus Industrie," pp. 2-3, 2-4.

122   Yoffie, "Collision Course in Commercial Aircraft: Boeing-Airbus-McDonnell Douglas 1991 (A)," p. 9.

123   Boeing Commercial Airplane Group, "European Targeting of the Commercial Aircraft Industry – Why Is Boeing Concerned?" p. 5.

124   U.S. House of Representatives, *Competitiveness of the U.S. Commercial Aircraft Industry*, Hearing before the Subcommittee on Commerce, Consumer Protection, and Competitiveness of the Committee on Energy and Commerce, pp. 4–5. Testimony of S. Bruce Smart, Undersecretary for International Trade, Department of Commerce. Emphasis added.

125   Congressional Research Service, "Airbus Industrie: An Economic and Trade Perspective," p. 58.

126   U.S. House of Representatives, *U.S. International Trade Performance and Outlook: Competitive Position in the Automotive, Aerospace, and Chemical and Pharmaceutical Sectors*, Hearings before the Subcommittee on Trade of the Committee on Ways and Means, p. 462. Emphasis added.

127   Hayward, *International Collaboration in Civil Aerospace*, p. 61.

128   Arnold and Porter, "U.S. Government Support of the U.S. Commercial Aircraft Industry," p. 3.

129   United States Trade Representative, "U.S. Government Response to the EC-Commissioned Report 'U.S. Government Support of the U.S. Commercial Aircraft Industry.' " See also David Weldon Thornton, *Airbus Industrie: The Politics of an International Industrial Collaboration* (New York: St. Martin's Press, 1995), p. 143.

130   On the global welfare effects of Airbus's entry, see Damien Neven and Paul Seabright, "European Industrial Policy: The Airbus Case," *Economic Policy* 21 (October 1995): 313–58.

131   Kendry et al., "The Economic and Industrial Importance of the Airbus Partnership," p. 24. Emphasis in the original.

132   Gellman Research Associates, "An Economic and Financial Review of Airbus Industrie," p. 5-5.

133   Airbus Industrie, "Report on U.S. Government Intervention in Sales of Civil Transport Aircraft" (Toulouse: Airbus Industrie, 1991).

134   Barbara Early, Peter Granatiero, Irene McKenna, and Sue Tysl, "Reevaluating Government Support in the Commercial Aircraft Industry" (Los Angeles: Loyola Marymount University, 1993), p. 5.

135   Klepper, "Industrial Policy in the Transport Aircraft Industry," p. 107; Otto Keck, "The National System for Technical Innovation in Germany," in Richard R. Nelson (ed.), *National Innovation Systems: A Comparative Analysis* (New York: Oxford University Press, 1993), p. 145; and Bundesministerium für Wirtschaft, "Die Konkurrenzsituation der deutschen Luft- und Raumfahrt im internationalen Vergleich," p. 23.

136   U.S. International Trade Commission, "Global Competitiveness of U.S. Advanced-Technology Manufacturing Industries," p. 5-11.

137   Commission of the European Communities, "Report on United States

Trade and Investment Barriers 1992: Problems of Doing Business with the U.S." (Brussels: Services of the Commission of the European Communities, 1992).

138 Airbus Industrie, "Presentation to the International Trade Commission" (Washington, DC: Airbus Industrie of North America, April 15, 1993).

139 See Stephen D. Krasner, "Global Communications and National Power: Life on the Pareto Frontier," *World Politics* 43.3 (1991): 336–66.

140 "Airbus Industrie: A Success Story," written remarks by Jean Pierson, Chief Executive Officer of Airbus Industrie, to the European Club of the Harvard Business School, March 6, 1991, p. 29.

4. The Semiconductor Rivalry

1 See National Advisory Committee on Semiconductors, "Attaining Preeminence in Semiconductors: Third Annual Report to the President and the Congress" (Washington, DC: GPO, 1992), p. 34; Michael Borrus, James Millstein, and John Zysman, "U.S.-Japanese Competition in the Semiconductor Industry: A Study in International Trade and Technology Development," University of California at Berkeley, Institute of International Studies Policy Papers in International Affairs No. 17 (1982), p. 111.

2 Richard Baldwin and Paul R. Krugman, "Market Access and International Competition: A Simulation Study of 16K Random Access Memories," Columbia Graduate School of Business, Center on Japanese Economy and Business Working Paper No. 2 (New York, 1986), p. 1.

3 Kenneth Flamm, "Policy and Politics in the International Semiconductor Industry," paper submitted into testimony, U.S. Congress, *Japan's Economic Challenge*, Hearings before the Joint Economic Committee, 101st Congress, 2nd Session, October 16, 18, and December 4, 6, 1990, pp. 257–9; and Robert W. Wilson, Peter K. Ashton, and Thomas P. Egan, *Innovation, Competition, and Government Policy in the Semiconductor Industry* (Lexington, MA: Lexington Books, 1980), pp. 151–3.

4 Daniel I. Okimoto, Takuo Sugano, and Franklin B. Weinstein (eds.), *Competitive Edge: The Semiconductor Industry in the U.S. and Japan* (Stanford: Stanford University Press, 1984), p. 84; and U.S. House of Representatives, *Industrial Policy*, Hearings before the Subcommittee on Economic Stabilization of the Committee on Banking, Finance, and Urban Affairs, 98th Congress, 1st Session [Part 3], August 2, 3, 4, 18, and 19, 1983, p. 521.

5 Congressional Budget Office, "The Benefits and Risks of Federal Funding for Sematech" (Washington, DC: CBO, 1987), p. 3.

6 On "import protection as export promotion," see Paul R. Krugman, *Rethinking International Trade* (Cambridge, MA: MIT Press, 1990), chap. 12.

7 Japan's import license controls were lifted in 1974, its restrictions on foreign direct investment in 1976, and its tariffs on chips in 1985.

8 Kenneth A. Froot and David B. Yoffie, "Trading Blocs and the Incentives

to Protect: Implications for Japan and East Asia," in Jeffrey A. Frankel and Miles Kahler (eds.), *Regionalism and Rivalry: Japan and the United States in Pacific Asia* (Chicago: University of Chicago Press, 1993), p. 143.

9   Laura D'Andrea Tyson and David B. Yoffie, "Semiconductors: From Manipulated to Managed Trade," in David B. Yoffie (ed.), *Beyond Free Trade* (Boston: Harvard Business School Press, 1993), p. 30; and F. M. Scherer, *International High-Technology Competition* (Cambridge, MA: Harvard University Press, 1992), p. 19.

10 Electronics Industries Association of Japan, "The Present Status and Future Outlook of the Semiconductor Memory Industry" (Tokyo: EIAJ, 1992), p. 22.

11 Congressional Budget Office, "The Benefits and Risks of Federal Funding for Sematech," p. 79.

12 David B. Yoffie, "Foreign Direct Investment in Semiconductors," in Kenneth A. Froot (ed.), *Foreign Direct Investment* (Chicago: University of Chicago Press, 1993), p. 199.

13 U.S. House of Representatives, *The Government Role in Joint Production Ventures,* Hearing before the Subcommittee on Science, Research and Technology of the Committee on Science, Space, and Technology, 101st Congress, 1st Session, September 19, 1989, p. 17.

14 Laura D'Andrea Tyson, *Who's Bashing Whom? Trade Conflict in High-Technology Industries* (Washington, DC: Institute for International Economics, 1992), p. 89; and U.S. House of Representatives, *Trade in Services and Trade in High Technology Products,* Hearing before the Subcommittee on Trade of the Committee on Ways and Means, 97th Congress, 2nd Session, May 24, 1982, p. 126.

15 Okimoto, Sugano, and Weinstein, *Competitive Edge: The Semiconductor Industry in the U.S. and Japan,* p. 41.

16 Semiconductor Industry Association, "The Semiconductor Producer-User Symbiosis of Japan Market Access" (Santa Clara, CA: SIA, 1987), p. 1.

17 U.S. House of Representatives, *U.S. Trade Policy Phase II: Private Sector,* Hearings before the Subcommittee on Trade of the Committee on Ways and Means, 97th Congress, 1st Session [Part A], December 10, 11, 14, 15, and 16, 1981, p. 576.

18 U.S. House of Representatives, *General Trade Policy,* Hearings before the Subcommittee on Commerce, Transportation, and Tourism of the Committee on Energy and Commerce, 98th Congress, 1st Session, March 15, April 5, May 25, and June 22, 1983, p. 303. Testimony of Alex Lidow on behalf of the SIA. Emphasis added.

19 U.S. House of Representatives, *Semiconductors: The Role of Consortia,* Hearing before the Subcommittee on Science, Space, and Technology, 102nd Congress, 1st Session, July 23, 1991, p. 70.

20 Congressional Budget Office, "The Benefits and Risks of Federal Funding for Sematech," p. 17.

21 Statement of Thomas W. Armstrong, President, Semiconductor Industry

Association, Hearing on U.S.-Japan Trade Relations before the Subcommittee on Trade of the Committee on Ways and Means, 104th Congress, 2nd Session, March 28, 1996 (text provided by the SIA); Electronics Industries Association of Japan, "Semiconductor Facts 1995" (Tokyo: EIAJ, 1995), p. 2-2; and U.S. House of Representatives, *Research and Development Joint Ventures*, Hearing before the Subcommittee on Science, Research and Technology of the Committee on Science and Technology, 98th Congress, 1st Session, July 12, 1983, p. 65.

22   U.S. Senate, *Semiconductors and the Electronics Industry*, Hearing before the Subcommittee on Science, Technology, and Space of the Committee on Commerce, Science, and Transportation, 101st Congress, 2nd Session, May 17, 1990, p. 3.

23   Electronics Industries Association of Japan, "The Present Status and Future Outlook of the Semiconductor Memory Industry," p. 27; and U.S. Senate, *Issues Confronting the Semiconductor Industry*, Hearings before the Subcommittee on Technology and the Law of the Committee on the Judiciary, 100th Congress, 1st Session, February 26 and March 3, 1987, p. 22.

24   Marco Iansiti and Jonathan West, "Learning, Experimentation, and Technology Integration: The Evolution of R&D in the Semiconductor Industry," Harvard Graduate School of Business Administration Working Paper No. 96-032 (Boston, 1996), p. 11.

25   U.S. House of Representatives, *Trade in Services and Trade in High Technology Products*, Hearing before the Subcommittee on Trade of the Committee on Ways and Means, p. 128.

26   U.S. Senate, *Renewal of the United States–Japan Semiconductor Agreement*, Hearing before the Subcommittee on International Trade of the Committee on Finance, 102nd Congress, 1st Session, March 22, 1991, p. 10.

27   Kenneth Flamm, *Mismanaged Trade? Strategic Policy and the Semiconductor Industry* (Washington, DC: Brookings, 1996).

28   Congressional Budget Office, "The Benefits and Risks of Federal Funding for Sematech," p. 44. Emphasis added.

29   U.S. Senate, *Competitive Challenge Facing U.S. Industry*, Hearings before the Committee on Commerce, Science, and Transportation, 100th Congress, 1st Session, January 20 and February 24, 1987, p. 144. Emphasis added.

30   National Advisory Committee on Semiconductors, "A National Strategy for Semiconductors: An Agenda for the President, the Congress, and the Industry" (Washington, DC: GPO, 1992), p. 3.

31   U.S. Senate, *The Future of the U.S. Semiconductor Industry and the Impact on Defense*, Hearing before the Subcommittee on Defense Industry and Technology of the Committee on Armed Services, 100th Congress, 1st Session, November 29, 1989, p. 4. Testimony of Ian Ross.

32   Daniel I. Okimoto, *Between MITI and the Market: Japanese Industrial Policy for High Technology* (Stanford: Stanford University Press, 1989), pp. 68-9.

33 Ministry of International Trade and Industry, "Sangyo Kagaku Gijyutsu no Doko to Kadai: Chikyu Kibo deno Gujyutsuteki Kyosei ni Mukete," trans. Tomoko Sugiyama (Tokyo: MITI, 1992), p. 182.

34 Baldwin and Krugman, "Market Access and International Competition: A Simulation Study of 16K Random Access Memories," p. 10.

35 Congressional Budget Office, "Using R&D Consortia for Commercial Innovation: Sematech, X-Ray Lithography, and High-Resolution Systems" (Washington, DC: CBO, 1990), p. 28.

36 Japanese Technology Evaluation Center, "JTEC Panel Report on Advanced Computing in Japan" (Springfield, VA: NTIS, 1990), p. 59.

37 U.S. Department of Defense, "Building U.S. Capabilities in Flat Panel Displays" (Washington, DC: Flat Panel Display Task Force, 1994), p. V-5; "Chip Equipment Makers Forge Alliances across Pacific," *Nikkei Weekly*, February 1, 1992, p. 8; "Uncle Sam's Helping Hand," *Economist*, April 2nd-8th, 1994, p. 79; and U.S. House of Representatives, *Decline of U.S. Semiconductor Infrastructure*, Hearing before the Subcommittee on Commerce, 101st Congress, 2nd Session, May 9, 1990, p. 45.

38 Office of Technology Assessment, "The Big Picture: HDTV and High-Resolution Systems," OTA-BP-CIT-64 (Washington, DC: GPO, 1990), pp. 67–8.

39 U.S. Department of Commerce, "A Competitive Assessment of the U.S. Semiconductor Manufacturing Equipment Industry" (Washington, DC: GPO, 1985), p. 38.

40 U.S. Department of Commerce, *1989 U.S. Industrial Outlook* (Washington, DC: ITA, 1989), p. 30-9.

41 National Advisory Committee on Semiconductors, "A Strategic Industry at Risk: A Report to the President and the Congress from the National Advisory Committee on Semiconductors" (Washington, DC: GPO, 1989). Emphasis added.

42 Robert E. Falstad, "High-Tech Research Consortia: Sematech's Experience" (Houston, TX: Sematech, 1990), p. 4.

43 U.S. House of Representatives, *Decline of U.S. Semiconductor Infrastructure*, Hearing before the Subcommittee on Commerce, p. 4.

44 U.S. Senate, *Semiconductors and the Electronics Industry*, Hearing before the Subcommittee on Science, Technology, and Space of the Committee on Commerce, Science, and Transportation, p. 64.

45 "Japan Leads in Optics, U.S. in Life Sciences," *Japan Economic Journal*, January 22, 1988, p. 17; "Gallium Arsenide Increasingly Popular for Special Applications," *Japan Economic Journal*, June 28, 1986, p. 27; and Okimoto, Sugano, and Weinstein, *Competitive Edge: The Semiconductor Industry in the U.S. and Japan*, p. 44.

46 U.S. Senate, *Competitiveness and Antitrust*, Hearings before the Committee on the Judiciary, 100th Congress, 1st Session, May 6 and 7, 1987, pp. 178–9.

47 U.S. Senate, *Issues Confronting the Semiconductor Industry*, Hearings be-

fore the Subcommittee on Technology and the Law of the Committee on the Judiciary, p. 89. Testimony of Charles H. Ferguson, MIT.

48 Sematech, "Sematech: Strategic Overview," (Austin, TX: Sematech, 1991), p. 2–2.

49 Congressional Budget Office, "The Benefits and Risks of Federal Funding for Sematech," p. 37. Emphasis added.

50 Office of Technology Assessment, "Competing Economies: America, Europe, and the Pacific Rim," OTA-ITE-498 (Washington, DC: GPO, 1991), p. 249. Emphasis added.

51 Electronics Industries Association of Japan, "Facts and Figures on the Japanese Electronics Industry: 1993 Edition" (Tokyo: EIAJ, 1993), p. 78; and Sematech, "Sematech Success: 1992 Annual Report" (Austin, TX: Sematech, 1993), p. 6.

52 Ministry of International Trade and Industry, "On the Japan-U.S. Semiconductor Arrangement" (Tokyo: MITI, 1996).

53 Congressional Budget Office, "The Benefits and Risks of Federal Funding for Sematech," p. 33.

54 Congressional Budget Office, "The Scope of the High-Definition Television Market and Its Implications for Competitiveness" (Washington, DC: GPO, 1989), pp. 26–7.

55 U.S. House of Representatives, *Competitiveness of the U.S. Semiconductor Industry*, Hearing before the Subcommittee on Commerce, Consumer Protection and Competitiveness of the Committee on Energy and Commerce, 100th Congress, 1st Session, June 9, 1987, p. 34.

56 U.S. Senate, *Semiconductors and the Electronics Industry*, Hearing before the Subcommittee on Science, Technology, and Space of the Committee on Commerce, Science, and Transportation, p. 74.

57 U.S. Congress, *U.S.-Japan Economic Relations*, Hearings before the Subcommittee on International Trade and Finance, and Security of the Joint Economic Committee, 97th Congress, 1st Session, June 19 and July 9 and 13, 1981, p. 92. Testimony of George Scalise on behalf of the SIA.

58 Okimoto, Sugano, and Weinstein, *Competitive Edge: The Semiconductor Industry in the U.S. and Japan*, p. 18.

59 Jeffrey A. Hart, *Rival Capitalists: International Competitiveness in the United States, Japan, and Western Europe* (Ithaca, NY: Cornell University Press, 1992), p. 72; John Stopford, Susan Strange, and John S. Henley, *Rival States, Rival Firms: Competition for World Market Shares* (Cambridge: Cambridge University Press, 1991), p. 87; and Geoffrey Carliner, "Industrial Policies for Emerging Industries," in Paul R. Krugman (ed.), *Strategic Trade Policy and the New International Economics* (Cambridge, MA: MIT Press, 1986), p. 156.

60 Office of Technology Assessment, "Competing Economies: America, Europe, and the Pacific Rim," p. 263.

61 Electronics Industries Association of Japan, "The Present Status and Future Outlook of the Semiconductor Memory Industry," p. 13.

62   Ministry of International Trade and Industry, "Kyujyunedndai no Densi Sangyo Bijyon," trans. Tomoko Sugiyama (Tokyo: MITI, 1992), p. 109; and Borrus, Millstein, and Zysman, "U.S.-Japanese Competition in the Semiconductor Industry: A Study in International Trade and Technology Development," pp. 67–71.

63   J. K. Paul, *High Technology International Trade and Competition* (Park Ridge, NJ: Noyce, 1984), p. 64.

64   Kent E. Calder, *Strategic Capitalism: Private Business and Public Purpose in Japanese Industrial Finance* (Princeton: Princeton University Press, 1993), pp. 172–3; U.S. Senate, *Trade Agreements Compliance Act*, Hearing before the Subcommittee on International Trade of the Committee on Finance, 101st Congress, 2nd Session, July 13, 1990, pp. 30–1; and U.S. Congress, *Impact of Unfair Foreign Trade Practices*, Hearing before the Subcommittee on Economic Goals and Intergovernmental Policy of the Joint Economic Committee, 98th Congress, 1st Session, March 20, 1985, p. 49.

65   Terutomo Ozawa, *Japan's Technological Challenge to the West, 1950– 1974: Motivation and Accomplishments* (Cambridge, MA: MIT Press, 1974), p. 62.

66   U.S. Congress, *Impact of Unfair Foreign Trade Practices*, Hearing before the Subcommittee on Economic Goals and Intergovernmental Policy of the Joint Economic Committee, p. 57.

67   Sheridan M. Tatsuno, *Created in Japan: From Imitators to World-Class Innovators* (New York: Harper & Row, 1990), pp. 167–76.

68   "U.S. Misses Golden Opportunity," *Japan Economic Journal*, April 9, 1988, p. 2. Tomihiro Matsumura, Senior Vice-President, NEC, sketched this argument.

69   Ministry of International Trade and Industry, "Kyujyunendai no Densi Sangyo Bijyon," pp. 112–13.

70   John E. Tilton, *International Diffusion of Technology: The Case of Semiconductors* (Washington, DC: Brookings, 1971).

71   U.S. House of Representatives, *Industrial Policy*, Hearings before the Subcommittee on Economic Stabilization of the Committee on Banking, Finance and Urban Affairs, p. 524. Emphasis added.

72   Congressional Budget Office, "The Benefits and Risks of Federal Funding for Sematech," p. xxi. Emphasis added.

73   U.S. House of Representatives, *International Technology Transfer: Who Is Minding the Store?* Hearing before the Subcommittee on International Scientific Cooperation of the Committee on Science, Space, and Technology, 101st Congress, 1st Session, July 19, 1989, p. 23. Emphasis added.

74   National Advisory Committee on Semiconductors, "A National Strategy for Semiconductors: An Agenda for the President, the Congress, and the Industry," pp. 3–4. Emphasis added. See also Douglas A. Irwin and Peter J. Klenow, "Learning-By-Doing Spillovers in the Semiconductor Industry," *Journal of Political Economy* 102.6 (1994): 1200–27; and Tyson and Yoffie, "Semiconductors: From Manipulated to Managed Trade," p. 38.

75 Daniel I. Okimoto, "Regime Characteristics of Japanese Industrial Policy," in Hugh Patrick (ed.), *Japan's High-Technology Industries: Lessons and Limitations of Industrial Policy* (Seattle: University of Washington Press, 1986), p. 57.

76 It is estimated that VLSI gave rise to over 1,000 patents, most of which were evaluated at conferences in Europe and the United States.

77 Martin Fransman, *The Market and Beyond: Information Technology in Japan* (Cambridge: Cambridge University Press, 1990), pp. 247, 249, 257, 264, 280.

78 Quoted in U.S. House of Representatives, *Reciprocal Trade and Market Access Legislation*, Hearing before the Subcommittee on Trade of the Committee on Ways and Means, 97th Congress, 2nd Session, July 26, 1982, p. 102.

79 U.S. Department of Commerce, "A Competitive Assessment of the U.S. Semiconductor Manufacturing Equipment Industry," pp. 48, 61.

80 C. Fred Bergsten and Marcus Noland, *Reconcilable Differences? United States-Japan Economic Conflict* (Washington, DC: Institute for International Economics, 1993), p. 130.

81 Congressional Budget Office, "The Benefits and Risks of Federal Funding for Sematech," pp. xxi, 47.

82 Jay S. Stowsky, "Weak Links, Strong Bonds: U.S.-Japanese Competition in Semiconductor Production Equipment," in Chalmers Johnson, Laura D'Andrea Tyson, and John Zysman (eds.), *Politics and Productivity: The Real Story of Why Japan Works* (New York: Harper Business, 1989), p. 243; and U.S. Department of Commerce, *1989 U.S. Industrial Outlook*, p. 30-9.

83 U.S. Department of Commerce, "A Competitive Assessment of the U.S. Semiconductor Manufacturing Equipment Industry," p. 94.

84 U.S. Congress, *U.S.-Japan Economic Relations*, Hearings before the Subcommittee on International Trade and Finance, and Security of the Joint Economic Committee, p. 93. See, for example, the testimony of George Scalise, Senior Vice-President, Advanced Micro Devices, on behalf of the SIA.

85 John J. Coleman, "The Semiconductor Industry Association and the Trade Dispute with Japan (B)," Harvard Business School Case No. 9-387-195 (Cambridge, MA, 1987–8), p. 1.

86 Electronics Industries Association of Japan, "Semiconductor Facts 1995," p. 4-1.

87 "Chip Makers Reject 'Techno-Nationalism,'" *Nikkei Weekly*, July 25, 1992, p. 8.

88 U.S. Congress, *U.S.-Japan Economic Relations*, Hearings before the Subcommittee on International Trade and Finance. Testimony of George Scalise, Senior Vice-President, AMD, on behalf of the SIA.

89 Sematech, "Sematech: Strategic Overview," pp. 1–2.

90 "In Brief: Matsushita Electric, Intel Refine Chip Etching," *Nikkei Weekly*, May 24, 1993, p. 9.

91 See Boyan Jovanovic and Glenn M. MacDonald, "Competitive Diffusion," *Journal of Political Economy* 102.1 (1994): 27.

92 Edwin Mansfield, "Appropriating the Returns from Investments in R&D Capital," in Karel Cool, Damien J. Neven, and Ingo Walter (eds.), *European Industrial Restructuring in the 1990s* (New York: New York University Press, 1992), p. 346.

93 Martin Fransman, *Japan's Computer and Communications Industry* (New York: Oxford University Press, 1995), p. 173.

94 Okimoto, Sugano, and Weinstein, *Competitive Edge: The Semiconductor Industry in the U.S. and Japan*, p. 49.

95 Japanese Technology Evaluation Center, "JTEC Panel Report on Advanced Computing in Japan," p. 46.

96 U.S. Senate, *Issues Confronting the Semiconductor Industry*, Hearings before the Subcommittee on Technology and the Law of the Committee on the Judiciary, p. 58.

97 "Microprocessors: From 'Second-Sourcing' to Self Development," *Japan Economic Journal*, June 14, 1986, p. 17; and Alan Wm. Wolff et al., "Japanese Market Barriers in Microelectronics: Memorandum in Support of a Petition Pursuant to Section 301 of the Trade Act of 1974 As Amended" (Cupertino, CA: SIA, 1985), p. 67.

98 U.S. Senate, *Competitiveness and Antitrust*, Hearings before the Committee on the Judiciary, p. 179.

99 U.S. Congress, *Impact of Unfair Foreign Trade Practices*, Hearing before the Subcommittee on Economic Goals and Intergovernmental Policy of the Joint Economic Committee, p. 124.

100 U.S. Department of Commerce, *1994 U.S. Industrial Outlook*, p. 15–4.

101 "Hitachi Files Lawsuit against TI over 256K," *Japan Economic Journal*, October 18, 1986, p. 17. Earlier, TI had filed against these and other Japanese firms for license arrangements concerning various memory chips.

102 Nihon Keizai Shimbun, "Japan Economic Almanac 1996" (Tokyo: Nihon Keizai Shimbun, 1996), p. 89; and Japanese Technology Evaluation Center, "JTEC Panel Report on Advanced Computing in Japan," pp. 35–43.

103 "Japan Chipmakers Are 'Co-Developers,' " *Nikkei Weekly*, December 7, 1991, p. 8.

104 Clyde V. Prestowitz Jr., Naotaka Matsukata, and Andrew Szamosszegi, "Prospects for U.S. Japanese Semiconductor Trade in the 21st Century" (Washington, DC: Economic Strategy Institute, 1996), p. 11.

105 Sematech, "Sematech Success: 1992 Annual Report," p. 7.

106 Council on Competitiveness, *Roadmap for Results: Trade Policy, Technology and American Competitiveness* (Washington, DC: Council on Competitiveness, 1993), p. 51; and U.S. Senate, *Review of Ongoing Trade Negotiations and Completed Trade Agreements*, Hearing before the Subcommittee on International Trade of the Committee on Finance, 102nd Congress, 1st Session, August 2, 1991.

107 Statement of Bill Spencer, President and CEO, Sematech, October 5, 1994, p. 5. Testimony courtesy of Sematech.

108 Electronics Industries Association of Japan, "Perspective on the Japanese Electronics Industry" (Tokyo: EIAJ, 1996).

109 U.S. Senate, *Impact of Imports and Foreign Investment on National Security*, Hearing before the Committee on Finance, 100th Congress, 1st Session, March 25, 1987, p. 105; and U.S. House of Representatives, *General Trade Policy*, Hearings before the Subcommittee on Commerce, Transportation, and Tourism of the Committee on Energy and Commerce, p. 309.

110 U.S. House of Representatives, *Trade in Services and Trade in High Technology Products*, Hearing before the Subcommittee on Trade of the Committee on Ways and Means, p. 123. Emphasis added.

111 U.S. House of Representatives, *U.S. Trade Policy Phase II: Private Sector*, Hearings before the Subcommittee on Trade of the Committee on Ways and Means, p. 577.

112 Helen V. Milner and David B. Yoffie, "Between Free Trade and Protectionism: Strategic Trade Policy and a Theory of Corporate Trade Demands," *International Organization* 43.2 (1989): 254.

113 U.S. House of Representatives, *Industrial Policy*, Hearings before the Subcommittee on Economic Stabilization of the Committee on Banking, Finance, and Urban Affairs, p. 527.

114 U.S. Congress, *U.S.-Japan Economic Relations*, Hearings before the Subcommittee on International Trade and Finance, p. 87.

115 Wolff et al., "Japanese Market Barriers in Microelectronics: Memorandum in Support of a Petition Pursuant to Section 301 of the Trade Act of 1974 As Amended," p. 75.

116 U.S. House of Representatives, *Acceleration of U.S. Technology Utilization and Commercialization*, Hearing before the Subcommittee on Technology and Competitiveness of the Committee on Science, Space, and Technology, 102nd Congress, 1st Session, May 7, 1991, p. 27; and U.S. House of Representatives, *Prospects for a New United States–Japan Semiconductor Agreement*, Hearing before the Subcommittee on International Economic Policy and Trade of the Committee on Foreign Affairs, 102nd Congress, 1st Session, March 20, 1991, p. 3.

117 U.S. House of Representatives, *Unfair Foreign Trade Practices*, Hearings before the Subcommittee on Oversight and Investigations of the Committee on Energy and Commerce, 101st Congress, 1st Session, March 1 and 2, 1989, p. 38.

118 U.S. House of Representatives, *U.S. Trade Policy Phase II: Private Sector*, Hearings before the Subcommittee on Trade of the Committee on Ways and Means, p. 602.

119 Masahiro Okuno-Fujiwara, "Industrial Policy in Japan: A Political Economy View," in Paul R. Krugman (ed.), *Trade with Japan: Has the Door Opened Wider?* (Chicago: University of Chicago Press, 1991), p. 287.

120 "Chip-Share Precedent Worries Tokyo," *Nikkei Weekly*, March 29, 1993, p. 1; and U.S. Congress, *Impact of Unfair Foreign Trade Practices*, Hearing before the Subcommittee on Economic Goals and Intergovernmental Policy of the Joint Economic Committee, p. 3. In the mid-1980s, for

example, U.S. market share in Japan versus U.S. world market share, stood at 3% versus 8% in pharmaceuticals; 4% versus 11% in telecommunications; 11% versus 53% in semiconductors; 27% versus 60% in computers; 5% versus 70% in software; 7% versus 23% in electronics components; and 8% versus 17% in medical devices. Yet as the *Nikkei Weekly* observes, "[t]he semiconductor accord has been the only trade arrangement in which Japan has agreed to a numerical target for increasing imports."

121   U.S. Congress, *Impact of Unfair Foreign Trade Practices*, Hearing before the Subcommittee on Economic Goals and Intergovernmental Policy of the Joint Economic Committee, p. 62.

122   Quoted in Wolff et al., "Japanese Market Barriers in Microelectronics: Memorandum in Support of a Petition Pursuant to Section 301 of the Trade Act of 1974 As Amended," p. 53. Emphasis added.

123   U.S. Senate, *Competitive Challenge Facing U.S. Industry*, Hearings before the Committee on Commerce, Science, and Transportation, p. 145; and U.S. Senate, *Impact of Imports and Foreign Investment on National Security*, Hearing before the Committee on Finance, pp. 105–9.

124   U.S. Senate, *Review of Ongoing Trade Negotiations and Completed Trade Agreements*, Hearing before the Subcommittee on International Trade of the Committee on Finance, p. 59.

125   See Kenneth Flamm, "Forward Pricing versus Fair Value: An Analytic Assessment of 'Dumping' in DRAMs," in Takatoshi Ito and Anne O. Krueger (eds.), *Trade and Protectionism* (Chicago: University of Chicago Press, 1993), pp. 49–93.

126   Semiconductor Industry Association, "The 1991 U.S.-Japan Semiconductor Agreement: 'Heading towards Crisis' " (San Jose: SIA, 1992), p. 19; "Japan, U.S. Reach Accord on Semiconductor Trade," *Japan Economic Journal*, August 9, 1986, p. 14; and "MITI to Monitor Domestic and Export Prices of ICs," *Japan Economic Journal*, May 3, 1986, pp. 1, 15.

127   Tyson, *Who's Bashing Whom?* p. 109; and "Japan, U.S. to End Chip Dispute," *Japan Economic Journal*, May 31, 1986, p. 4.

128   John J. Coleman, "The Semiconductor Industry Association and the Trade Dispute with Japan (A)," Harvard Business School Case No. 9-387-205 (Cambridge, MA, 1987–91), p. 3.

129   U.S. Senate, *Technology Policy and Competitiveness: The Federal Government's Role*, Hearing before the Subcommittee on Government Information and Regulation of the Committee on Governmental Affairs, 102nd Congress, 2nd Session, March 12, 1992, p. 24. Emphasis added.

130   U.S. House of Representatives, *Competitiveness of the U.S. Semiconductor Industry*, p. 35.

131   Ibid., p 37. Testimony of Lew Cramer, Acting Deputy Assistant Secretary, Science and Electronics, Department of Commerce.

132   Congressional Budget Office, "Using R&D Consortia for Commercial Innovation: Sematech, X-Ray Lithography, and High-Resolution Systems," p. 34.

133 U.S. House of Representatives, *Enforcement of the United States–Japan Semiconductor Agreement*, 101st Congress, 1st Session, May 24, 1989, p. 2.

134 Office of the United States Trade Representative, "Fact Sheet: U.S.-Japan Semiconductor Arrangement" (Washington, DC: USTR Release, May 27, 1992).

135 National Advisory Committee on Semiconductors, "A Strategic Industry at Risk: A Report to the President and the Congress from the National Advisory Committee on Semiconductors," p. 14.

136 U.S. Senate, *Trade Agreements Compliance Act*, Hearing before the Subcommittee on International Trade of the Committee on Finance, p. 30.

137 U.S. Senate, *Semiconductors and the Electronics Industry*, Hearing before the Subcommittee on Science, Technology, and Space of the Committee on Commerce, Science, and Transportation, p. 2. Emphasis added.

138 Flamm, *Mismanaged Trade?* p. 229.

139 Office of the United States Trade Representative, "Foreign Share of the Japanese Semiconductor Market Drops to 19.2 Percent in the Second Quarter" (Washington, DC: USTR Release, September 22, 1993); and Office of the United States Trade Representative, "No Improvement in Foreign Share of Japanese Semiconductor Market" (Washington, DC: USTR Release, December 29, 1992).

140 "Group Makes Ultra-Thin Chip in the U.S.," *New York Times*, January 22, 1993, p. D4; "U.S. Plans to Reduce Chip Funds," *New York Times*, August 18, 1992, pp. D1, D9.

141 Okimoto, *Between MITI and the Market*, p. 74; and U.S. House of Representatives, *General Trade Policy*, Hearings before the Subcommittee on Commerce, Transportation, and Tourism of the Committee on Energy and Commerce, p. 308.

142 Bergsten and Noland, *Reconcilable Differences?* p. 130; and Tyson and Yoffie, "Semiconductors: From Manipulated to Managed Trade," p. 58.

143 "MITI to Urge 226 Companies to Increase Microchip Imports," *Nikkei Weekly*, February 1, 1992, p. 3.

144 Quoted in U.S. Congress, *Japan's Economic Challenge*, Hearings before the Joint Economic Committee, p. 271.

145 "Government-Industry Body to Be Set Up for Developing SOR Equipment," *Japan Economic Journal*, May 17, 1986, p. 20. Public funding was estimated to be 70%.

146 Electronics Industries Association of Japan, "The Present Status and Future Outlook of the Semiconductor Memory Industry," p. 42; and "A Shakeout Is under Way for Japanese Chip Makers," *New York Times*, January 22, 1993, pp. D1, D7.

147 Flamm, *Mismanaged Trade?* p. 117.

148 Ibid., p. 229.

149 Coleman, "The Semiconductor Industry Association and the Trade Dispute with Japan (A)," p. 3.

150 Wolff et al., "Japanese Market Barriers in Microelectronics: Memoran-

dum in Support of a Petition Pursuant to Section 301 of the Trade Act of 1974 As Amended," and "MITI to Monitor Domestic and Export Prices of ICs," *Japan Economic Journal*, May 3, 1986, p. 15.

151 "Group Makes Ultra-Thin Chip in the U.S." *New York Times*, January 22, 1993, p. D4; and "U.S. Plans to Reduce Chip Funds," *New York Times*, August 18, 1992, pp. D1, D9.

152 It should be noted that Sematech's CEO, Bill Spencer, explained to Congress that it was Washington's decision to wean Sematech, and not Sematech's decision to go it alone. I thank Sematech for providing the text of Bill Spencer's testimony before Congress.

5. The High-Definition Television Rivalry

1   Laura D'Andrea Tyson, *Who's Bashing Whom? Trade Conflict in High-Technology Industries* (Washington, DC: Institute for International Economics, 1992), p. 238; Jean-Claude Derian, *America's Struggle for Leadership in Technology* (Cambridge, MA: MIT Press, 1990), p. 271; U.S. House of Representatives, *Industrial Policy*, Hearings before the Subcommittee on Economic Stabilization of the Committee on Banking, Finance, and Urban Affairs, 98th Congress, 1st Session [Part 3], August 2, 3, 4, 18, and 19, 1983, p. 522; and U.S. Senate, *Industrial Growth and Productivity*, Hearings before the Subcommittee on Industrial Growth and Productivity of the Committee on the Budget, 97th Congress, 1st Session, December 3, 5, 1980; January 26, 1981, p. 94.

2   "High-Definition Television: The World at War," *Economist*, August 4, 1991, p. 68.

3   Boston Consulting Group, "Development of a U.S.-Based ATV Industry" (Preliminary report prepared for the American Electronics Association, 1989), p. 8. See also U.S. Senate, *Department of Defense Authorizations for Appropriations for Fiscal Years 1990 and 1991*, Hearings before the Committee on Armed Services, 101st Congress, 1st Session, March 17; May 11, 16, 17, 31; June 2, 1989, p. 317.

4   U.S. House of Representatives, *High Definition Television*, Hearing before the Committee on Science, Space, and Technology, 101st Congress, 1st Session, March 22, 1989, p. 170.

5   Heather Hazard, "Zenith and High-Definition Television 1990," Harvard Business School Case No. 9-391-084 (Cambridge, MA, 1991), p. 9.

6   Hi-Vision Promotion Center, "Hi-Vision Almanac 1993" (Kanagawa, Japan: Hi-Vision Promotion Center, 1993), p. 11.

7   National Telecommunications and Information Administration, "Advanced Television, Related Technologies, and the National Interest" (Washington, DC: DOC, 1989), p. 1.

8   American Electronics Association, "ATV Task Force Findings" (Santa Clara, CA: AEA, 1989), p. 6.

9   Office of Technology Assessment, "The Big Picture: HDTV and High-

Resolution Systems," OTA-BP-CIT-64 (Washington, DC: GPO, 1990), p. 52.

10 Ronald K. Jurgen, "Chasing Japan in the HDTV Race," *IEEE Spectrum* 26.10 (1989): 27.

11 Boston Consulting Group, "Development of a U.S.-Based ATV Industry," p. 57. See also "Sony to Sell EDTVs in Europe, U.S." *Japan Economic Journal*, November 12, 1988, p. 12.

12 "Sharp Undercuts Rivals with New 'Home HDTV,' " *Nikkei Weekly*, February 8, 1992, p. 7. Sharp had introduced an $8,000 NTSC-compatible receiver, a third the cost of conventional receivers but not fully compatible with Japan's Hi-Vision.

13 Hazard, "Zenith and High Definition Television 1990," p. 9; and U.S. House of Representatives, *High Definition Television*, Hearing before the Committee on Science, Space, and Technology, p. 173.

14 U.S. Department of Commerce, "Japan-Plasma Display Production-IMI950901: Market Research Reports" (Washington, DC: ITA, 1996).

15 U.S. House of Representatives, *High Definition Television*, Hearing before the Committee on Science, Space, and Technology, p. 1. Emphasis added.

16 U.S. House of Representatives, *High Definition Television*, Hearings before the Subcommittee on Telecommunications and Finance of the Committee on Energy and Commerce, 101st Congress, 1st Session, March 8, 9, 1989, p. 14.

17 National Telecommunications and Information Administration, "Advanced Television, Related Technologies, and the National Interest," p. 1.

18 U.S. Senate, *Department of Commerce Technology Programs Authorization*, Hearing before the Committee on Commerce, Science, and Transportation, 101st Congress, 1st Session, June 6, 1989, p. 111.

19 U.S House of Representatives, *High Definition Television*, Hearing before the Subcommittee on Research and Development and the Subcommittee on Investigations of the Committee on Armed Services, 101st Congress, 1st Session, May 10, 1989, p. 34.

20 U.S. House of Representatives, *High Definition Television (Part 2)*, Hearing before the Subcommittee on Telecommunications and Finance of the Committee on Energy and Commerce, 101st Congress, 1st Session, September 13, 1989, p. 29.

21 American Electronics Association, "High Definition Television (HDTV): Economic Analysis of Impact" (Santa Clara, CA: AEA, 1988), p. 3-11.

22 U.S. House of Representatives, *High Definition Television*, Hearing before the Subcommittee on Research and Development and the Subcommittee on Investigations of the Committee on Armed Services, p. 66.

23 U.S. Senate, *Department of Defense Authorization for Appropriations for Fiscal Years 1990 and 1991*, Hearings before the Committee on Armed Services, p. 77.

24 National Telecommunications and Information Administration, "Advanced Television, Related Technologies, and the National Interest," p. 16.

25 Congressional Budget Office, "The Scope of the High-Definition Television Market and Its Implications for Competitiveness" (Washington, DC: CBO, 1989), p. 21.

26 Jeffrey A. Hart and Laura D'Andrea Tyson, "Responding to the Challenge of HDTV," *California Management Review* 31.4 (1989): 138.

27 U.S. Department of Commerce, *1994 U.S. Industrial Outlook* (Washington, DC: ITA, 1994), p. 36–16.

28 Congressional Budget Office, "The Scope of the High-Definition Television Market and Its Implications for Competitiveness," p. 23.

29 NHK Science and Technical Research Laboratories, *High Definition Television: Hi-Vision Technology*, trans. by James G. Parker (New York: Van Nostrand Reinhold, 1993), p. ix.

30 High Vision Broadcasting Research Committee, "High Vision Broadcasting Research Committee Report," trans. Tomoko Sugiyama (Tokyo: High Vision Broadcasting Research Committee, 1992), p. 61.

31 National Telecommunications and Information Administration, "Advanced Television, Related Technologies, and the National Interest," p. 16; and Electronic Industries Association of Japan, "Facts and Figures on the Japanese Electronics Industry" (Tokyo: EIAJ, 1993), p. 78.

32 U.S. Department of Commerce, *1989 U.S. Industrial Outlook* (Washington, DC: ITA, 1989), p. 30-3; and Therese Flaherty, "The Loss of U.S. Dominance in DRAMs: A Case History (1976–1984)," Harvard Business School Case No. 9-689-067 (Cambridge, MA, 1989), p. 3.

33 Semiconductor Industry Association, "The Semiconductor Producer-User Symbiosis of Japan Market Access" (Washington, DC: SIA, 1987).

34 National Advisory Committee on Semiconductors, "A Strategic Industry at Risk: A Report to the President and the Congress from the National Advisory Committee on Semiconductors" (Washington, DC: GPO, 1989), p. 3.

35 National Telecommunications and Information Administration, "Advanced Television, Related Technologies, and the National Interest," p. 15.

36 Ibid., p. 16.

37 Electronics Industries Association of Japan, "The Present Status and Future Outlook of the Semiconductor Memory Industry" (Tokyo: EIAJ, 1992), p. 6. Emphasis added.

38 U.S. House of Representatives, *High Definition Television*, Hearing before the Committee on Science, Space, and Technology, p. 96. Testimony of DARPA's Craig Fields.

39 TechSearch International Inc., "Japanese Developments in High Definition Television: HDTV Developments by Industry" (Austin, TX: TechSearch, 1989), pp. 13, 19.

40 U.S. Congress, *High Definition Television*, Hearing before the Committee on Science, Space, and Technology, p. 136; and U.S. Congress, *High Definition Television (Part 2)*, Hearing before the Subcommittee on Telecommunications and Finance of the Committee on Energy and Commerce, p. 11.

41 Office of Technology Assessment, "The Big Picture: HDTV and High-Resolution Systems," p. 61.

42 Congressional Budget Office, "The Scope of the High-Definition Television Market and Its Implications for Competitiveness," p. 16. Emphasis added.

43 U.S. Senate, *Prospects for Development of a U.S. HDTV Industry*, Hearing before the Committee on Governmental Affairs, 101st Congress, 1st Session, August 1, 1989, p. 16.

44 American Electronics Association, "News Release" (Washington, DC: AEA, 1989), p. 1.

45 Congressional Budget Office, "Using R&D Consortia for Commercial Innovation: Sematech, X-Ray Lithography, and High-Resolution Systems" (Washington, DC: CBO, 1990), p. 42.

46 Office of Technology Assessment, "The Big Picture: DHTV and High-Resolution Systems," p. 70.

47 NHK Science and Technical Research Laboratories, *High Definition Television: Hi-Vision Technology*, p. xiii.

48 U.S. Department of Defense, "Building U.S. Capabilities in Flat Panel Displays" DoD Flat Panel Display Task Force Final Report (Washington, DC, 1994), p. I-4. Emphasis in the original.

49 U.S. House of Representatives, *New Directions in Home Video*, Hearing before the Subcommittee on Science, Research and Technology of the Committee on Science, Space, and Technology, 100th Congress, 2nd Session, June 23, 1988, p. 19. Testimony of Don Ritter (R-Pennsylvania).

50 Correspondence of Sachio Fukuda, Deputy Director, HDTV Promotion Office, Satellite Broadcasting Division, Broadcasting Bureau, Ministry of Posts and Telecommunications, Tokyo, Japan.

51 Jean-Pierre Coffinet and Joseph Nemec Jr., "The Strategic Path for Achieving Market Leadership within an Innovation-Driven Industry – The HDTV Case Example," *Interfaces* 22.4 (1992): 54.

52 U.S. Department of Commerce, *1994 U.S. Industrial Outlook*, p. 15-23.

53 U.S. Department of Defense, "Building U.S. Capabilities in Flat Panel Displays."

54 TechSearch International Inc., "Japanese Developments in High Definition Television: HDTV Developments by Industry," pp. 20, 25–6.

55 Office of Technology Assessment, "The Big Picture: HDTV and High-Resolution Systems," p. 74.

56 U.S. Senate, *Prospects for Development of a U.S. HDTV Industry*, Hearing before the Committee on Governmental Affairs, p. 17. Emphasis added.

57 Ibid., p. 25.

58 U.S. House of Representatives, *High Definition Television*, Hearing before the Committee on Science, Space, and Technology, p. 2. Testimony of Robert A. Roe, Chair, Committee on Science, Space, and Technology. See also Michael Depagne, "High-Definition Television: A Policy Framework to Revive U.S. Leadership in Consumer Electronics," *Information Society* 7.1 (1990): 54; and "The U.S. Electronics Industry Can Be Reinvigorated," *Aviation Week and Space Technology*, December 18–25, 1989, p. 40.

59 U.S. Senate, *Department of Commerce Technology Programs Authorization*, Hearing before the Committee on Commerce, Science, and Transportation, p. 104.

60 Jeffrey A. Hart, "Strategic Impacts of High Definition Television for U.S. Manufacturing" (Ann Arbor, MI: National Center for Manufacturing Sciences, 1989), p. 40.

61 Similar assessments are offered in Tyson, *Who's Bashing Whom?* p. 244; and Cynthia A. Beltz, *High-Technology Maneuvers: Industrial Policy Lessons of HDTV* (Washington, DC: American Enterprise Institute Press, 1991), p. 80.

62 Office of Technology Assessment, "The Big Picture: HDTV and High-Resolution Systems," p. 64.

63 C. Fred Bergsten and Marcus Noland, *Reconcilable Differences? United States–Japan Economic Conflict* (Washington, DC: Institute for International Economics, 1993), p. 158; and U.S. Senate, *Review of Ongoing Trade Negotiations and Completed Trade Agreements*, Hearing before the Subcommittee on International Trade of the Committee on Finance, 102nd Congress, 1st Session, August 2, 1991, p. 59.

64 Hi-Vision Promotion Center, "Hi-Vision Almanac 1993," p. 5; HDTV Semiconductor Cooperation Committee, "The Progress Report of the HDTV Semiconductor Cooperation Committee" (Tokyo: SIA/EIAJ HDSCC, 1993), p. 4; and Semiconductor Industry Association, "The 1991 U.S.-Japan Semiconductor Agreement: 'Heading Toward Crisis' " (San Jose: SIA, 1992), p. 5. See also U.S. House of Representatives, *Prospects for a New United States–Japan Semiconductor Agreement*, Hearing before the Subcommittee on International Economic Policy and Trade of the Committee on Foreign Affairs, 102nd Congress, 1st Session, March 20, 1991, p. 4.

65 Robert B. Nathan Associates, "Television Manufacturing in the United States: Economic Contributions – Past, Present, and Future" (Washington, DC: EIA, 1989), paper submitted into testimony, U.S. Senate, *Prospects for Development of a U.S. HDTV Industry*, Hearing before the Committee on Governmental Affairs, pp. 46–9.

66 U.S. House of Representatives, *New Directions in Home Video*, Hearing before the Subcommittee on Science, Research and Technology of the Committee on Science, Space, and Technology, p. 106.

67 Thomas Gale Moore, "The Promise of High-Definition Television: Hype and the Reality," *Policy Analysis*, no. 123, August 30, 1989, p. 9.

68 Hart, "Strategic Impacts of High Definition Television for U.S. Manufacturing," p. 8.

69 U.S. Department of Commerce, "Japan-Plasma Display Production-IMI950901: Market Research Reports."

70 U.S. Department of Commerce, "U.S. Research Facilities of Foreign Companies" (Washington, DC: ITA, 1994), appendix A.

71 John D. Aram, Leonard H. Lynn, and N. Mohan Reddy, "Institutional Relationships and Technology Commercialization: Limitations of Market-Based Policy," *Research Policy* 21.5 (1992): 413.

72 U.S. House of Representatives, *High Definition Television*, Hearings before

the Subcommittee on Telecommunications and Finance of the Committee on Energy and Commerce, p. 414.

73 U.S. House of Representatives, *High Definition Television (Part 2)*, Hearing before the Subcommittee on Telecommunications and Finance of the Committee on Energy and Commerce, p. 30. Emphasis added.

74 U.S. House of Representatives, *High Definition Television*, Hearing before the Committee on Science, Space, and Technology, p. 136.

75 Kozo Yamamura, "Caveat Emptor: The Industrial Policy of Japan," in Paul R. Krugman (ed.), *Strategic Trade Policy and the New International Economics* (Cambridge, MA: MIT Press, 1986), p. 180.

76 U.S. Department of Defense, "Building U.S. Capabilities in Flat Panel Displays," pp. IV-6, IV-7.

77 Electronics Industries Association of Japan, "Perspective on the Japanese Electronics Industry" (Tokyo: EIAJ, 1996).

78 TechSearch International Inc., "Japanese Developments in High Definition Television: HDTV Developments by Industry," p. 10. The MUSE "family" includes two HDTV-quality standards, MUSE-T (for satellite transmission), and MUSE (for direct broadcast, cable, and VCR), as well as three Advanced Definition Television (ADTV) standards, Narrow-MUSE (which meets FCC simulcast requirements and can be made compatible with MUSE, but is not NTSC-compatible), MUSE-6 (which is transmitted within a single 6-MHz radio frequency and is fully NTSC-compatible), and MUSE-9 (which is also fully NTSC-compatible, and adds a 3-MHz augmentation channel to MUSE-6).

79 Joseph Farrell and Carl Shapiro, "Standard Setting in High Definition Television," *Brookings Papers on Economic Activity: Microeconomics 1992*, p. 12. SECAM is 825 lines by 50 frames, PAL is 625 lines by 50 frames, and NTSC 525 lines by 59.94 frames. Interestingly, HD-MAC would not be compatible with either SECAM or PAL. To accommodate these standards, D-MAC and D2–MAC were to bridge SECAM and PAL with HD-MAC, respectively.

80 Hi-Vision Promotion Center, "Hi-Vision Almanac 1993," p. 4. See also "Companies Set Battle Lines in HDTV Chip Competition," *Nikkei Weekly*, November 23, 1991, pp. 1, 23; and Sheridan M. Tatsuno, *Created in Japan: From Imitators to World-Class Innovators* (New York: Harper & Row, 1990), p. 144.

81 Xiudian Dai, Alan Cawson, and Peter Holmes, "The Rise and Fall of High-Definition Television: The Impact of European Technology Policy," *Journal of Common Market Studies* 34.2 (1996): 149–66; and Tyson, *Who's Bashing Whom?* p. 241.

82 "HDTV: High Definition Debate," *Europe*, October 1993, p. 34; and "Britain Right in Digital Debate," *Management Today*, March 1993, p. 17.

83 U.S. House of Representatives, *FCC and NTIA Authorizations*, Hearings before the Subcommittee on Telecommunications and Finance of the Committee on Energy and Commerce, 101st Congress, 1st Session, September 14, 21, 1989, p. 5.

84 "Broadcasting System to Become Digital," *Japan Times*, May 13, 1994, p.

12; "Posts Official Backpedals on HDTV," *Japan Times*, February 24, 1994, p. 7; and Council on Competitiveness, *Roadmap for Results: Trade Policy, Technology and American Competitiveness* (Washington, DC: Council on Competitiveness, 1993), p. 173.

85 Federal Communications Commission, "Fourth Report and Order" (Washington, DC: FCC, 1996).

86 Depagne, "High-Definition Television: A Policy Framework to Revive U.S. Leadership in Consumer Electronics," pp. 66–7.

87 U.S. Senate, *Department of Defense Authorization for Appropriations for Fiscal Years 1990 and 1991*, Hearings before the Committee on Armed Services p. 10.

88 U.S. House of Representatives, *High Definition Television*, Hearing before the Committee on Science, Space, and Technology, p. 10.

89 U.S. Senate, *Department of Defense Authorization for Appropriations for Fiscal Years 1990 and 1991*, Hearings before the Committee on Armed Services, p. 314.

90 Wade Roush, "Science and Technology in the 101st Congress," *Technology Review* 93.8 (1990): 62.

91 Government Accounting Office, *Federal Awareness of the Development of High Definition Television*, Report to the Chairman, Subcommittee on Technology and National Security, Joint Economic Committee (Washington, DC: GAO, 1990), p. 2.

92 U.S. House of Representatives, *High Definition Television*, Hearing before the Subcommittee on Telecommunications and Finance of the Committee on Energy and Commerce, p. 2. Testimony of Edward J. Markey, Chair, Subcommittee on Telecommunications and Finance.

93 U.S. House of Representatives, *New Directions in Home Video*, Hearing before the Subcommittee on Science, Research and Technology of the Committee on Science, Space, and Technology, pp. 8–9. Testimony of Mel Levine (D-California).

94 U.S. House of Representatives, *High Definition Television (Part 2)*, Hearing before the Subcommittee on Telecommunications and Finance of the Committee on Energy and Commerce, p. 9. Testimony of Don Ritter (R-Pennsylvania).

95 U.S. House of Representatives, *High Definition Television*, Hearing before the Subcommittee on Research and Development and the Subcommittee on Investigations of the Committee on Armed Services, p. 34.

96 American Electronics Association, "ATV Task Force Findings," pp. 29–34.

97 Council on Competitiveness, *Roadmap for Results: Trade Policy, Technology and American Competitiveness*, p. 170; Aram et al., "Institutional Relationships and Technology Commercialization: Limitations of Market-Based Policy," p. 416; and Hazard, "Zenith and High-Definition Television 1990," p. 11.

98 Norioki Kobayashi, "U.S.-Japan Technological Friction," *Management Japan* 24.2 (1991): 12.

99 TechSearch International, Inc. "Japanese Developments in High Definition

Television: NHK and Government Policies" (Austin, TX: TechSearch, 1989), pp. 17–48.

100 Office of Technology Assessment, "The Big Picture: HDTV and High-Resolution Systems," p. 28.

101 TechSearch International Inc., "Japanese Developments in High Definition Television: HDTV Developments by Industry," p. 29.

102 Farrell and Shapiro, "Standard Setting in High Definition Television," p. 7; National Telecommunications and Information Administration, "Advanced Television, Related Technologies and the National Interest," pp. 18–24; and U.S. House of Representatives, *High Definition Television*, Hearing before the Committee on Science, Space and Technology, p. 9.

103 Office of Technology Assessment, "The Big Picture: HDTV and High-Resolution Systems," p. 30.

104 TechSearch International Inc., "Japanese Developments in High Definition Television: Executive Summary" (Austin, TX: TechSearch, 1989), p. 5.

6. Robotics, Superconductors, and Wheat

1 See, for example, Marie Thursby, "Strategic Models, Market Structure, and State Trading: An Application to Agriculture," in Robert E. Baldwin (ed.), *Trade Policy Issues and Empirical Analysis* (Chicago: University of Chicago Press, 1988), pp. 79–105.

2 Committee on Computing, Information, and Communications, "Computing, Information, and Communications: Technologies for the 21st Century" (Washington, DC: National Science and Technology Council, 1998).

3 Lester Thurow, *Head to Head: The Coming Economic Battle among Japan, Europe, and America* (New York: Morrow, 1992), p. 45; and Edwin Mansfield, "Innovation, R and D, and Firm Growth in Robotics: Japan and the United States," in Ake E. Andersson, David F. Batten, and Charlie Karlsson (eds.), *Knowledge and Industrial Organization* (Berlin: Springer-Verlag, 1989), p. 143.

4 Courtesy of the Robotic Industries Association. While this definition is widely cited in studies of robotics, definitions differ across countries, making international comparisons somewhat difficult.

5 B. Bowonder and T. Miyake, "Creating and Sustaining Competitiveness: An Analysis of the Japanese Robotics Industry," *International Journal of Technology Management* 9.5–7 (1994): 578.

6 United Nations, *World Industrial Robots, 1997* (New York: United Nations, 1997), p. 24; and United Nations, *World Industrial Robots, 1995* (New York: United Nations, 1995), p. 14. Differences in the definitions of robotics across the United States and Japan should be kept in mind in weighing these figures.

7 Robotic Industries Association, "Robot Orders Top $1 Billion in 1996, Smashing Previous Records," a report available on the web from the RIA at http://www.robotics.org/htdocs/whatshot/robot.html; and Asian Technology Information Program, "Robots and Use in Japanese Industry," a

report available from ATIP on the web at http://www.atip.or.jp/public/atip.reports.91/robots.html. The figure pertaining to the percentage of U.S. shipments exported was provided by Jeff Burnstein of the Robotic Industries Association.

8   U.S. Department of Commerce, "A Competitive Assessment of the U.S. Manufacturing Automation Equipment Industries" (Washington, DC: ITA, 1984), p. 73.

9   National Science Board, "Science and Engineering Indicators 1993" (Washington, DC: National Science Foundation, 1993), p. 79; and U.S. Department of Commerce, "A Competitive Assessment of the U.S. Robotics Industry" (Washington, DC: GPO, 1987), pp. 20, 25.

10 The quotation is from U.S. House of Representatives, *Critical Technologies: Machine Tools, Robotics, and Manufacturing,* Hearing before the Subcommittee on Technology and Competitiveness of the Committee on Science, Space, and Technology, 102nd Congress, 1st Session, May 2, 1991, p. 9. Testimony of Joseph Engleberger, Transitions Research Corporation.

11 Uwe R. Zimmer, Thomas Christaller, and Christfried Webers, "Recent Developments in Japanese Robotics Research: Notes of a Japan Tour," German National Research Institute, GMD Technical Report No. 1077 (Sankt Augustin, Germany, 1997), p. 2.

12 See, for example, Japanese Technology Evaluation Center, "Human-Computer Interaction Technologies in Japan" (Baltimore: Loyola College, 1996).

13 U.S. Department of Commerce, *1994 U.S. Industrial Outlook* (Washington, DC: ITA, 1994), pp. 17-7, 17-9.

14 U.S. Department of Commerce, *U.S. Industry and Trade Outlook '98* (New York: DRI/McGraw-Hill, 1998), p. 17-3.

15 See Michael L. Dertouzos, Richard K. Lester, and Robert M. Solow, *Made in America: Regaining the Productive Edge* (New York: HarperPerennial, 1989), pp. 20–1.

16 Japanese Technology Evaluation Center, "JTEC Panel Report on Mechatronics in Japan" (La Jolla, CA: Science Applications International Corp., 1985), p. 1-1.

17 Congressional Budget Office, "The Benefits and Risks of Federal Funding for Sematech" (Washington, DC: CBO, 1987), p. 17.

18 Japanese Technology Evaluation Center, "JTEC Panel Report on Mechatronics in Japan," p. 1-2.

19 Japanese Technology Evaluation Center, "Human-Computer Interaction Technologies in Japan," p. xiii.

20 Japanese Technology Evaluation Center, "JTEC Panel Report on Space Robotics in Japan" (Baltimore: Loyola College, 1991).

21 Office of Science and Technology Policy, "National Critical Technologies Report" (Washington, DC: OSTP, 1995), chap. 6, p. 2 of 14, figure 6.1. This report is available from the OSTP on the web at http://www.whitehouse.gov/WH/OSTP/CTIformatted/.

22 Office of Technology Assessment, "Computerized Manufacturing Automa-

tion: Employment, Education, and the Workplace," OTA-CIT-235 (Washington, DC: OTA, 1984), pp. 292, 299. Emphasis added.

23 See Michael E. Porter, *The Competitive Advantage of Nations* (New York: Free Press, 1990), p. 238.

24 Office of Technology Assessment, "Computerized Manufacturing Automation: Employment, Education, and the Workplace," p. 321.

25 Ibid., p. 325; and U.S. House of Representatives, *The Role of Automation and Robotics in Advancing United States Competitiveness*, Hearing before the Subcommittee on Science, Research and Technology of the Committee on Science and Technology, 99th Congress, 1st Session, October 7, 1985, p. 143.

26 Japanese Technology Evaluation Center, "JTEC Panel Report on Space Robotics in Japan," p. 20.

27 U.S. Department of Commerce, "A Competitive Assessment of the U.S. Robotics Industry," pp. 32–3.

28 Office of Technology Assessment, "Computerized Manufacturing Automation: Employment, Education, and the Workplace," p. 307.

29 Data from the RAND Corporation's RaDiUS database. My thanks to Caroline Wagner, Critical Technologies Institute, the RAND Corporation.

30 Data from the RAND Corporation's RaDiUS database. My thanks to Carl Shephard, Office of Technology Policy, Department of Commerce.

31 This figure provided by Howard Moraff, Program Director, Robotics and Human Augmentation, National Science Foundation.

32 Japanese Technology Evaluation Center, "JTEC Panel Report on Space Robotics in Japan," p. 3.

33 Zimmer, Christaller, and Webers, "Recent Developments in Japanese Robotics Research: Notes of a Japan Tour," pp. 9–10; Japanese Technology Evaluation Center, "JTEC Panel Report on Space Robotics in Japan," pp. 192–3.

34 Data from the MITI budget provided by the Japan Science and Technology Corporation.

35 Asian Technology Information Program, "Robots and Use in Japanese Industry," p. 3; U.S. Department of Commerce, "A Competitive Assessment of the U.S. Robotics Industry," p. 40; Japanese Technology Evaluation Center, "JTEC Panel Report on Mechatronics in Japan," pp. 3–39, 3–40; and U.S. Department of Commerce, "A Competitive Assessment of the U.S. Manufacturing Automation Equipment Industries," p. 57.

36 My thanks to the Japan Robot Association for bringing the human-friendly network robotics project to my attention.

37 Office of Technology Assessment, "High-Temperature Superconductivity in Perspective," OTA-E-440 (Washington, DC: U.S. GPO, 1990), appendix 2A.

38 U.S. House of Representatives, *Superconductivity*, Hearing before the Subcommittee on Transportation, Aviation and Materials of the Committee on Science, Space, and Technology, 101st Congress, 2nd Session, February 21,

1990, p. 28. Testimony of Dr. Allan Bromley, Director, Office of Science and Technology Policy.

39   Office of Technology Assessment, "Commercializing High-Temperature Superconductivity," OTA-ITE-388 (Washington, DC: GPO, 1988), p. 4.

40   U.S. Department of Commerce, "A Competitive Assessment of the U.S. Electric Power Generating Equipment Industry" (Washington, DC: ITA, 1985).

41   World Technology Evaluation Center, "Panel Report on Power Applications of Superconductivity in Japan and Germany" (Baltimore: Loyola College, 1997).

42   Office of Technology Assessment, "R&D in the Maritime Industry: A Supplement to an Assessment of Maritime Trade and Technology," OTA-BP-O-35 (Washington, DC: GPO, 1985).

43   For background on this industry, see Dong Sung Cho and Michael E. Porter, "Changing Global Industry Leadership: The Case of Shipbuilding," in Porter (ed.), *Competition in Global Industries* (Boston: Harvard Business School Press, 1986), pp. 539–67.

44   Office of Technology Assessment, "High-Temperature Superconductivity in Perspective," pp. 47–8.

45   Ibid., chap. 3.

46   Office of Technology Assessment, "Commercializing High-Temperature Superconductivity," p. 117.

47   World Technology Evaluation Center, "WTEC Panel Report on Power Applications of Superconductivity in Japan and Germany," p. xii.

48   The data were provided by Bill Oosterhuis, Team Leader, Solid State and Materials Chemistry, Division of Materials Sciences, U.S. Department of Energy.

49   National Commission on Superconductivity, "Report of the National Commission on Superconductivity" (Washington, DC: National Commission on Superconductivity, 1990), p. 7.

50   U.S. Department of Energy, "Superconductivity for Electric Systems Program Plan FY1996–FY2000" (Washington, DC: DOE, 1996), pp. 22–3.

51   "Low-Calorie, High-Energy," *IEEE Spectrum*, July 1997, p. 40. See also "Hitachi Turns Superconducting Power Up a Notch," *Nikkei Weekly*, February 2, 1998, p. 6.

52   Japanese Technology Evaluation Center, "High Temperature Superconductivity in Japan" (Baltimore: Loyola College, 1989).

53   World Technology Evaluation Center, "Panel Report on Power Applications of Superconductivity in Japan and Germany," p. xi.

54   U.S. Department of Energy, Materials Technology Subcommittee Communications Group on Superconductivity, "Federal Research Programs in Superconductivity" (Washington, DC: DoE, 1994), p. iii.

55   Communiqué issued by the Fifth International Superconductivity Industry Summit, available on the web at http://nehan.sendai.kopas.co.jp/ISTEC/SUMMIT/E5summit.html.

56   Bruce L. Gardner, "The Political Economy of U.S. Export Subsidies for

Wheat," in Anne O. Krueger (ed.), *The Political Economy of American Trade Policy* (Chicago: University of Chicago Press, 1996), p. 299.

57 Robert L. Paarlberg, *Fixing Farm Trade: Policy Options for the United States* (Cambridge, MA: Ballinger, 1988), pp. 91–3.

58 Ronald T. Libby, *Protecting Markets: U.S. Policy and the World Grain Trade* (Ithaca, NY: Cornell University Press, 1992), p. 58.

59 Political tensions over the exclusion and later inclusion of China and the Soviet Union stand out in this regard.

60 Robert L. Paarlberg, "Does the GATT Agreement Promote Export Subsidies?" *Choices* (Fourth Quarter 1995), p. 11.

61 Robert L. Paarlberg, "The Mysterious Popularity of the EEP," *Choices* (Second Quarter 1990): 16.

62 Libby, *Protecting Markets: U.S. Policy and the World Grain Trade*, p. 81.

63 Gardner, "The Political Economy of U.S. Export Subsidies for Wheat," p. 301.

64 Ibid., p. 327.

65 My thanks to Robert Paarlberg for sharing with me his expert insights into this case.

7. Conclusion

1 Bundesministerium für Wirtschaft, "Report by the Coordinator for German Aerospace Affairs in 1996" (Bonn: Federal Ministry of Economics, 1996), p. 5.

2 Paul Krugman, *Geography and Trade* (Cambridge, MA: MIT Press, 1991).

3 Anne O. Krueger, *Political Economy of Policy Reform in Developing Countries* (Cambridge, MA: MIT Press, 1993).

4 Richard N. Cooper, "US Response to Foreign Industrial Policies," in Dominick Salvatore (ed.), *Protection and World Welfare* (Cambridge: Cambridge University Press, 1993), pp. 131–59; and William Diebold Jr., *Industrial Policy as an International Issue* (New York: McGraw-Hill, 1980).

5 See, for example, Lisa L. Martin, *Coercive Cooperation: Explaining Multilateral Economic Sanctions* (Princeton: Princeton University Press, 1992).

6 Robert Powell, "Anarchy in International Relations Theory: The Neorealist-Neoliberal Debate," *International Organization* 48.2 (1994): 330.

7 Duncan Snidal, "International Cooperation among Relative Gains Maximizers," *International Studies Quarterly* 35.4 (1991): 387–402.

8 Richard Pomfret, "Voluntary Export Restraints in the Presence of Monopoly Power," *Kyklos* 42.1 (1989): 61–72.

9 See, for example, Jean Tirole, *Theory of Industrial Organization* (Cambridge, MA: MIT Press, 1988), p. 209; and Elhanan Helpman and Paul R. Krugman, *Market Structure and Foreign Trade* (Cambridge, MA: MIT Press, 1985), p. 35.

10 S. Lael Brainard and David Martimort, "Strategic Trade Policy with Incompletely Informed Policymakers," National Bureau of Economic Research Working Paper No. 4069 (Cambridge, MA, 1992).

11 John A. C. Conybeare, "The Use of Deterrent Threats in International Trade Conflicts," in Paul C. Stern, Robert Axelrod, Robert Jervis, and Roy Radner (eds.), *Perspectives on Deterrence* (New York: Oxford University Press, 1989), p. 204.

12 Judith Goldstein, "Ideas, Institutions, and American Trade Policy," *International Organization* 42.1 (1988): 179–218; Ronald Rogowski, "Trade and the Variety of Democratic Institutions," *International Organization* 41.2 (1987): 203–23; and Peter Hall, *Governing the Economy: The Politics of State Intervention in Britain and France* (New York: Oxford University Press, 1986).

13 Avinash Dixit, "How Should the United States Respond to Other Countries' Trade Policies?" in Robert M. Stern (ed.), *U.S. Trade Policies in a Changing World Economy* (Cambridge, MA: MIT Press, 1987), p. 246.

Select Bibliography

Aerospace Industries Association. "National Benefits of Aerospace Exports." Washington, DC: AIA, 1983.

"Does the United States Support Its Commercial Transport Manufacturers like Europe Supports Airbus?" Washington, DC: AIA, 1985.

"Technology Diffusion – The Movement of Technology between Aerospace and Other Industries." Washington, DC: AIA, 1985.

"Maintaining Technological Leadership: The Critical Role of IR&D/B&P." Washington, DC: AIA, 1989.

"U.S. Aerospace Technology Development: Stepping Up the Pace." Washington, DC: AIA, 1989.

"The Importance of Aerospace to the Nation's Economy." Washington, DC: AIA, 1992.

"Tools of the Trade: Why Offsets, Outsourcing, and Joint Ventures Are Crucial to U.S. Aerospace." Washington, DC: AIA, 1996.

Aggarwal, Vinod K., Robert O. Keohane, and David B. Yoffie. "The Dynamics of Negotiated Protectionism." *American Political Science Review* 81.2 (1987): 345–66.

Airbus Industrie. "Report on U.S. Government Intervention in Sales of Civil Transport Aircraft." Toulouse: Airbus Industrie, 1991.

"An Introduction to Airbus Industrie." Washington, DC: Airbus Industrie North America, 1992.

American Electronics Association. "High Definition Television (HDTV): Economic Analysis of Impact." Santa Clara, CA: AEA, 1988.

"ATV Task Force Findings." Santa Clara, CA: AEA, 1989.

Arnold and Porter. "U.S. Government Support of the U.S. Commercial Aircraft Industry." Washington, DC: Prepared for the Commission of European Communities, 1991.

Baldwin, Richard, and Paul R. Krugman. "Market Access and International Competition: A Simulation Study of 16K Random Access Memories." Columbia Graduate School of Business, Center on Japanese Economy and Business Working Paper No. 2. New York, 1986.

"Industrial Policy and International Competition in Wide-Bodied Jet Aircraft," In Robert E. Baldwin (ed.), *Trade Policy Issues and Empirical Analysis*, pp. 45–71. Chicago: University of Chicago Press, 1988.

191

Barber, Randy, and Robert E. Scott. "Jobs on the Wing: Trading Away the Future of the U.S. Aerospace Industry." Washington, DC: Economic Policy Institute, 1995.

Beltz, Cynthia A. *High-Tech Maneuvers: Industrial Policy Lessons of HDTV.* Washington, DC: American Enterprise Institute, 1991.

Bendesministerium für Wirtschaft. "Report by the Coordinator for German Aerospace Affairs in 1996." Bonn: Federal Ministry of Economics, 1996.

Bergsten, C. Fred, and Marcus Noland. *Reconcilable Differences? United States-Japan Economic Conflict.* Washington, DC: Institute for International Economics, 1993.

Bernstein, Jeffrey I. "Costs of Production, Intra- and Interindustry R&D Spillovers: Canadian Evidence." *Canadian Journal of Economics* 21.2 (1988): 324–47.

Bernstein, Jeffrey I., and M. Ishaq Nadiri. "Interindustry R&D Spillovers, Rates of Return, and Production in High-Tech Industries." *American Economic Review* 78.2 (1988): 429–34.

Bhagwati, Jagdish. *Protectionism.* Cambridge, MA: MIT Press, 1988.

Boeing Commercial Airplane Group. "European Targeting of the Commercial Aircraft Industry – Why Is Boeing Concerned?" Seattle: Boeing, 1991.

Current Market Outlook: World Market Demand and Airplane Supply Requirements, 1992. Seattle: Boeing, 1992.

Borrus, Michael, James Millstein, and John Zysman. "U.S.-Japanese Competition in the Semiconductor Industry: A Study in International Trade and Technology Development." University of California at Berkeley, Institute of International Studies Policy Papers in International Affairs No. 17. 1982.

Boston Consulting Group. "Development of a U.S.-Based ATV Industry." Preliminary report prepared for the American Electronics Association, 1989.

Bowonder, B., and T. Miyake. "Creating and Sustaining Competitiveness: An Analysis of the Japanese Robotics Industry." *International Journal of Technology Management* 9.5–7 (1994): 575–611.

Bowonder, B., and S. V. Ramana Rao. "Creating and Sustaining Competitiveness – An Analysis of the World Civil Aircraft Industry." *World Competition: Law and Economics Review* 16.4 (1993): 5–47.

Brainard, S. Lael, and David Martimort. "Strategic Trade Policy with Incompletely Informed Policymakers." National Bureau of Economic Research Working Paper No. 4069. Cambridge, MA: 1992.

Brander, James A. "Rationales for Strategic Trade and Industrial Policy." In Paul R. Krugman (ed.), *Strategic Trade Policy and the New International Economics*, pp. 23–46. Cambridge, MA: MIT Press, 1986.

Brander, James A., and Barbara J. Spencer. "Export Subsidies and International Market Share Rivalry." *Journal of International Economics* 18 (1985): 83–100.

Branscomb, Lewis M. "The National Technology Policy Debate." In Branscomb (ed.), *Empowering Technology: Implementing a U.S. Strategy*, pp. 1–35. Cambridge, MA: MIT Press, 1993.

Bundesministerium für Wirtschaft. "Die Konkurrenzsituation der deutschen

Luft- und Raumfahrt im internationalen Vergleich." Bonn: Bundesminister-ium für Wirtschaft, 1988.

Busch, Marc L., and Eric Reinhardt. "Industrial Location and Protection: The Political and Economic Geography of U.S. Nontariff Barriers." *American Journal of Political Science* (forthcoming).

Caballero, Richard J., and Richard K. Lyons. "External Effects and Europe's Integration." In L. Alan Winters and Anthony Venables (eds.), *European Integration: Trade and Industry*, pp. 34–51. Cambridge: Cambridge University Press, 1991.

Calder, Kent E. *Strategic Capitalism: Private Business and Public Purpose in Japanese Industrial Finance*. Princeton: Princeton University Press, 1993.

Carliner, Geoffrey. "Industrial Policies for Emerging Industries." In Paul R. Krugman (ed.), *Strategic Trade Policy and the New International Econom-ics*, pp. 147–68. Cambridge, MA: MIT Press, 1986.

Caves, Richard E. "Economic Models of Political Choice: Canada's Tariff Struc-ture." *Canadian Journal of Economics* 9.2 (1977): 278–300.

Cho, Dong Sung, and Michael E. Porter. "Changing Global Industry Leadership: The Case of Shipbuilding." In Michael E. Porter (ed.), *Competition in Global Industries*, pp. 539–67. Boston: Harvard Business School Press, 1986.

Ciccone, Antonio, and Robert E. Hall. "Productivity and the Density of Eco-nomic Activity." *American Economic Review* 86.1 (1996): 54–70.

Coe, David T., and Elhanan Helpman. "International R&D Spillovers." Centre for Economic Policy Research Discussion Paper No. 840. London, 1993.

Coe, David T., Elhanan Helpman, and Alexander W. Hoffmaister. "North-South R&D Spillovers," Centre for Economic Policy Research Discussion Paper No. 1133. London, 1995.

Cohen, Wesley M., and Richard C. Levin. "Empirical Studies of Innovation and Market Share." In Richard Schmalensee and Robert D. Willig (eds.), *Hand-book of Industrial Organization*, vol. 2, pp. 1059–1107. Amsterdam: North Holland, 1989.

Commission of the European Communities. "Demand Prospects for Civil Trans-port Aircraft." Brussels: Commission of the European Communities, 1975.

"A Competitive European Aeronautical Industry." Brussels: Commission of the European Communities, 1990.

"Report on United States Trade and Investment Barriers 1992: Problems of Doing Business with the U.S." Brussels: Services of the Commission of the European Communities, 1992.

Committee on Computing, Information, and Communications. "Computing, Information, and Communications: Technologies for the 21st Century." Washington, DC: National Science and Technology Council, 1998.

Congressional Budget Office. "Federal Financial Support for High-Technology Industries." Washington, DC: GPO, 1985.

"The Benefits and Risks of Federal Funding for Sematech." Washington, DC: GPO, 1987.

"The Scope of the High-Definition Television Market and Its Implications for Competitiveness." Washington, DC: GPO, 1989.

"Using R&D Consortia for Commercial Innovation: Sematech, X-Ray Lithography, and High-Resolution Systems." Washington, DC: CBO, 1990.

Congressional Research Service. "Airbus Industrie: An Economic and Trade Perspective." Report prepared for the Subcommittee on Technology and Competitiveness, transmitted to the Committee on Science, Space, and Technology, 102nd Congress, 2nd Session, March 1992.

Conybeare, John A. C. *Trade Wars: The Theory and Practice of International Commercial Rivalry*. New York: Columbia University Press, 1987.

"The Use of Deterrent Threats in International Trade Conflicts." In Paul C. Stern, Robert Axelrod, Robert Jervis, and Roy Radner (eds.), *Perspectives on Deterrence*, pp. 191–210. New York: Oxford University Press, 1989.

"Voting for Protection: An Electoral Model of Tariff Policy." *International Organization* 45.1 (1991): 57–82.

Cooper, Richard N. "US Response to Foreign Industrial Policies." In Dominick Salvatore (ed.), *Protection and World Welfare*, pp. 131–59. Cambridge: Cambridge University Press, 1993.

Dai, Xiudian, Alan Cawson, and Peter Holmes. "The Rise and Fall of High-Definition Television: The Impact of European Technology Policy." *Journal of Common Market Studies* 34.2 (1996): 149–66.

de la Potterie, Bruno van Pottelsberghe. "Inter-Industry Technological Spillovers and the Rate of Return on R&D." MITI Discussion Paper No. 96-DOF-23. Tokyo, 1996.

Derian, Jean-Claude. *America's Struggle for Leadership in Technology*. Cambridge, MA: MIT Press, 1990.

Dertouzos, Michael L., Richard K. Lester, and Robert M. Solow. *Made in America: Regaining the Productive Edge*. New York: HarperPerennial, 1989.

Diebold, William, Jr. *Industrial Policy as an International Issue*. New York: McGraw-Hill, 1980.

Dixit, Avinash. "How Should the United States Respond to Other Countries' Trade Policies?" In Robert M. Stern (ed.), *U.S. Trade Policies in a Changing World Economy*, pp. 245–82. Cambridge, MA: MIT Press, 1987.

Early, Barbara, Perry Granatiero, Irene McKenna, and Sue Tysl. "Re-evaluating Government Support in the Commercial Aircraft Industry." Los Angeles: Loyola Marymount University, 1993.

Electronics Industries Association of Japan. "The Present Status and Future Outlook of the Semiconductor Memory Industry." Tokyo: EIAJ, 1992.

European Commission. "The Aeronautics Task Force: Interim Report." Brussels: EC Directorate-General III/D Industry, 1995.

Falstad, Robert E. "High-Tech Research Consortia: Sematech's Experience." Houston, TX: Sematech, 1990.

Farrell, Joseph, and Carl Shapiro. "Standard Setting in High Definition Television." *Brookings Papers on Economic Activity: Microeconomics 1992*: 1–77.

Fecher, Fabian, and Sergio Perelman. "Productivity Growth and Technical Efficiency in OECD Industrial Activities." In Richard E. Caves (ed.), *Industrial Efficiency in Six Nations*, pp. 459–88. Cambridge, MA: MIT Press, 1992.

Federal Communications Commission. "Fourth Report and Order." Washington, DC: FCC, 1996.

Flamm, Kenneth. "Policy and Politics in the International Semiconductor Industry." Paper submitted into testimony, U.S. Congress, *Japan's Economic Challenge*. Hearings before the Joint Economic Committee, 101st Congress, 2nd Session, October 16, 18, and December 4, 6, 1990.

"Forward Pricing versus Fair Value: An Analytic Assessment of 'Dumping' in DRAMs." In Takatoshi Ito and Anne O. Krueger (eds.), *Trade and Protectionism*, pp. 47–93. Chicago: University of Chicago Press, 1993.

Mismanaged Trade? Strategic Policy and the Semiconductor Industry. Washington, DC: Brookings, 1996.

Ford, Robert, and Win Swyker. "Industrial Subsidies in the OECD Economies." *OECD Economic Studies* 15 (1990): 37–81.

Fransman, Martin. *The Market and Beyond: Information Technology in Japan.* Cambridge: Cambridge University Press, 1990.

Japan's Computer and Communications Industry. New York: Oxford University Press, 1995.

Frieden, Jeffry A. *Debt, Development, and Democracy: Modern Political Economy and Latin America, 1965–1985.* Princeton: Princeton University Press, 1991.

Friedman, David B., and Richard J. Samuels. "How to Succeed without Really Flying: The Japanese Aircraft Industry and Japan's Technology Ideology." In Jeffrey A. Frankel and Miles Kahler (eds.), *Regionalism and Rivalry: Japan and the United States in Pacific Asia*, pp. 251–317. Chicago: University of Chicago Press, 1993.

Froot, Kenneth A., and David B. Yoffie. "Trading Blocs and the Incentives to Protect: Implications for Japan and East Asia." In Jeffrey A. Frankel and Miles Kahler (eds.), *Regionalism and Rivalry: Japan and the United States in Pacific Asia*, pp. 125–52. Chicago: University of Chicago Press, 1993.

Gansler, Jacques S. *The Defense Industry.* Cambridge, MA: MIT Press, 1980.

Gardner, Bruce L. "The Political Economy of U.S. Export Subsidies for Wheat." In Anne O. Krueger (ed.), *The Political Economy of American Trade Policy*, pp. 291–331. Chicago: University of Chicago Press, 1996.

Gellman Research Associates. "An Economic and Financial Review of Airbus Industrie." Report prepared for the U.S. Department of Commerce, International Trade Administration. Jenkintown, PA, 1990.

Goldstein, Judith. "Ideas, Institutions, and American Trade Policy." *International Organization* 42.1 (1988): 179–218.

Golich, Vicki L. "From Competition to Collaboration: The Challenge of Commercial-Class Aircraft Manufacturing." *International Organization* 46.4 (1992): 899–934.

Government Accounting Office. *Federal Awareness of the Development of High Definition Television.* Report to the Chairman, Subcommittee on Technology and National Security, Joint Economic Committee. Washington, DC: GAO, 1990.

Gowa, Joanne. "Rational Hegemons, Excludable Goods, and Small Groups: An Epitaph for Hegemonic Stability Theory?" *World Politics* 41.3 (1989): 307–24.

Gowa, Joanne, and Edward D. Mansfield. "Power Politics and International Trade." *American Political Science Review* 87.2 (1993): 408–20.

Grossman, Gene M. "Promoting New Industrial Activities: A Survey of Recent Arguments and Evidence." *OECD Economic Studies* 11 (1988): 87–125.

Grossman, Gene M., and Elhanan Helpman. "Protection for Sale." *American Economic Review* 84.4 (1994): 833–50.

"Endogenous Innovation in the Theory of Growth." *Journal of Economic Perspectives* 8.1 (1994): 23–44.

"Trade Wars and Trade Talks." *Journal of Political Economy* 103.4 (1995): 675–708.

Grossman, Gene M., and J. David Richardson. "Strategic Trade Policy: A Survey of Issues and Early Analysis." Princeton University: Special Papers in International Economics No. 15. Princeton, 1985.

Haberler, Gottfried. "Strategic Trade Policy and the New International Economics: A Critical Analysis." In Ronald W. Jones and Anne O. Krueger (eds.), *The Political Economy of International Trade: Essays in Honor of Robert E. Baldwin*, pp. 25–30. Cambridge, MA: Blackwell, 1990.

Hall, Peter. *Governing the Economy: The Politics of State Intervention in Britain and France*. New York: Oxford University Press, 1986.

Hansen, John Mark. *Gaining Access: Congress and the Farm Lobby, 1919–1981*. Chicago: University of Chicago Press, 1991.

Hansen, Wendy L., and Kee Ok Park. "Nation-State and Pluralistic Decision Making in Trade Policy: The Case of the International Trade Administration." *International Studies Quarterly* 39.2 (1995): 181–212.

Hart, Jeffrey A. "Strategic Impacts of High Definition Television for U.S. Manufacturing." Ann Arbor, MI: National Center for Manufacturing Sciences, 1989.

Rival Capitalists: International Competitiveness in the United States, Japan, and Western Europe. Ithaca, NY: Cornell University Press, 1992.

Hart, Jeffrey A., and Laura D'Andrea Tyson. "Responding to the Challenge of HDTV." *California Management Review* 31.4 (1989): 132–45.

Hayward, Keith. *International Collaboration in Civil Aerospace*. New York: St. Martin's, 1986.

The British Aircraft Industry. Manchester: Manchester University Press, 1989.

HDTV Semiconductor Cooperation Committee. "The Progress Report of the HDTV Semiconductor Cooperation Committee." Tokyo: SIA/EIAJ HDSCC, 1993.

Helpman, Elhanan, and Paul R. Krugman. *Market Structure and Foreign Trade*. Cambridge, MA: MIT Press, 1985.

Hickie, Desmond. "Airbus Industrie: A Case Study in European High Technology Cooperation." In Ulrich Hilpert (ed.), *State Policies and Techno-Industrial Innovation*, pp. 187–212. New York: Routledge, 1991.

High Vision Broadcasting Research Committee. "High Vision Broadcasting Research Committee Report." Trans. Tomoko Sugiyama. Tokyo: High Vision Broadcasting Research Committee, 1992.

Hillman, Arye L. "Protection, Politics, and Market Structure." In Elhanan Helpman and Assaf Razin (eds.), *International Trade and Trade Policy*, pp. 118–40. Cambridge, MA: MIT Press, 1991.

Hwang, Hae-Sin, and Craig T. Schulma. "Strategic Non-Intervention and the Choice of Trade Policy for International Oligopoly." *Journal of International Economics* 34 (1993): 74–93.

Iansiti, Marco, and Jonathan West. "Learning, Experimentation, and Technology Integration: The Evolution of R&D in the Semiconductor Industry." Harvard Graduate School of Business Administration Working Paper No. 96-032. Boston, 1996.

Irwin, Douglas A., and Peter J. Klenow. "Learning-By-Doing Spillovers in the Semiconductor Industry." *Journal of Political Economy* 102.6 (1994): 1200–27.

Japanese Technology Evaluation Center. "JTEC Panel Report on Mechatronics in Japan." La Jolla, CA: Science Applications International Corp., 1985.

"High Temperature Superconductivity in Japan." Baltimore: Loyola College, 1989.

"JTEC Panel Report on Advanced Computing in Japan." Springfield, VA: NTIS, 1990.

"JTEC Panel Report on Space Robotics in Japan." Baltimore: Loyola College, 1991.

"Human-Computer Interaction Technologies in Japan." Baltimore: Loyola College, 1996.

Johnson, Harry G. *International Trade and Economic Growth: Studies in Pure Theory*. Cambridge, MA: Harvard University Press, 1967.

Jovanovic, Boyan, and Glenn M. MacDonald. "Competitive Diffusion," *Journal of Political Economy* 102.1 (1994): 24–52.

Keck, Otto. "The National System for Technical Innovation in Germany." In Richard R. Nelson (ed.), *National Innovation Systems: A Comparative Analysis*, pp. 115–57. New York: Oxford University Press, 1993.

Kendry, Adrian, Peter Duffield, and John Butler. "The Economic and Industrial Importance of the Airbus Partnership." Bristol: Centre for Social and Economic Research, 1995.

Keohane, Robert O. *After Hegemony: Cooperation and Discord in the World Political Economy*. Princeton: Princeton University Press, 1984.

Klepper, Gernot. "Industrial Policy in the Transport Aircraft Industry." In Paul R. Krugman and Alasdair Smith (eds.), *Empirical Studies of Strategic Trade Policy*, pp. 101–29. Chicago: University of Chicago Press, 1994.

Klepper, Gernot, Robert W. Crandall, and Didier Laussel. "Entry into the Market for Large Transport Aircraft." *European Economic Review* 34.4 (1990): 775–803.

Knight, Jack. *Institutions and Social Conflict.* Cambridge: Cambridge University Press, 1992.

Krasner, Stephen D. "Global Communications and National Power: Life on the Pareto Frontier." *World Politics* 43.3 (1991): 336–66.

Krueger, Anne O. *Political Economy of Policy Reform in Developing Countries.* Cambridge, MA: MIT Press, 1993.

Krugman, Paul R. "Strategic Sectors and International Competition." In Robert M. Stern (ed.), *U.S. Trade Policies in a Changing World Economy,* pp. 207–32. Cambridge, MA: MIT Press, 1987.

"Technology-Intensive Goods." In Michael Finder and Andrej Olechowski (eds.), *The Uruguay Round: A Handbook for the Multilateral Trade Negotiations,* pp. 191–97. Washington, DC: World Bank, 1987.

Rethinking International Trade. Cambridge, MA: MIT Press, 1990.

Geography and Trade. Cambridge, MA: MIT Press, 1991.

"Introduction." In Paul R. Krugman and Alasdair Smith (eds.), *Empirical Studies of Strategic Trade Policy,* pp. 1–9. Chicago: University of Chicago Press, 1994.

Lake, David A. *Power, Protection and Free Trade: International Sources of U.S. Commercial Strategy, 1887–1939.* Ithaca, NY: Cornell University Press, 1988.

"Leadership, Hegemony, and the International Economy: Naked Emperor or Tattered Monarch with Potential." *International Studies Quarterly* 37.4 (1993): 459–89.

Libby, Ronald T. *Protecting Markets: U.S. Policy and the World Grain Trade.* Ithaca, NY: Cornell University Press, 1992.

Lichtenberg, Frank R. "R&D Investment and International Productivity Differences." National Bureau of Economic Research Working Paper No. 4161. Cambridge, MA, 1992.

Lieberman, Marvin B. "The Learning Curve and Pricing in the Chemical Processing Industries." *Rand Journal of Economics* 15.2 (1984): 213–28.

Long-Term Credit Bank of Japan. "The Japanese Aircraft Industry: Entering a Period of Progress Spurred by International Joint Development." LTCB Research Special Issue on Japan's High-Technology Industries No. 6. Tokyo, 1986.

Lorell, Mark A. "Multinational Development of Large Aircraft: The European Experience." Rand Corporation Document R-2596-DR&E. Santa Monica, CA, 1980.

Lynn, Matthew. *Birds of Prey: The War between Boeing and Airbus.* London: Heinemann, 1995.

Magee, Stephen P., William A. Brock, and Leslie Young. *Black Hole Tariffs and Endogenous Policy Theory: Political Economy in General Equilibrium.* Cambridge: Cambridge University Press, 1989.

Mansfield, Edward D., and Marc L. Busch. "The Political Economy of Nontariff Barriers: A Cross-National Analysis." *International Organization* 49.4 (1995): 723–49.

Mansfield, Edwin. "How Rapidly Does New Industrial Technology Leak Out?" *Journal of Industrial Economics* 34.2 (1985): 217–23.

"Innovation, R and D, and Firm Growth in Robotics: Japan and the United States." In Ake E. Andersson, David F. Batten, and Charlie Karlsson (eds.), *Knowledge and Industrial Organization*, pp. 145–55. Berlin: Springer-Verlag, 1989.

"Appropriating the Returns from Investments in R&D Capital." In Karel Cool, Damien J. Neven, and Ingo Walter (eds.), *European Industrial Restructuring in the 1990s*, pp. 331–56. New York: New York University Press, 1992.

Martin, Lisa L. *Coercive Cooperation: Explaining Multilateral Economic Sanctions*. Princeton: Princeton University Press, 1992.

McIntyre, Ian. *Dogfight: The Transatlantic Battle over Airbus*. Westport, CT: Praeger, 1992.

Milner, Helen V. *Resisting Protectionism: Global Industries and the Politics of International Trade*. Princeton: Princeton University Press, 1988.

Interests, Institutions, and Information: Domestic Politics and International Relations. Princeton: Princeton University Press, 1997.

Milner, Helen V., and David B. Yoffie. "Between Free Trade and Protectionism: Strategic Trade Policy and a Theory of Corporate Trade Demands." *International Organization* 43.2 (1989): 239–71.

Moravcsik, Andrew. "Armaments among Allies: European Weapons Collaboration, 1975–1985." In Peter B. Evans, Harold K. Jacobson, and Robert D. Putnam (eds.), *Double-Edged Diplomacy: International Bargaining and Domestic Politics*, pp. 128–67. Berkeley: University of California Press, 1993.

Mowery, David C. *Alliance Politics and Economics: Multinational Joint Ventures in Commercial Aircraft*. Cambridge, MA: Ballinger, 1987.

Mowery, David C., and Nathan Rosenberg. *Technology and the Pursuit of Economic Growth*. Cambridge: Cambridge University Press, 1989.

National Academy of Engineering. *The Competitive Status of the U.S. Civil Aviation Manufacturing Industry: A Study of the Influences of Technology in Determining International Industrial Competitive Advantage*. Washington, DC: National Academy Press, 1985.

National Advisory Committee on Semiconductors. "A Strategic Industry at Risk: A Report to the President and the Congress from the National Advisory Committee on Semiconductors." Washington, DC: GPO, 1989.

"A National Strategy for Semiconductors: An Agenda for the President, the Congress, and the Industry." Washington, DC: GPO, 1992.

"Attaining Preeminence in Semiconductors: Third Annual Report to the President and the Congress." Washington, DC: GPO, 1992.

National Commission on Superconductivity. "Report of the National Commission on Superconductivity." Washington, DC: National Commission on Superconductivity, 1990.

National Science Board. "Science and Engineering Indicators 1993." Washington, DC: National Science Foundation, 1993.

National Telecommunications and Information Administration. "Advanced Television, Related Technologies, and the National Interest." Washington, DC: DOC, 1989.

Nelson, Richard R. *High-Technology Policies: A Five Nation Comparison.* Washington, DC: American Enterprise Institute, 1984.

Newhouse, John. *The Sporty Game: The High-Risk Competitive Business of Making and Selling Commercial Airlines.* New York: Knopf, 1982.

NHK Science and Technical Research Laboratories. *High Definition Television: Hi-Vision Technology.* Trans. James G. Parker. New York: Van Nostrand Reinhold, 1993.

Office of Science and Technology Policy. "National Critical Technologies Report." Washington, DC: OSTP, 1995.

Office of Technology Assessment. "Computerized Manufacturing Automation: Employment, Education, and the Workplace." OTA-CIT-235. Washington, DC: OTA, 1984.

"R&D in the Maritime Industry: A Supplement to an Assessment of Maritime Trade and Technology." OTA-BP-O-35. Washington, DC: GPO, 1985.

"Commercializing High-Temperature Superconductivity." OTA-ITE-388. Washington, DC: GPO, 1988.

"High-Temperature Superconductivity in Perspective." OTA-E-440. Washington, DC: GPO, 1990.

"The Big Picture: HDTV and High-Resolution Systems." OTA-BP-CIT-64. Washington, DC: GPO, 1990.

"Competing Economies: America, Europe, and the Pacific Rim." OTA-ITE-498. Washington, DC: GPO, 1991.

"Government Support of the Large Commercial Aircraft Industries of Japan, Europe, and the United States." Washington, DC: OTA Contractor Report, 1991.

Office of the United States Trade Representative. "1992 National Trade Estimate Report on Foreign Trade Barriers." Washington, DC: GPO, 1992.

"1992 Trade Policy Agenda and 1991 Annual Report of the President of the United States on the Trade Agreements Program." Washington, DC: GPO, 1992.

Okimoto, Daniel I. "Regime Characteristics of Japanese Industrial Policy." In Hugh Patrick (ed.), *Japan's High-Technology Industries: Lessons and Limitations of Industrial Policy*, pp. 35–95. Seattle: University of Washington Press, 1986.

Between MITI and the Market: Japanese Industrial Policy for High Technology. Stanford: Stanford University Press, 1989.

Okuno-Fujiwara, Masahiro. "Industrial Policy in Japan: A Political Economy View." In Paul R. Krugman (ed.), *Trade with Japan: Has the Door Opened Wider?*, pp. 271–303. Chicago: University of Chicago Press, 1991.

Organisation for Economic Co-operation and Development. *Technology and the Economy: The Key Relationship.* Paris: OECD, 1992.

Technology and Industrial Performance. Paris: OECD, 1996.

Ostry, Sylvia, and Richard R. Nelson. *Techno-Nationalism and Techno-Globalism: Conflict and Cooperation.* Washington, DC: Brookings, 1995.

Ozawa, Terutomo. *Japan's Technological Challenge to the West, 1950–1974: Motivation and Accomplishments.* Cambridge, MA: MIT Press, 1974.

Paarlberg, Robert L. *Fixing Farm Trade: Policy Options for the United States.* Cambridge, MA: Ballinger, 1988.

Patrick, Hugh. "Japanese High Technology Policy in Comparative Context." Columbia University Graduate School of Business, Center on Japanese Economy and Business Working Paper No. 1. New York, 1986.

Paul, J. K. *High Technology International Trade and Competition.* Park Ridge, NJ: Noyce, 1984.

Pomfret, Richard. "Voluntary Export Restraints in the Presence of Monopoly Power." *Kyklos* 42.1 (1989): 61–72.

"The New Trade Theories, Rent Snatching and Jet Aircraft." *World Economy* 14.3 (1991): 269–77.

Porter, Michael E. *The Competitive Advantage of Nations.* New York: Free Press, 1990.

Powell, Robert. "Anarchy in International Relations Theory: The Neorealist-Neoliberal Debate." *International Organization* 48.2 (1994): 313–34.

Richardson, J. David. "The Political Economy of Strategic Trade Policy." *International Organization* 44.1 (1990): 107–35.

Sizing-Up U.S. Export Disincentives. Washington, DC: Institute for International Economics, 1993.

Robert B. Nathan Associates. "Television Manufacturing in the United States: Economic Contributions – Past, Present, and Future." Washington, DC: EIA, 1989.

Rogowski, Ronald. "Trade and the Variety of Democratic Institutions." *International Organization* 41.2 (1987): 203–23.

Romer, Paul M. "The Origins of Endogenous Growth." *Journal of Economic Perspectives* 8.1 (1994): 3–22.

Saxenian, Annalee. *Regional Advantage: Culture and Competition in Silicon Valley and Route 128.* Cambridge, MA: Harvard University Press, 1994.

Scherer, F. M. *International High-Technology Competition.* Cambridge, MA: Harvard University Press, 1992.

Schoenhardt-Bailey, Cheryl. "Lessons in Lobbying for Free Trade in 19th Century Britain: To Concentrate or Not." *American Political Science Review* 85.1 (1991): 37–58.

Science and Technology Agency. "White Paper on Science and Technology 1988 (Summary): Towards the Establishment of a New Creative Research Environment." Tokyo: Science and Technology Agency, 1988.

Semiconductor Industry Association. "The Semiconductor Producer-User Symbiosis of Japan Market Access." Washington, DC: SIA, 1987.

"The 1991 U.S.-Japan Semiconductor Agreement: 'Heading towards Crisis.'" San Jose: SIA, 1992.

Snidal, Duncan. "International Cooperation among Relative Gains Maximizers." *International Studies Quarterly* 35.4 (1991): 387–402.

Stegemann, Klaus. "Policy Rivalry among Industrial States: What Can We Learn from Models of Strategic Trade Policy?" *International Organization* 43.1 (1989): 73–100.

Stopford, John, Susan Strange, and John S. Henley. *Rival States, Rival Firms: Competition for World Market Shares.* Cambridge: Cambridge University Press, 1991.

Stowsky, Jay S. "Weak Links, Strong Bonds: U.S.-Japanese Competition in Semiconductor Production Equipment." In Chalmers Johnson, Laura D'Andrea Tyson, and John Zysman (eds.), *Politics and Productivity: The Real Story of Why Japan Works*, pp. 241–74. New York: Harper Business, 1989.

Tatsuno, Sheridan M. *Created in Japan: From Imitators to World-Class Innovators.* New York: Harper & Row, 1990.

TechSearch International Inc. "Japanese Developments in High Definition Television: Executive Summary." Austin, TX: TechSearch, 1989.

"Japanese Developments in High Definition Television: HDTV Developments by Industry." Austin, TX: TechSearch, 1989.

"Japanese Developments in High Definition Television: NHK and Government Policies." Austin, TX: TechSearch, 1989.

Thornton, David Weldon. *Airbus Industrie: The Politics of an International Industrial Collaboration.* New York: St. Martin's Press, 1995.

Thurow, Lester. *Head to Head: The Coming Economic Battle among Japan, Europe, and America.* New York: Morrow, 1992.

Thursby, Marie. "Strategic Models, Market Structure, and State Trading: An Application to Agriculture." In Robert E. Baldwin (ed.), *Trade Policy Issues and Empirical Analysis*, pp. 79–105. Chicago: University of Chicago Press, 1988.

Tilton, John E. *International Diffusion of Technology: The Case of Semiconductors.* Washington, DC: Brookings, 1971.

Tirole, Jean. *Theory of Industrial Organization.* Cambridge, MA: MIT Press, 1988.

"The Internal Organization of Government." *Oxford Economic Papers* 46 (1994): 1–29.

Todd, Daniel, and Jamie Simpson. *The World Aircraft Industry.* London: Croom Helm, 1986.

Trefler, Daniel. "Trade Liberalization and the Theory of Endogenous Protection: An Econometric Study of U.S. Import Policy." *Journal of Political Economy* 101.1 (1993): 138–60.

Tyson, Laura D'Andrea. *Who's Bashing Whom? Trade Conflict in High-Technology Industries.* Washington, DC: Institute for International Economics, 1992.

Tyson, Laura D'Andrea, and David B. Yoffie. "Semiconductors: From Manipulated to Managed Trade." In David B. Yoffie (ed.), *Beyond Free Trade*, pp. 29–78. Boston: Harvard Business School Press, 1993.

U.S. Congress. *U.S.-Japan Economic Relations.* Hearings before the Subcommittee on International Trade and Finance, and Security of the Joint Economic Committee, 97th Congress, 1st Session, June 19 and July 9 and 13, 1981.

U.S. Department of Commerce. "A Competitive Assessment of the U.S. Manufacturing Automation Equipment Industries." Washington, DC: International Trade Administration, 1984.

"A Competitive Assessment of the U.S. Electric Power Generating Equipment Industry." Washington, DC: ITA, 1985.

"A Competitive Assessment of the U.S. Semiconductor Manufacturing Equipment Industry." Washington, DC: GPO, 1985.

A Competitive Assessment of the U.S. Civil Aircraft Industry. Boulder, CO: Westview Press, 1986.

"A Competitive Assessment of the U.S. Robotics Industry." Washington, DC: GPO, 1987.

"U.S. Research Facilities of Foreign Companies." Washington, DC: ITA, 1994.

"Japan-Plasma Display Production-IMI950901: Market Research Reports." Washington, DC: ITA, 1996.

U.S. Department of Defense. "Building U.S. Capabilities in Flat Panel Displays." DoD Flat Panel Display Task Force Final Report. Washington, DC, 1994.

U.S. Department of Energy, Materials Technology Subcommittee Communications Group on Superconductivity. "Federal Research Programs in Superconductivity." Washington, DC: DOE, 1994.

"Superconductivity for Electric Systems Program Plan FY1996–FY2000." Washington, DC: DOE, 1996.

U.S. House of Representatives. *U.S. Trade Policy Phase II: Private Sector.* Hearings before the Subcommittee on Trade of the Committee on Ways and Means, 97th Congress, 1st Session [Part A], December 10, 11, 14, 15, and 16, 1981.

Trade in Services and Trade in High Technology Products. Hearing before the Subcommittee on Trade of the Committee on Ways and Means, 97th Congress, 2nd Session, May 24, 1982.

Reciprocal Trade and Market Access Legislation. Hearing before the Subcommittee on Trade of the Committee on Ways and Means, 97th Congress, 2nd Session, July 26, 1982.

General Trade Policy. Hearings before the Subcommittee on Commerce, Transportation, and Tourism of the Committee on Energy and Commerce, 98th Congress, 1st Session, March 15, April 5, May 25, and June 22, 1983.

Research and Development Joint Ventures. Hearing before the Subcommittee on Science, Research and Technology of the Committee on Science and Technology, 98th Congress, 1st Session, July 12, 1983.

Industrial Policy. Hearings before the Subcommittee on Economic Stabilization of the Committee on Banking, Finance, and Urban Affairs, 98th Congress, 2nd Session, July 13, 14, 18, and 26–8, 1983.

Industrial Policy. Hearings before the Subcommittee on Economic Stabilization of the Committee on Banking, Finance, and Urban Affairs, 98th Congress, 1st Session [Part 3], August 2, 3, 4, 18, and 19, 1983.

The Role of Automation and Robotics in Advancing United States Competitiveness. Hearing before the Subcommittee on Science, Research and Technology of the Committee on Science and Technology, 99th Congress, 1st Session, October 7, 1985.

Competitiveness of the U.S. Semiconductor Industry. Hearing before the Subcommittee on Commerce, Consumer Protection, and Competitiveness of the Committee on Energy and Commerce, 100th Congress, 1st Session, June 9, 1987.

Competitiveness of U.S. Commercial Aircraft Industry. Hearing before the Subcommittee on Commerce, Consumer Protection and Competitiveness of the Committee on Energy and Commerce, 100th Congress, 1st Session, June 23, 1987.

Major Issues in United States European Community Trade. Staff report prepared for the use of the Subcommittee on Oversight and Investigations of the Committee on Energy and Commerce, July 1987.

New Directions in Home Video. Hearing before the Subcommittee on Science, Research and Technology of the Committee on Science, Space, and Technology, 100th Congress, 2nd Session, June 23, 1988.

Unfair Foreign Trade Practices. Hearings before the Subcommittee on Oversight and Investigations of the Committee on Energy and Commerce, 101st Congress, 1st Session, March 1 and 2, 1989.

High Definition Television. Hearings before the Subcommittee on Telecommunications and Finance of the Committee on Energy and Commerce, 101st Congress, 1st Session, March 8, 9, 1989.

High Definition Television. Hearing before the Committee on Science, Space, and Technology, 101st Congress, 1st Session, March 22, 1989.

Proposed Joint Development of the FSX Fighter with Japan. Hearings before the Subcommittee of the Committee on Banking, Finance, and Urban Affairs, 101st Congress, 1st Session, April 15 and May 5, 1989.

High Definition Television. Hearing before the Subcommittee on Research and Development and the Subcommittee on Investigations of the Committee on Armed Services, 101st Congress, 1st Session, May 10, 1989.

Enforcement of the United States-Japan Semiconductor Agreement. 101st Congress, 1st Session, May 24, 1989.

International Technology Transfer: Who Is Minding the Store? Hearing before the Subcommittee on International Scientific Cooperation of the Committee on Science, Space, and Technology, 101st Congress, 1st Session, July 19, 1989.

High Definition Television (Part 2). Hearing before the Subcommittee on Telecommunications and Finance of the Committee on Energy and Commerce, 101st Congress, 1st Session, September 13, 1989.

FCC and NTIA Authorizations. Hearings before the Subcommittee on Telecommunications and Finance of the Committee on Energy and Commerce, 101st Congress, 1st Session, September 14, 21, 1989.

The Government Role in Joint Production Ventures. Hearing before the Subcommittee on Science, Research and Technology of the Committee on Science, Space, and Technology, 101st Congress, 1st Session, September 19, 1989.

Superconductivity. Hearing before the Subcommittee on Transportation, Aviation and Materials of the Committee on Science, Space, and Technology, 101st Congress, 2nd Session, February 21, 1990.

International Science and Technology and Foreign Policy. Hearings before the Subcommittee on International Science Cooperation of the Committee on Science, Space, and Technology, 101st Congress, 2nd Session, April 4, 26, 1990.

Decline of U.S. Semiconductor Infrastructure. Hearing before the Subcommittee on Commerce, 101st Congress, 2nd Session, May 9, 1990.

The Future of the U.S. Space Program. Hearing before the Subcommittee on Space and Science Applications of the Committee on Science, Space, and Technology, 101st Congress, 2nd Session, July 23, 1990.

Prospects for a New United States-Japan Semiconductor Agreement. Hearing before the Subcommittee on International Economic Policy and Trade of the Committee on Foreign Affairs, 102nd Congress, 1st Session, March 20, 1991.

Critical Technologies: Machine Tools, Robotics, and Manufacturing. Hearing before the Subcommittee on Technology and Competitiveness of the Committee on Science, Space, and Technology, 102nd Congress, 1st Session, May 2, 1991.

Acceleration of U.S. Technology Utilization and Commercialization. Hearing before the Subcommittee on Technology and Competitiveness of the Committee on Science, Space, and Technology, 102nd Congress, 1st Session, May 7, 1991.

The Role of Basic Research in Economic Competitiveness. Hearing before the Subcommittee on Science of the Committee on Science, Space, and Technology, 102nd Congress, 1st Session, June 20, 1991.

Semiconductors: The Role of Consortia. Hearing before the Subcommittee on Science, Space, and Technology, 102nd Congress, 1st Session, July 23, 1991.

Europe and the United States: Competition and Cooperation in the 1990s. Study papers submitted to the Subcommittee on International Economic Policy and Trade and the Subcommittee on Europe and the Middle East of the Committee on Foreign Affairs. Washington, DC: GPO, 1992.

U.S. International Trade Performance and Outlook: Competitive Position in the Automotive, Aerospace, and Chemical and Pharmaceutical Sectors. Hearings before the Subcommittee on Trade of the Committee on Ways and Means, 102nd Congress, 2nd Session, March 11, 23, 30, 31, and April 7, 1992.

U.S. International Trade Commission. "Global Competitiveness of U.S. Advanced-Technology Manufacturing Industries: Large Civil Aircraft." Washington, DC: ITC, 1993.

U.S. Senate. *Space Benefits – The Secondary Application of Aerospace Technology in Other Sectors of the Economy*. Prepared for the Committee on Aeronautical and Space Sciences, April 16, 1975.

Industrial Growth and Productivity. Hearings before the Subcommittee on Industrial Growth and Productivity of the Committee on the Budget, 97th Congress, 1st Session, December 3, 5, 1980; January 26, 1981.

Export-Import Bank Amendments of 1983. Hearings before the Subcommittee on International Finance and Monetary Policy of the Committee on Banking, Housing, and Urban Affairs, 98th Congress, 1st Session, March 22 and 24, 1983.

Competitive Challenge Facing U.S. Industry. Hearings before the Committee on Commerce, Science, and Transportation, 100th Congress, 1st Session, January 20 and February 24, 1987.

Issues Confronting the Semiconductor Industry. Hearings before the Subcommittee on Technology and the Law of the Committee on the Judiciary, 100th Congress, 1st Session, February 26 and March 3, 1987.

Impact of Imports and Foreign Investment on National Security. Hearing before the Committee on Finance, 100th Congress, 1st Session, March 25, 1987.

Competitiveness and Antitrust. Hearings before the Committee on the Judiciary, 100th Congress, 1st Session, May 6 and 7, 1987.

Department of Defense Authorization for Appropriations for Fiscal Years 1990 and 1991. Hearings before the Committee on Armed Services, 101st Congress, 1st Session, March 17; May 11, 16, 17, 31; June 2, 1989.

Department of Commerce Technology Programs Authorization. Hearing before the Committee on Commerce, Science, and Transportation, 101st Congress, 1st Session, June 6, 1989.

Prospects for Development of a U.S. HDTV Industry. Hearing before the Committee on Governmental Affairs, 101st Congress, 1st Session, August 1, 1989.

The Future of the U.S. Semiconductor Industry and the Impact on Defense. Hearing before the Subcommittee on Defense Industry and Technology of the Committee on Armed Services, 100th Congress, 1st Session, November 29, 1989.

Semiconductors and the Electronics Industry. Hearing before the Subcommittee on Science, Technology, and Space of the Committee on Commerce, Science, and Transportation, 101st Congress, 2nd Session, May 17, 1990.

Trade Agreements Compliance Act. Hearing before the Subcommittee on International Trade of the Committee on Finance, 101st Congress, 2nd Session, July 13, 1990.

Renewal of the United States-Japan Semiconductor Agreement. Hearing before the Subcommittee on International Trade of the Committee on Finance, 102nd Congress, 1st Session, March 22, 1991.

Review of Ongoing Trade Negotiations and Completed Trade Agreements. Hearing before the Subcommittee on International Trade of the Committee on Finance, 102nd Congress, 1st Session, August 2, 1991.

Technology Policy and Competitiveness: The Federal Government's Role. Hearing before the Subcommittee on Government Information and Regulation of the Committee on Governmental Affairs, 102nd Congress, 2nd Session, March 12, 1992.

United States Trade Commission. "Operation of the Trade Agreements Program 41st Report." Washington, DC: GPO, 1989.

United States Trade Representative. "U.S. Government Response to the EC-Commissioned Report 'U.S. Government Support of the U.S. Commercial Aircraft Industry.' " Washington, DC: USTR, 1992.

Uriu, Robert M. *Troubled Industries: Confronting Economic Change in Japan.* Ithaca, New York: Cornell University Press, 1996.

von Hippel, Eric. *The Sources of Innovation.* New York: Oxford University Press, 1988.

Wade, Robert. *Governing the Market: Economic Theory and the Role of Government in East Asian Industrialization.* Princeton: Princeton University Press, 1990.

Wilbur Smith Associates. "The Economic Impact of Civil Aviation on the U.S. Economy: Update '91." Columbia, SC: Prepared for Martin Marietta Corporation, 1993.

Wilson, Robert W., Peter K. Ashton, and Thomas P. Egan. *Innovation, Competition, and Government Policy in the Semiconductor Industry.* Lexington, MA: Lexington Books, 1980.

Wolff, Alan Wm., et al. "Japanese Market Barriers in Microelectronics: Memorandum in Support of a Petition Pursuant to Section 301 of the Trade Act of 1974 As Amended." Cupertino, CA: SIA, 1985.

World Technology Evaluation Center. "WTEC Panel Report on Power Applications of Superconductivity in Japan and Germany." Baltimore: Loyola College, 1997.

Yamamura, Kozo. "Caveat Emptor: The Industrial Policy of Japan." In Paul R. Krugman (ed.), *Strategic Trade Policy and the New International Economics*, pp. 169–209. Cambridge, MA: MIT Press, 1986.

Yoffie, David B. "Foreign Direct Investment in Semiconductors." In Kenneth A. Froot (ed.), *Foreign Direct Investment*, pp. 197–222. Chicago: University of Chicago Press, 1993.

Yoshino, M. Y. "Global Competition in a Salient Industry: The Case of Civil Aircraft." In Michael E. Porter (ed.), *Competition in Global Industries*, pp. 517–38. Boston: Harvard Business School Press, 1986.

Zimmer, Uwe R., Thomas Christaller, and Christfried Webers. "Recent Developments in Japanese Robotics Research: Notes of a Japan Tour." German National Research Institute, GMD Technical Report No. 1077. Sankt Augustin, Germany, 1997.

Zimmerman, Martin B. "Learning Effects and the Commercialization of New Energy Technologies: The Case of Nuclear Power." *Bell Journal of Economics* 13.2 (1982): 297–310.

Index

209